Praise for *Sin* AND Syntax

"Probably the hippest grammar guide ever written, this book shows how to write for results, wholesome or subversive."

—*American Way*

"Move over, grumpy schoolmarms everywhere. Your time has come. For the writer or wannabe, *Sin and Syntax* is an urgently needed, updated, and hip guide to modern language and writing. Nobody but Connie Hale could make the elements of twenty-first-century style so much fun."

—Jon Katz, media critic and author of
Running to the Mountain and *Virtuous Reality*

"*Sin and Syntax* is one of the rare books that recognizes—and even celebrates—the fact that good writing has little to do with 'rules' and much to do with a true understanding of effective prose. Connie Hale provides us an invaluable service by showing us what works and what doesn't in the real world, regardless of what the pedants say."

—Jesse Sheidlower, editor at large of the
Oxford English Dictionary and author of *The F-Word*

"This new grammar book is light-years ahead of what you'd read in eighth-grade English: With vivid, contemporary examples of what to do and what not to do, it's fun to read."

—*Charlotte Observer*

"In *Sin and Syntax: How to Craft Wicked Good Prose,* Constance Hale provides a plugged-in, cutting-edge alternative to the musty prescriptions of Strunk and White. Here you will find an open-minded, exuberant approach to style that is intelligent and refreshing."

—Charles Harrington Elster, in the *San Diego Union-Tribune*

"Hale has put together a writing/grammar manual that is fresh and fun. The basic rules are here, and they are well explained. The 'sin' from the title is partly advice on when and how to break these rules. The other sins are examples of oft-repeated mistakes . . . this guide will help [readers] use effective and artful language. The examples range from Dr. Seuss books to John F. Kennedy's speeches to commercials. . . . Easy to understand and appealing to a broad range of readers, this book is highly recommended for all libraries."

—Alisa J. Cihlar, Monroe P.L., WI, in *Library Journal*

"This is a wonderful how-to book about writing stuff people want to read. Those who have studied the subject might think of Hale as a peacemaker between the Strunk and White tribe devoted to precision and the more entertaining descendants of Henry Mencken, full of energy and inventions. Nonwriters who just want advice that won't put them to sleep will find sentences they can dance to."

—Mike Maza, in the *Dallas Morning News*

"Constance Hale, in *Sin and Syntax: How to Craft Wicked Good Prose*, is the first grammarian I've seen in a long time brave enough to revive diagramming."

—Ed Gray, in the *Arkansas Democrat-Gazette*

"Hale's analyses of texts, from Faulkner's *Absalom, Absalom!* to the jargon-laden prose of government and corporate documents, are full of insight because she lets the reader in on how language has the power to move us or confuse us."

—Charles K. Bultman, in *California Lawyer*

"Hale [is] good at explaining rules, and she provides a lot of examples of writing that really is sinfully good. Osmosis alone should help you here."

—Gary Kaufman, in *Salon*

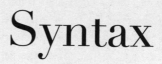

Sin

A N D

Syntax

Sin

AND

Syntax

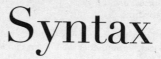

HOW TO CRAFT

WICKED

GOOD PROSE

Constance Hale

THREE RIVERS PRESS
NEW YORK

To Madeleine Carter Mayher,
who gave me her love
of the mother tongue

Library of Congress Cataloging-in-Publication Data is available upon request.

ISBN 978-0-385-34689-4
eISBN 978-0-385-34693-1

Printed in the United States of America

Cover design by Maria Elias

16 15 14 13 12 11 10 9

Second Paperback Edition

Contents

PART 2

SENTENCES

PART 3

MUSIC

Introduction

Driven by some combustible mix of passion (for the power of words) and desperation (so many snags in your sentences!), you've picked up a book called *Sin and Syntax*. What, you're wondering, does *syntax* (that collection of prissy rules telling us how to put words together) have to do with *sin* (the reckless urge to flout propriety)?

Sin and Syntax plays with dynamic tensions in language: The underlying codes that give prose its clarities yet fail to explain its beauties. The sludge that muddles writing. The delight in the wacky. *Sin and Syntax* is about the skill that allows you, the writer, to harness such complexities, to create prose that thrills.

Are you ready to turn syntax from a minefield into a stamping ground—*your* stamping ground? Forget schoolmarmish rules. Forget grammar as it was drilled in grade school. Rest assured, you'll get your grammar here, on the theory that it's best to know the rules before you break them. This book will indeed show you how to avoid red-pen comments, but, more important, it'll show you how to make some sinful mischief.

IF ALL THIS SEEMS paradoxical, get used to it. Language *is* paradox.

Sin and Syntax dwells in contradictions. It dabbles in the eloquence of tradition, the intelligence of creoles, the decadence of slang. We'll root around where language is most playful: in the pop, the vernacular, the mongrel tongues. We'll examine how the highbrow and the lowbrow define the edges of prose and how the middlebrow dooms it to mediocrity. We'll diss legalese and computerese and ditch the lifeless rhythms of Standard Written English.

We'll also summon the spirit of renegades who ignore taboos and make the language sing, from Shakespeare to Shake 'n Bake and from Joan Didion to Junot Díaz. With a little Bob Dylan and Nicki Minaj thrown in. We'll wallow with Walt Whitman, who ridiculed the "dictionary makers," insisting that language has its base "broad and low, close to the ground." We'll accept English as a robust, swarthy tongue, capable of surviving tumult and thriving on change.

T. S. Eliot once argued that a language with identical spoken and written forms would be "practically intolerable," since no one would listen to the first or read the second. Eliot was cool, but let's not be seduced by false dichotomies. Insisting on strict or stuffy words in writing means you may miss the shifting brilliances of the colloquial. On the other hand, glorifying the spoken, demanding that people "write as they speak," can put a higher premium on the pedestrian than on grace, style, and richness. A passion for new terms and easy abbreviation makes for readable emails, but discretion, sensitivity, and metaphor still matter.

In figuring out how to write better, let's look to the ways the spoken and the written cross-pollinate. Let's look to texts like the *Book of Common Prayer*, which was written to be read out loud, and to orators like Winston Churchill, who wrote and rewrote and practiced and repracticed before he ever addressed a public. Let's look to the voices of cyberspace and to the rhythms of rap, celebrating the syntax and sounds that make narratives come alive.

Books on prose style, of course, are as old as sin—or at least as old as Aristotle, who launched the industry with *Poetics* and *Rhetoric*. You'll see the names of Aristotle's descendants mentioned throughout the book: Henry Fowler, Sir Arthur Quiller-Couch, George Orwell, Sir Ernest Gowers. These men have refined the rules of style and usage over the centuries, their efforts culminating in the terse commandments of William Strunk and E. B. White (*Use the active voice. Omit needless words. Avoid foreign languages*). We'll hear from more recent gods and goddesses of grammar, too, like Karen Elizabeth Gordon, Patricia O'Conner, Ben Yagoda, and Mignon Fogarty.

But this book is really more about great writing than good grammar. We pay homage to that guru of prose style, William Zinsser, who distilled the wisdom of the ancients into what he called, in his classic *On Writing Well*, "four articles of faith": clarity, simplicity, brevity, and humanity.

Sin and Syntax accepts the high bar set by Zinsser—then reimagines both the parts of speech and the parts of the sentence so that you can clear that bar. *Sin and Syntax* holds that the flesh of prose gets its shape and strength from the bones of grammar, and that sinfully good writing depends on understanding both the arcana of syntax and the art of musical sentences.

But adding a little illicit activity to such "articles of faith," *Sin and Syntax* offers five new principles of prose:

Relish every word.
Aim deep, but be simple.
Take risks.
Seek beauty.
Find the right pitch.

Moving from the basic to the sophisticated, *Sin and Syntax* covers the parts of speech and how to exploit them (in "Words"), shows the parts of a sentence and how to arrange them (in "Sentences"), and reveals how melody, rhythm, lyricism, and voice give prose its mystery (in "Music").

Within these three parts, each of the book's chapters is broken into five sections:

- "Bones" is the grammar sermonette, giving you simple keys rather than rigid rules. Learn the sensible system, if only to know how to escape it in flights of creative fancy (it's more flexible than English teachers would have you believe).
- "Flesh" contains the lesson on writing. Linking grammar to prose, it shows how the parts of speech, the elements of sentences, and the techniques of music give us our most riveting stories.
- "Cardinal Sins" catalogs true transgressions: errors made in ignorance. This section will set you straight, exposing the disaster

that lurks in mangled syntax. "Cardinal Sins" also debunks myths and shibboleths that often substitute for a real understanding of the underpinnings of language. (*Don't use the passive voice. Don't start a sentence with a conjunction. Don't end a sentence with a preposition.*)

- "Carnal Pleasures" shows how, sometimes, writing works because it hews to the underlying codes of language. And how, sometimes, writing works because it defies the codes—or seems to. "Carnal Pleasures" contains playful, riotous, and sometimes exquisite pieces of writing. It shows how breaking the rules can lead to breakthrough prose.
- "Catechism" puts the lessons into practice. It is the instructional piece at the end of the week, or, in this case, of the chapter. Some simple exercises will test your understanding of grammatical or stylistic ideas, and writing prompts will encourage you to stretch new muscles. Keys to the answers, when relevant, are given by chapter in the Appendix.

Sin and Syntax is designed so that a novice can march from chapter to chapter in orderly fashion, learning how to sync the parts one at a time. But it is also designed so that a prose veteran can head directly to troublesome areas for a refresher course in grammar and a reliable list of do's and don'ts.

Straightening out grammar and syntax is of course not the be-all and end-all of writing. But a writer needs a command of language as much as a commanding idea. When style complements substance, when technique is put into the service of a good tale, prose can pulse with life.

PART I

Words

The French mime Étienne Decroux used to remind his students, "One pearl is better than a whole necklace of potatoes." What is true for that wordless art form applies equally to writing: well-crafted prose depends on the writer's ability to distinguish between pearls and potatoes. Only *some* words are fit to be strung into a given sentence.

Great writers are meticulous with their pearls, sifting through piles of them and stringing only perfect specimens upon the thread of syntax. The careful execution of beautiful, powerful prose through beautiful, powerful words is guided by my five principles.

RELISH EVERY WORD

True prose stylists carry on an impassioned lifelong love affair with words, banishing mediocre ones like so many uninteresting suitors, burnishing the good ones till they shimmer. Be infatuated, be seduced, be obsessed.

But be smart about words, too. "All words are pegs to hang ideas on," wrote the nineteenth-century essayist Henry Ward Beecher: words not linked to ideas are not worthy of writing—or reading. Once you've committed your words to paper (or to the screen), test each term. Does it carry your idea? Does it express, exactly, that once inchoate thought?

Sensitize yourself to denotation and connotation. *Denotation,* the dictionary definition of a word, refers to its explicit or literal meanings.

Connotation, the suggestive power of a word, refers to its implicit or latent meanings. The denotations of *peach* (a single-seeded fruit with tangy yellowish pulp and downy skin that goes from yellow to red) and *mango* (a single-seeded fruit with a tangy yellowish pulp and firm skin mottled with greens, yellows, and reds) differ only slightly. But whereas *peach* summons hot summers in Georgia and the cheeks of a Southern belle, *mango* conjures images of India and Mexico and the paintings of Gauguin. Wouldn't it be a mistake to swap in *mango* when writing about, say, the dusty-peach *chambres* of a grande dame with a thing for Louis XVI?

Beyond the sense of a word is its sensuousness: its sound, its cadence, its spirit. The sounds of *peach* and *mango* differ, letting you play in different ways with surrounding words. In turning a phrase, we want the words to build like a jazz riff, with the melodies of one word playing off the melodies of the others.

AIM DEEP, BUT BE SIMPLE

"People used to call me a good writer," mused John Ruskin, a giant of the nineteenth-century essay. "Now they say I can't write at all; because, for instance, if I think anybody's house is on fire, I only say, 'Sir, your house is on fire.' . . . I used to say, 'Sir, the abode in which you probably passed the delightful days of youth is in a state of inflammation.'"

Verbose is not a synonym for *literary.* Let's not forsake short, common words that name big things—*hope* and *pride,* for example—or simple couplings that leave strong impressions, like William Carlos Williams's "red wheel barrow" or Prince's "little red Corvette."

It's not enough, though, just to be simple. "Nine pounds where three are sufficient is obesity," said Frank Lloyd Wright. "But to eliminate expressive words in speaking or writing—words that intensify or vivify meaning—is not simplicity. It may be, or usually is, stupidity."

Studying manuscript changes is one of the best ways to get a sense of how great writers arrive at "words that intensify or vivify meaning." John Updike's manuscripts are housed in Houghton Library, Harvard University's manuscript repository. Updike was known for writing fluently and revising little, but the archive reveals the care he took to excise unnecessary words and to recast necessary ones, and, in doing so, to craft the tone of his sentences.

The *New York Times Book Review* editor Sam Tanenhaus called Updike's sentences "lathe-turned." Take, for example, the opening scene of Updike's *Rabbit at Rest*. In a first, handwritten stab, Updike begins the novel with this sentence, scrawled across the page:

> The Southwest Florida Regional Airport is relatively new and you drive to it off Exit 21 of Federal 75.

The next draft, typed, opens anew, as the author resequences the initial paragraphs to create a less linear, more interior effect:

> Standing amid the tan loud, post-Christmas crowd at the Southwest-ern Florida Regional Airport, Rabbit Angstrom has a funny sudden feeling that what he has come to meet, what's floating in unseen about to land, is not his son Nelson and wife and children but some-thing more ominous and intimately his, his own death, shaped vaguely like an airplane. The sensation chills and oppresses him, above and beyond the air-conditioning. But then he has been feeling uneasy with Nelson for thirty years.
>
> The airport is relatively new; you drive to it off Exit 21 of Federal 75 down three miles of divided highway that for all the skinny palms and groomed green at its sides seems to lead nowhere.

Then Updike continues to refine, discarding the adjective "tan" and changing "vaguely" and "with." The most interesting change, though, is in the sentence "The sensation chills and oppresses him, above and be-yond the air-conditioning." Updike removes the second verb and adds "terminal" before "air-conditioning"—making a pun that underscores his theme of impending death and sharpening the image: "The sensa-tion chills him, above and beyond the terminal air-conditioning."

Updike continued to craft, to tweak, to fret over words. The open-ing, with "tan" restored and "loud" replaced, appears in the published book this way:

Standing amid the tan, excited post-Christmas crowd at the South-western Florida Regional Airport, Rabbit Angstrom has a funny sudden feeling that what he has come to meet, what's floating in unseen about to land, is not his son Nelson and daughter-in-law Pru and their two children but something more ominous and intimately his: his own death, shaped vaguely like an airplane. The sensation chills him, above and beyond the terminal air-conditioning. But then facing Nelson has made him feel uneasy for thirty years.

The airport is relatively new. You drive to it off Exit 21 off Interstate 75 down three miles of divided highway that for all the skinny palms in rows and groomed too-green flat-bladed grass at its sides seems to lead nowhere.

As Updike shows, even the smallest words (*loud* or *excited*? *Bermuda grass* or *flat-bladed grass*?) matter. Updike kept refining in every draft. He relished every word.

TAKE RISKS

After having suffered the hyperactive red pens of schoolmarms and the hypercorrect rules of inflexible pedagogues, too many of us have retreated to the realm of the safe, the standard, the unimaginative. We stick to common words—or, worse, pull out a hackneyed phrase. We yield to the conventions of a profession rather than pushing ourselves to be unconventional. We use jargon rather than coming up with original language.

Hidden in such prefab prose is a fear of going to the edge. But it's romping on the fringes of language that gives writing its frisson. The right word might be snagged off the street, snatched from another language, or hatched in the sand tray of the imagination. Dive into the polyglot English tongue, taking a cue from Walt Whitman, that high priest of the rambunctious:

I like limber, lasting, fierce words. I like them applied to myself—and I like them in newspapers, courts, debates, Congress. Do you suppose the liberties and the brawn of These States have to do only with delicate lady-words? with gloved gentleman words? Bad presidents, bad judges, bad clients, bad editors, owners of slaves, and the long ranks of Northern political suckers (robbers, traitors, suborned), monopolists, infidels . . . shaved persons, supplejacks, ecclesiastics, men not fond of women, women not fond of men, cry down the use of strong, cutting, beautiful rude words. [But] to the manly instincts of the People they will be forever welcome.

Whitman's American English scarfs up words from other languages with gusto. If someone's bugging you, you can go the Anglo-Saxon route and *shun* her; or you can *avoid* her (Latin); or you can *eschew* her (French). Or you can tell her to *get outta your face*. Don't shun slang, especially when it's vivid and musical and fills a gap in the lexicon.

A word not in the dictionary is not out of bounds. H. L. Mencken carried on about coinages bubbling up out of the American experience; one of his favorites, *rubberneck*, he called "almost a complete treatise on American psychology." That simple word, he wrote, conveyed a characteristically American boldness and contempt: "the grotesque humor of the country, the delight in devastating opprobriums, and the acute feeling for the succinct and savory."

More modern neologists have kept up the mischief, giving us gems like *snarky*, *snail mail*, *chump change*, *game changer*, *de-ice*, *de-friend*, *sexting*, *supersize*, *rollerblade*, *blog*, and, my favorite, *babelicious*.

SEEK BEAUTY

Brevity isn't everything. Winston Churchill, who generally endorsed short and simple words, chose *flocculent* over *woolly* in describing the mental process of certain people in his treatise *The Second World War*. Why? *Flocculent* carries an edge of contempt, echoing words like *flop*, *flap*, *flaccid*, *flimsy*, *flabby*, and *flatulent*. Churchill knew that sounds can make words sing.

It's not just sound that gives a word beauty. It's also precision. In our media-driven age, when the succinct sound bite and the skeletal headline push us to ever more elliptical expression, we need to make space for meaning. The constrictive columns on the newspaper's front page make *probe* a popular synonym for *investigation, inquiry,* or *hearing,* but check out the unintended ambiguity of this regrettable headline: "City's Housing Chief Probed." (Did he say "Ouch"?)

Some editors dumb down copy for mass audiences, preferring the short word to the long. I once filed a story on a California town celebrating its determination to come back after an earthquake by holding a party at 5:04 P.M., exactly a year after the Loma Prieta temblor. "If earthquakes give you the willies," I wrote in my lead, "Gilroy has come up with a palliative you're going to love." The city editor changed *palliative* to *cure,* arguing that "no one knows the meaning of *palliative.*" But there is no cure for earthquake anxiety. *Palliative* really was the right word, even if *cure* was shorter, simpler, and more common.

FOR INSPIRATION, GO ON literary adventures with novelists like Djuna Barnes, William Faulkner, Vladimir Nabokov, or Toni Morrison—none of whom uses lowest-common-denominator diction. Faulkner's *Absalom, Absalom!* delivers monologues like this one, by Mississippi spinster Rosa Coldfield. The sixty-five-year-old "widowed virgin" reflects bitterly on her adolescent flowering, which was driven underground when, at fourteen, she fell in love only to be jilted. Faulkner's rich words have all the pungency of emotions that have been on low simmer for half a century:

> Once there was (they cannot have told you this) a summer of wistaria. It was a pervading everywhere of wistaria (I was fourteen then) as though of all springs yet to capitulate condensed into one spring, one summer: the spring and summertime which is every female's who breathed above dust, beholden of all betrayed springs held over from all irrevocable time, repercussed, bloomed again. It was a vintage year of wistaria: vintage year being that sweet conjunction of root bloom and urge and hour and weather; and I (I was fourteen)—I will not insist on bloom, at whom no man had yet to look—nor would ever—twice. . . . But root and urge I do insist and claim, for had I not heired too from all the unsistered Eves since the Snake? Yes, urge I

do: warped chrysalis of what blind perfect seed: for who shall say what gnarled forgotten root might not bloom yet with some globed concentrate more globed and concentrate and heady-perfect because the neglected root was planted warped and lay not dead but merely slept forgot?

Language doesn't have to be Faulknerian to be luscious. In *Sula*, Toni Morrison also focuses on a summer of "root bloom and urge and hour and weather." But in her case, the adolescents Sula and Nel live in Medallion, Ohio:

> Then summer came. A summer limp with the weight of blossomed things. Heavy sunflowers weeping over fences; iris curling and browning at the edges far away from their purple hearts; ears of corn letting their auburn hair wind down to their stalks. And the boys. The beautiful, beautiful boys who dotted the landscape like jewels, split the air with their shouts in the field, and thickened the river with their shining wet backs. Even their footsteps left a smell of smoke behind.
>
> It was in that summer, the summer of their twelfth year, the summer of the beautiful black boys, that they became skittish, frightened and bold—all at the same time.

Morrison's paragraph starts with tight sentences and breaks open like the blossoms they describe. Her participles pour out. The words themselves glisten.

FIND THE RIGHT PITCH

Prose is an intimate exchange between writer and reader. Always think about your reader; hold your audience in your mind. Don't talk to readers as if they are strangers, or as if they are beneath you.

In music, pitch has to do with the position of a sound within the complete range of sound. But even in music, pitch is not cut and dried—sound registers in the mind of the listener. In writing, pitch might be thought of as tilt, slant, cant, spiel, delivery, or act of persuasion—it has to do with how a writer combines meaning, melody, and tone to touch a reader.

The best children's book authors are masters of pitch, because they need to write lines that appeal simultaneously to those equally fearsome critics—children and their easily bored parents. If children are lulled to sleep by the soft lines and easy rhymes of *Goodnight Moon* ("Goodnight stars. Goodnight air. Goodnight noises everywhere"), adults ride the swells of sound and never tire of the story, no matter how many times they read it. If children love the topsy-turvy sentences of Dr. Seuss's *Green Eggs and Ham* ("I am Sam. Sam I am"), adults appreciate the subversive humor ("I will eat them in the rain. And in the dark. And on a train").

Years ago, when I was tutoring children in order to support my writing habit, I had occasion to discuss the progress of a seven-year-old student with her father, a man of many academic degrees. I'll never forget his mentioning a "colloquy" he had had with Annie the night before. It struck me as an example of imperfect pitch, because the word was so out of keeping with the child we were talking about and our work together. Pompous phrasing often serves no purpose other than to puff up the speaker.

Academic treatises often contain such tone-deaf writing. When we learn to write English papers in high school we are often rewarded for big words. Unfortunately, these habits only get worse in Ph.D. programs, which seem to breed abstract language like cultures in a Petri dish. The best academic writers impress us not just with their scholarship, but with their ability to find the right pitch—think of the English professor Henry Louis Gates, Jr., for example, the scientist Jared Diamond, the media studies professor Camille Paglia, the linguist Noam Chomsky, and the historians Jill Lepore and Annette Gordon-Reed.

Pretentious diction, of course, is rife in many professions besides academia. Take the legal field. No attorney goes home and says at the dinner table, "Please pass the green beans. Said green beans are excellent." So why does she write contracts and letters that sound so unnatural? The best attorneys know how to "talk to the jury." Celebrated legal writers like Oliver Wendell Holmes, Clarence Darrow, Barbara Jordan, and Antonin Scalia know to adjust pitch to a wide audience.

Jargon—the technical words and code phrases that professionals use to talk to one another in shorthand—can keep a layperson in the dark. When one computer programmer tells another to "type 'hash bang slash user slash local slash bin slash perl'" (i.e., "!/usr/local/bin/perl"), that coders' jargon serves a purpose, helping two people work together efficiently. But when marketing mavens promote hardware and software to the public, their words are softer than software: *implementation, functionality, interoperability,* and even *ease of use* are just a bunch of junk words. Jargon can reflect institutions more than it does the real humans they serve. Even if it gets to the mercenary point, "monetizing" is no better than "finding a way to make money." If you want to write eloquently as a professional, you need to do it with good words. Universal words.

TO FIND THE RIGHT pitch is to be human, to have a sense of the street, while still reaching for the lofty. It means resisting the kind of language that suits cogs in a machine better than sentient beings. George Orwell, in his 1946 essay "Politics and the English Language," concocted this impenetrable sentence to show what happens when we lose an ear for our own voices:

> Objective consideration of contemporary phenomena compels the conclusion that success or failure in competitive activities exhibits no tendency to be commensurate with innate capacity, but that a considerable element of the unpredictable must invariably be taken into account.

Orwell's sentence, with its inflated abstractions, makes a mess of a statement that started out as the epitome of simplicity, clarity, and humanity. The sentence comes from Ecclesiastes, and it shows how well the seventeenth-century scholars who translated the Bible into English understood the notion of pitch:

I returned and saw under the sun, that the race is not to the swift, nor the battle to the strong, neither yet bread to the wise, nor yet riches to men of understanding, nor yet favor to men of skill; but time and chance happeneth to them all.

Every word in that sentence is a pearl, and every word helps set a pitch that is at once humble and eloquent.

CHAPTER 1

Nouns

Bones

What would a grammar book be if it didn't lounge around in a little Latin? Let's take the word *noun,* which derives from *nomen,* for "name." This useful Latin trivia tells us exactly why nouns exist: to name the things in our world. But before we focus on nouns, let's take a quick trip down memory lane to refresh our understanding about *all* the parts of speech.

Many of us first learned about the different categories of words in grade school, or—depending on our age—from the TV series *School-house Rock!,* which defines the parts of speech with catchy ditties. The song about the noun tells us that it is "a special kind of word" ("It's any name you ever heard") and that it is "quite interesting" ("a person, place, or thing").

But nouns are even more "interesting" than that, especially the ones we want to use in writing that skews older than elementary school. It's true that nouns name people, places, and things-you-can-taste-touch-see-smell-or-hear. But a noun can also name intangible things, like concepts, emotions, or ideas. *Math* is a noun; so are *melancholy* and *myth.* The linguist Steven Pinker calls a noun "simply a word that does nouny things; it is the kind of word that comes after an article, can have an 's stuck onto it, and so on."

Just to complicate things, Pinker and linguists categorize words differently than do most grammar teachers. Where grammarians see eight parts of speech, linguists see four major "word classes" (nouns, verbs, adjectives, and adverbs) and a few minors (including pronouns, conjunctions, and prepositions). As for interjections—well, we'll take those up later.

Word buckets

The idea that there are "parts of speech" goes back to the ancient Greeks and Romans, but eighteenth-century British grammarians settled on *nouns, pronouns, verbs, adjectives, adverbs, conjunctions, prepositions,* and *interjections.* These eight parts of speech have been generally accepted for the last two and a half centuries by schoolteachers and lexicographers, in spite of the fact that some words don't fit neatly into syntactical buckets: Is *nonetheless,* for example, an adverb, a conjunction, a conjunctive adverb, or just a "transitional expression"? (Answer: it depends on who's answering.) Other words fit into multiple categories depending on their function in a sentence: I can *fancy* (verb) a pair of leather boots, choose *fancy* (adjective) high heels, and entertain a *fancy* (noun) about being chic. Perfect fit or not, the parts of speech still give us a way to talk about words.

ALMOST EVERY ENGLISH SENTENCE contains at least one noun. They are indispensible when it comes to portraying a character or painting a scene.

Let's take a look at a paragraph from *The Pillars of Hercules* in which the travel writer Paul Theroux describes "The 7:20 Express to Latakia":

There was undoubtedly a more hallucinogenic **experience** available in poppy-growing **Turkey** than a long **bus ride** through **Central Anatolia**, though it was hard for me to imagine what this might be after a twenty-three-hour **trip** in the sulfurous **interior** of a **bus** of chain-smoking **Turks**, as **day** became **twilight**, turned to **night**, the **moon** passing from one **side** of the **bus** to the other, gleaming briefly in the **snow** of the **Galatia highlands**, **fog** settling and dispersing like **phantasms**, **glimpses** of **dervishes**, **day** dawning again, another **stop**, more **yogurt**, **children** crying in the **backseats**, full **daylight** in **Iskenderun**, **rain** in **Antioch**, all **windows** shut, the stale **smoke** condensing in brown bitter **slime** on the closed **windows** as fresh blue **fumes** rose from forty-nine burning **cigarettes** in this sleepless **acid trip** on the **slipstream** of secondhand **smoke**.

Like any effective scene description, this one is packed with "person, place, concrete thing, intangible thing" words.

- People: *Turks, dervishes, children*
- Places: *Turkey, Central Anatolia, interior (of a bus), Iskenderun*
- Concrete things: *bus, day, night, moon, snow, fog, yogurt, backseats, rain, windows, smoke, slime, fumes, cigarettes*
- Intangible things: *experience, phantasms, glimpses, acid trip, slipstream*

Some of these nouns—like *bus ride, twilight, phantasms*—slide back and forth between tangible and intangible, depending on the writer's use and the reader's frame of mind.

Theroux's passage gives us a chance to look at other facets of nouns, too.

A **common noun** refers generically to people, places, or things. It might be vague or it might be specific, but it is always written in lowercase letters (*bus, day, moon, snow, yogurt, phantasms, dervishes*). It may also be abstract (*glimpses, twilight*).

A **proper noun** is more specific, in that it refers to one and only one person, place, or thing. It might name an individual (*Paul Theroux*), a geographical place (*Turkey, Iskenderun, Antioch*), or a particular train line (*7:20 Express to Latakia*). Proper nouns are written with initial capital letters (and when they are brand names they might even contain interior capital letters, as in iPhone and YouTube).

In **compound nouns**, words double up to express a whole that is more than the sum of its parts. They can be made of common nouns (*bus ride*), proper nouns (*Central Anatolia*), or both (*Galatia highlands*). They can be "open compounds" (*acid trip*) or closed ones (*daylight, slipstream*). Compounding has been common throughout the history of English, but writers and their editors don't always agree on when and whether to splice words together. (Theroux went with *backseat,* which is now Webster's preferred form, but Raymond Carver and Richard Ford—in their short stories "Cathedral" and "Rock Springs"—prefer *back seat.*)

Flesh

If we need to introduce ourselves to others, we rely on nouns, whether proper (*Edmund*) or common (*a farmer's son*). We put them on our business cards (*doctor, lawyer, merchant, chief*), we use them for Web sites and Twitter handles (*prosedoctors.com, @Dr.WhoOnline*), and we let them animate real or made-up epitaphs (*"Here lies Dr. Keene, the good Bishop of Chester, / Who ate up a fat goose, but could not digest her"*).

The lesser mortals among us use generic nouns when we are grasping for words to say who we are (*woman, doctor, athlete*). The writers among us want to say as much as we can in as few words as possible, so we find specific, revealing nouns (*mother, cardiologist, kayaker*). Nouns like *soccer mom, mother hen,* or *matron* say even more—because they give clues about age and attitude.

The best nouns are concrete rather than abstract, specific rather than general. They are also evocative. Consider the difference between a *demonstration of affection,* a *hug,* and a *caress.* Slang and regionalisms can be part of the mix, too. You keep your "domestic partner"; I'll clutch my *babe* or my *baby mama.* You might drive off in "an automobile" or "a sport utility vehicle"; we'll skip town in a Mustang with the top down.

Those paragons of style William Strunk and E. B. White may have favored words that are familiar, short, and standard, but let's push back. Think about how many times you've let "house" sit there in your copy. O.K., it's familiar, it's short, it's standard, but is it the most potent word? Riff through the choices, which include *cottage, duplex, dacha, shack, bungalow, A-frame, Tudor, Victorian, hacienda, manor,* and *wickiup.* (Don't even think about colorless words like *abode, dwelling, domicile,* or *residence.*) Create analogies: Is that pile of wood and steel a *poor man's Fallingwater?* a *Tony Smith on stilts?* a *Bauhaus mineshaft?*

Choosing the right noun means exploring the layers of a word. First, it must precisely render an image: pick *bungalow* if you're describing a one-story house with a low-pitched roof. Second, your noun must be evocative, its connotations conjuring a realm of emotion or sensation: stay with *bungalow* (or perhaps choose *cottage*) if you're capturing coziness, a homey atmosphere. Finally, your noun must be apt—its associations, its links to other words and ideas, must complement your meaning. Are the occupants a bunch of frat boys? Then *crash pad* might work better.

Great writers understand the richness of the English lexicon, and they take time to choose their words carefully, especially when revising. Once, curious to see how Mark Twain worked his nouns, I pored over manuscripts at the University of California's Bancroft Library. In the manuscript of *Pudd'nhead Wilson,* Twain had crossed out "flower beds" in a description of a Missouri house, replacing it with "potted geraniums." The change made the flowers burst red into my imagination. (By the book's publication the image had become even more concrete: "A breed of geranium whose spread of intensely red blossoms accented the prevailing pink tint of the rose-clad house-front like an explosion of flame.")

Jo Ann Beard, in the short story "Cousins," does Twain one better. She makes the effect of the geraniums even more graphic:

Their house has a face on it, two windows with the shades half down, a brown slot of a door, and a glaring mouthful of railing with a few pickets missing. Pink geraniums grow like earrings on either side of the porch. It's August and the grass is golden and spiky against our ankles, the geraniums small like dust.

NOUNS CAN BE PLAYFUL as well as precise. When Ferdinand LeMenthe (leader of the Red Hot Peppers) was upstaged by a comedian calling himself "Swect Papa Cream Puff right out of the bakery shop," the early jazzman rechristened himself "Sweet Papa Jelly Roll, with stovepipes in my hips and all the women in town dyin' to turn my damper down." According to J. L. Dillard in *American English,* LeMenthe was rolling together myriad associations: *jeli* in the African Mandingo language is a minstrel popular with women because of his skill with words and music; in the Caribbean, *jelly* refers to the meat of the coconut when it is still white and viscous, resembling semen; in Harlem, street associations for the gooey pastry have included *lover* and *sex* itself.

With his new name, Jelly Roll Morton was branding himself for his avid fans. Brand names, when they work, are pithy and packed with meaning. Memorable brands are nouns so evocative that they become synonymous with the thing they name, whether a store (7-Eleven), a soft drink (Red Bull), or a laundry detergent (Tide). Sometimes brands are plays on words. In 1989, Apple hit upon PowerBook, starting with the terms *laptop* and *notebook.* The coinage combines the notion of a small product brimming with information and the suggestion of pure computing muscle.

The name that launched a zillion tweets

When the reporters Lisa Chow and Jim Colgan of WNYC News interviewed Jack Dorsey about how his company got its name, here's how the Twitter co-founder described the process:

> We wanted a name that evoked what we did. We wanted something that was tangible. And we looked at what we were doing and when you received a tweet over SMS, your phone would buzz. It would jitter. It would twitch. And those were the early names, Jitter and Twitch. And neither one of them

really inspired the best sort of imagery. . . . One of the guys who was helping us build and create the system, Noah Glass, took the word Twitch, and he went down the dictionary. And we all looked at the Oxford English Dictionary at the T-W's, and we found the word Twitter, [meaning] a short inconsequential burst of information, chirps from birds. And we were like, that describes exactly what we're doing here. . . . Twit is not necessarily associated with the best things. But it has been amazing in terms of building the brand because the users have taken it and invented their own vernacular around it, like tweet and twitterpated.

SOMETIMES NOUNS PINWHEEL AROUND a subject, giving it a multicolored vitality. Francis X. Clines, in *The New York Times*, referred to Judge Kenneth Starr's style as "part Garbo, part Inspector Javert." Adding alliteration to the formula, I once began a profile of Rosalie Sorrels by calling the folksinger "part poet, part parent, part pioneer, part provocateur."

Descriptions require powerhouse nouns. Good character sketches focus on concrete details, as does this profile of Dizzy Gillespie from *The New Yorker*. The writer, Whitney Balliett, starts with Gillespie's duds, focusing next on the jewelry, the cheeks, the mouth, and finally the eyes:

Gillespie, who is not a **clotheshorse**, was wearing a **Sherlock Holmes hat**, houndstooth **jacket**, rumpled striped brown **pants**, a navy-blue **T-shirt**, and a couple of **medallions** suspended from a long gold **neck chain**. He hasn't changed much in the last ten years. He has a medium-length grayish **Afro**, and he looks grizzly. His huge and celebrated **cheeks** are **broadsides** in repose and **spinnakers** in action, and he has a **scimitar smile** and a thousand tiny, even **teeth**. He likes to smile and roll his **eyes** in mock **surprise**, but most of the time his **eyes** are narrowed; they take in much and send out little, and when he puts on his dark-rimmed, two-ton **glasses** they disappear.

Balliett's precise images give us a clear snapshot of Gillespie, and the perfectly pitched metaphors (cheeks that are "broadsides in repose and spinnakers in action") make the portrait breathe.

Most of us, if we close our eyes, can conjure an image of the actor Harrison Ford. But that doesn't mean we can describe him well. To do so requires some hard looking, some deep thinking, and some careful crafting. Dave Kehr, in *The New York Times*, did all three:

> If America had a face, it would be Harrison Ford's. It is a comfortable, creased, familiar face, a face of no particular ethnicity (Mr. Ford's father was of Irish Catholic descent, his mother Russian Jewish) and no particular region (Mr. Ford grew up in Park Ridge, Ill., a nondescript, middle-class suburb of Chicago). It is the face of someone you know and always have known—a solid, stalwart person, someone who can be relied on to do a good job, to be a good husband, to bring up good kids. It's a face for cereal boxes and dollar bills, the face of someone you would select, as Mr. Ford was recently, to read excerpts from the Declaration of Independence during the national broadcast of Macy's Fourth of July fireworks.
>
> But there's something else in that face—something in the eyes that's fearful and easily hurt, something in the off-angled mouth that's sardonic, even a bit cruel. The disarming, boyish smile shades into a sneer with only the tiniest twist of a facial muscle.

Kehr starts with the generic noun *face,* but he also gives us very specific ethnicity (Irish Catholic, Russian Jewish) and geography (Park Ridge, Illinois). This is the face of "a solid, stalwart person"—a good husband and a good father. Then the concrete nouns give way to one idea after another: we get fear, hurt, sardonicism, cruelty, and a sneer.

This is what great character descriptions do: they give us precise information as well as ideas, physical traits as well as psychological ones, and sometimes the psychological embedded in the physical.

IN CRAFTING SCENES, MANY writers make the mistake of loading up adjectives. But nouns can do the detail work, too. They name particulars of a place or culture. In his memoir of his years in the U.S. Air Force, *Burning the Days*, James Salter goes far beyond the generic "West Point cadet's uniform," offering his reader hard-as-metal nouns that add up to an anthropology of military culture:

> For parade and inspections we wore eighteenth-century **accessories**, crossed white **belts** and dummy **cartridge box**, with **breastplate** and **belt buckle** shined to a mirrorlike **finish**. In the doorway of the room at night, before taps, we sat feverishly polishing them. **Pencil erasers** and **jeweler's rouge** were used to painstakingly rub away small **imperfections**, and the rest was done with a constantly re-folded **polishing cloth**. It took hours. The terrible **ring** of **metal** on the floor—a **breastplate** that had slipped from someone's hand—was like the dropping of an **heirloom**.

Salter gives us not just the glimmering "breastplate and belt buckle," but the "pencil erasers" and "jeweler's rouge" that burnish them. And in one noun—"heirloom"—he conveys an entire centuries-old legacy.

Half a world away—in more ways than one—is the world described by the Indian writer Arundhati Roy in *The God of Small Things*:

> **May** in **Ayemenem** is a hot, brooding **month**. The **days** are long and humid. The **river** shrinks and black **crows** gorge on bright **mangoes** in still, **dustgreen trees**. **Red bananas** ripen. **Jackfruits** burst. Dissolute **bluebottles** hum vacuously in the fruity **air**. Then they stun themselves against clear **windowpanes** and die, fatly baffled in the **sun**.
>
> The **nights** are clear, but suffused with **sloth** and sullen **expectation**.

Of course, Roy uses adjectives along with the nouns, but she grounds us in a specific time and place (*May, Ayemenem*) and she fills the scene with concrete things (*crows, mangoes, dustgreen trees, red bananas, jackfruits, bluebottles*). She also uses nouns to give us big ideas (*sloth* and *expectation*).

Cardinal Sins

Nouns were big in Gregory the Great's *Moralia,* which first warned people at the end of the sixth century of the dangers of Pride, Envy, Anger, Lust, Gluttony, Covetousness, and Sloth. Lurking in more contemporary texts are the seven deadly sins committed with nouns: Sloth, Fog, Gluttony, Gobbledygook, Jargon, Pride, and Euphemism. We can simplify that list into five broad categories: Imprecision, Abstraction, Groupspeak, Pretense, and Euphemism.

IMPRECISION

If you can't be bothered to look up a word in a dictionary, pick up a thesaurus, or spend time mulling the perfect word, you are not a prose stylist. You are a hack. Writerly "sloth" means grabbing the closest shop-worn words without a glimmer of guilt, or creating ugly nouns out of other nouns, verbs, or even inelegant suffixes. "Fog" can be translated as "terminal vagueness." And "gluttony" means that you load up on empty verbal calories instead of insisting on linguistic flavor and nutrition.

Remember, concrete nouns are the stuff of precise images and vivid sentences. They animate nursery rhymes (*Two little blackbirds sitting on a hill*) and adult poetry (*Two roads diverged in a yellow wood*). But writers sometimes forget that the primary role of nouns is to paint a clear picture. Instead, they pile up vague nouns (*domicile, abode,* or *residence* instead of *bungalow*). Lazy writers leave us clueless as to the individual nature of the people, places, things, or ideas they are writing about.

Clichés—trite phrases blanched of meaning by overuse—also signal sloth. They may start life as vivid metaphors. Whoever uttered "It's raining cats and dogs" for the first time found a catchy way to convey anarchy in the sky. Shakespeare's *green-eyed jealousy* must have been brilliant the first time it was uttered in the Globe, but "green with envy" has gone around the Anglophone globe so many times it's lost all color. In today's magazines (*Wired* being one of them), "Holy Grail" is a favorite. The problem is, it's more medieval than modern.

Political clichés often start as plays on words, then become stale:

Watergate was the name of an apartment complex and a political scandal that started there; Billygate was a decent shorthand for Jimmy Carter's brother problems; but after Nannygate, Troopergate, and Tasergate, the wordplay had no play left in it. Some political clichés don't even have bragging rights as metaphors. "Flip-flopping" stopped being clever after the 2004 Bush-Kerry campaign; after the 2012 Obama-Romney race, we should send *offshoring* offshore.

Watch out for the mindless slapping together of prefixes on prefixes, suffixes on suffixes—don't create clunkers like *disintermediation, decentralization, effectualization, finalization, scrutinization,* and that horrid replacement for "use," *utilization*. Enough with the suffix cut-and-paste acts.

Sometimes the culprits are conventions that we use without thinking. Go no farther than the nearest business memo to find these hollow organization men: *your consideration of this matter, the aforementioned point,* and the corporate secretary's favorite, *the above-referenced matter.*

Here's another example from the business world that a slothful writer might not think to question:

> Work in a consulting relationship with internal and external customers to decompose complex business problems and create information and education products.

Use concrete nouns, or your prose might decompose. We could recompose that sentence to read *We'll work with you and your customers to solve business problems and create new products.*

Some companies seem to be in the business of manufacturing fog: GreenTree Nutrition, Inc., called its Web site hawking health news, diet tips, and vitamins "a business model focused on content-enabled commerce"; a press release the company put out bragged about the "deep Internet and nutraceutical industry knowledge" of its investors and called its site the "wellness hub people will come to for its deep, consumer-focused content and brand-agnostic wellness product superstore." That sentence could send even the healthy running for aspirin.

Don't be lazy. Work to find the precise concrete noun.

ABSTRACTION

Abstraction often rises from a kind of gluttony: the word gourmand's urge to use five words where one would do. Gluttons yammer about "adverse climatic conditions" instead of calling bad weather just that; rain is *rain,* not "precipitation activity" or "a thunderstorm probability situation." "The phenomenon of an economic crisis" should be trimmed to, simply, *recession.* Its opposite, "Increased labor market participation rates," just means *more people working again.*

Abstractions like *condition, precipitation,* and *phenomenon* are set-ups. Beware of Greek- and Latin-based words, especially those ending in *-ion.* Don't be tempted to prettify a blunt noun like "a drunk" with a staggering noun phrase like "a person in an intoxicated condition." Other words that lead to waterlogged phrases include *case, character, degree, element, instance, kind, nature,* and *persuasion.* These will lead you to roundabout prepositional phrases instead of straight nouns and verbs:

- "His complaints are of a very far-reaching character." (*His complaints ranged from leaky faucets to noises in his head.*)
- "Voters showed a greater degree of interest in the electoral process this year." (*Citizens voted in droves.*)
- "The wages will be low owing to the unremunerative nature of the work." (*You're a teacher? Don't expect to get rich.*)
- "People of the artistic persuasion require an exceptional degree of autonomy." (*Artists need freedom.*)

The tendency to use a pileup of abstract nouns when one or two concrete ones would do is especially strong in government. A Marine Corps officer who works in the Pentagon wrote me about working on a document intended to give soldiers strategic guidance. Its title: "Global Force Management Implementation Guidance." (Unfortunately, the content was classified, so I couldn't help him defog even that title.)

Sometimes abstraction comes in the form of redundant pairs. "Efficiency and effectiveness" is a favorite of business book authors, who argue that the words mean different things but often use them reflexively. Ditto "attitude and mindset." Such redundancy is common in academic writing, like a history tome that uses "crisis and instability," "networks of the wealthy and influential," and "an affluent lifestyle and a certain level of conspicuous consumption." Can you spot the redundancies there?

GROUPSPEAK

Will we ever forgive Warren G. Harding for taking the perfectly good noun *normality* and perverting it into *normalcy*? Of course, taking a perfectly good noun and mangling it didn't start or end with Harding. Soon words like this become common and people stop to even question them. Groupspeak might mean "gobbledygook," "bureaucratese," or "jargon"—but it's all goop.

A New York State fire officer who wrote this monthly progress report clearly wasn't in a rush to put out any flames:

> Heavy rains throughout most of the State have given an optimistic outlook for lessened fire danger for the rest of the season. However, an abundance of lightning maintains a certain amount of hazard in isolated areas that have not received an excessive amount of rain. We were pleased to have been able to help Nevada with the suppression of their conflagration.

That paragraph was quoted in the Bureau of Land Management's *Gobbledygook Has Gotta Go*. Look how easy it is to edit it down to plain talk and add a few strong nouns and verbs:

> Heavy rains throughout most of the State have ~~given an optimistic outlook for~~ lessened fire danger for the rest of the season. However, ~~an abundance of~~ lightning ~~maintains a certain amount of hazard in~~ **threatens** isolated **dry** areas. ~~that have not received an excessive amount of rain.~~ We were pleased to help ~~have been able to~~ Nevada **fight their fires**. ~~with the suppression of their conflagration.~~

Sometimes we load up on so many nouns that we end up with writing that is all empty carbohydrates—just Wonder Bread. A year is "twelve calendar months," orders are "directives," down payments are "capitalized cost reductions," and a weapons wonk is "a specialist in arms control and security issues."

Bureaucratese gives us sentences like this, from a government memo:

> Consistent with such a strategy should be a commitment from the Federal Government for comprehensive planning.

Who's the doer in that sentence? The Feds, right? What's the action buried in nouns like *commitment* and *planning*? The sentence is just trying to say *The Federal Government should support comprehensive planning*. Lean words focus a sentence on its drama and give us the chance for cleaner rhythms. With fewer syllabic stumbling blocks, sentences are easier to say or read.

Public officials have periodically launched campaigns to eradicate gobbledygook. Jimmy Carter called for "keeping it simple" in 1978; Bill Clinton signed a similar executive order twenty years later. Things got so bad at the Justice Department in the early nineties that Attorney General Janet Reno urged the nation's lawyers to find "small, old words that all people understand—words like 'right' and 'wrong' and 'justice.'"

Nevertheless, in 2006, U.S. Attorney General Alberto Gonzales appeared before the Senate Judiciary Committee and forgot simplicity. When Senator Edward Kennedy pressed him for specific reasons why seven U.S. attorneys were fired on December 7, 2006, Gonzales said:

> Senator, I have in my mind a recollection as to knowing as to some of these United States attorneys. There are two that I do not recall knowing in my mind what I understood to be the reasons for the removal.

Here's how Gonzales might have answered: "Senator, I believe I knew the reasons for some of the firings. For two of them, I had no idea."

RENO AND OTHERS MAY be fighting an uphill battle in taming the Justice Department, but they'd need to clone themselves five times over to police the language in the national bar association. Like other professionals, lawyers rely on jargon—agreed-upon argot and technical lingo. A staple of every work conversation, jargon makes for a shorthand that lets professionals banter precisely and efficiently. Lawyers' terms like *plaintiff*, *ex parte*, *hearsay*, *felony*, *prima facie*, and *habeas corpus* are, indeed, precise. But what about all those *aforesaids*, *hereofs*, and *hereinafters*? That's not just jargon. It's junk. Legalese.

Is it necessary to say "Now comes the above named John Doe, plaintiff herein, by and through Smith & Jones, his attorneys of record, and shows unto this Honorable Court as follows . . ."? Why not just "The plaintiff complains that . . ."?

Similarly, why write "I have received your letter and thank you for the information contained therein" when "Thank you for your letter" does the job?

A parody in a lawyers' magazine once launched the story of "Jack and the Beanstalk" like this: "Once on or about a time, there was a minor named John or 'Jack' (as he will hereinafter be designated), other name or names to your relator unknown."

When it comes to impenetrability, legal writing is only the most notorious. Doctors, dictators, seamen, CEOs—they've all got their own jargon and they should all avoid it when trying to communicate with clients or write for the lay public. As Steve Mirsky points out in *Scientific American*, the doctors with "bedside manner" know that a gift for the vernacular helps them communicate with patients—and write memorably about their field. The term *tennis elbow* beats *lateral epicondylitis* in a piece intended for general readership. *Chauffeur's fracture* sticks better than *a break to the radial styloid*—even if it means explaining that the name for this wrist injury pays homage to those drivers of old who hurt themselves turning a hand crank to rev up the Studebaker.

PRETENSE

Is it powermongering? Is it insecurity? Is it arrogance? Why do so many professors and professionals resort to pompous, ponderous, or just imponderable nouns?

The worst offenders are surely academics—and they're the ones teaching students how to write! Just try to decipher this beaut from Eric Voegelin's *The New Science of Politics*:

> The problems of an eidos in history, hence, arises only when Christian transcendental fulfillment becomes immanentized. Such an immanentist hypostasis of the eschaton, however, is a theoretical fallacy.

Did you catch the subject-verb disagreement there? (Problems . . . arises?) Even Voegelin lost track of his point!

And here's the Russian poet and Dante scholar Osip Mandelstam, quoted in *The Guardian*, writing about *The Divine Comedy*:

> . . . in its most densely foliated aspect is oriented toward authority, it is most densely rustling, most concertante just when it is caressed by dogma, by canon, by the firm chrysostomatic word. But the whole trouble is that in authority—or, to put it more precisely, in authoritarianism—we see only insurance against error, and we fail to perceive anything in that grandiose music of trustfulness, of trust, in the nuances—delicate as an alpine rainbow—of probability and conviction, which Dante has at his command.

Now, perhaps we should blame Mandelstam's translator, but I suspect the original contains impenetrable language even to speakers of Russian. The most absurdly ridiculous abstract noun in that paragraph is *chrysostomatic*. If you can find it in a dictionary, you'll see that it means "eloquent"—something the paragraph certainly isn't.

If such language stayed in the Ivory Tower it might not be such a worry. But academic writing is on the creep. That may be because many of us learn to write in English and history classes, where we get points for speaking in abstractions and using "dictionary" words. Perhaps this is why so many professionals co-opt the professors' tricks (or tics).

If you're not sure which words will get you labeled "pretentious," check out Pompous Ass Words, a Web site dedicated to identifying words that will make you sound like a pompous ass. Dan Fejes and others track highfalutin words they come across in news stories and must look up in the dictionary—only to find that they have put down their reading for a word that was chosen for no purpose other than to befuddle them. In each case, the obscure word means little or nothing more than what another legitimate, common word means. For example, *tendentious* could be replaced with *biased* without a loss of meaning. Or *puissant* with *powerful*. Or *risible* with *laughable*.

In a book by an author whose literary brand screams "cool adventure jock," it's strange to see a word like *casuistry*, which means "rationalization." But there it is, in Jon Krakauer's *Under the Banner of Heaven*:

When this casuistry came to light, it unleashed a nationwide howl of indignation.

There's a time and a place for ornate language. Pretense results when a writer preoccupied with his or her own diction loses sight of the primary goal: communicating with an audience. Whenever you've got a choice, go with the plain talk.

EUPHEMISM

Discretion is indeed the better part of valor, and civility and tact are certainly worth cultivating. We have all experienced the compassionate desire to address unbearable pain or embarrassment—the death of a beloved, say, or a distressing medical condition—without causing someone else even more pain and embarrassment.

Euphemisms (descriptions of unpleasant behavior through more pleasant terms) are the province of people who want to soften something harsh—whether an untimely death (Lucille Ball's "pushing up daisies"), a tasteless publicity stunt (Justin Timberlake's "wardrobe malfunction"), or a politician's peccadillo (South Carolina governor Mark Sanford's "hiking the Appalachian trail"). But euphemisms don't make for powerful prose.

Pushing up daisies

I'm generally anti-euphemism, but they can be funny, especially when they involve wit or metaphor. "What are your favorite euphemisms for death?" I once asked my Facebook friends. The writers among them replied:

My uncle, the late Beverly Hills attorney Simon Taub, and others in LA always said "took a cab" for "died." (Arthur Plotnik)

I remember a book where the grandmother used to say "When I take off" in referring to her death. I always loved that and imagined her peeling out in a VW bus, though maybe it's not what you're looking for." (Leslie Lang)

Tommy Lee Jones's character, Deputy Marshal Samuel Gerard, says in *The Fugitive,* about Harrison Ford's Dr. Richard Kimble, "The guy did a Peter Pan right off of this dam, right here." (Nancy Devine)

Poignancy comes when writers cut to the unvarnished truth. "Political language is designed to make lies sound truthful and murder respectable, and to give an appearance of solidity to pure wind," wrote George Orwell in "Politics and the English Language." Orwell could do little to discourage the powers that be from substituting mild expressions for harsh ones, though. An air attaché at the U.S. embassy in Phnom Penh once admonished reporters: "You always write it's bombing, bombing, bombing. It's not bombing. It's air support." In the 1980s, Ronald Reagan dubbed the MX missile the "Peacekeeper," in hopes of making the nuclear weapon more palatable. President George W. Bush preferred "weapons of mass destruction."

Such euphemism isn't reserved for arms, obviously. In 2008, President Bush won the Doublespeak Award from the National Council of Teachers of English for using the term "aspirational goal" in place of a *deadline* for withdrawal of troops from Iraq. Likewise, members of the Asia Pacific Economic Cooperation forum and others have set "aspirational goals" for reducing carbon emissions and slowing global warming. (Aspirations and goals are the same thing; yet combined, the terms cancel each other out, producing a phrase that means, in effect, a goal to which one does not aspire *all that much*.)

Even salesmen in this age of telemarketing wrap themselves in euphemisms: the Willy Lomans of yesteryear are now *advisers, associates, specialists,* or *consultants.* At Comcast, they are *customer service representatives,* and at United Airlines, *employee owners.* Speaking of airlines, have you noticed how filled with euphemism airlinespeak is? Nothing is free, but everything is "complimentary." Instructions are "friendly reminders." Your buoyant cushion is "a flotation device."

In the corporate world, euphemism allows boardroom bullies to call massive firings *layoffs, downsizing, rightsizing,* and *reshaping.* In the fall of 2011, Bank of America chief executive Brian T. Moynihan called the company's executive shake-ups part of a "delayering" process. Such euphemism is merely a cowardly attempt by bosses to pass the buck in the firing process, a code way of saying "Blame the organization, not me!"

It's hardly new: Digital Equipment Corporation once resorted to the ridiculous "involuntary methodologies." One plant shutdown at General Motors was a "volume-related production-schedule adjustment." And when game maker Milton Bradley closed a Scrabble plant in Fairfax, Vermont, a spokesman for Hasbro, the corporate parent, made this statement:

> This is all part of our global improvement product enhancement program.

That five-word euphemism is as big a blank as a Scrabble tile without a letter.

Carnal Pleasures

Lest you still think nouns are too crisp and concrete to have fun with, let's look at the creative mischief we can make with them.

The online world is full of writers who flout the rules and flaunt their wit, starting with the denizens of Twitter. Picking a Twitter handle and writing a 140-character profile may not seem like a literary adventure, but some writers treat these tasks as exercises in flexing their noun muscles. Take these, for example:

@geminiwrites:

Freelance editor. Writer. Native NYer missing home. Published a little. Anglophile, oenophile, lifeophile. Hashtag addict and all-around short & funny person.

@siskanna:

Writer; dreamer; teacher; professor; runner; sister; daughter; mother; lover; friend; seeker; star gazer; chicken-soup-maker.

A Twitter handle is like a personal brand name, and the subversive spellings are mimicked elsewhere in social media. Vowels are dropped (*Tumblr*), consonants are doubled (*Digg*), and words are pinned together with abandon (*Pinterest*). According to the linguist and naming expert Christopher Johnson, in *Microstyle,* professional brand makers become adept at misspelling nouns, which makes it easier to register and protect a name as a trademark as well as to search for it online.

But say you aren't satisfied with 140-character posts. Say you have a more serious purpose. You want to write something that lasts. Where do nouns fit in?

In 1839, Henry David Thoreau made a trip with his brother, John, along two New England rivers. He recorded what he saw, mixing detailed description with poetic citations as well as reflections on the relationship of man and nature. *A Week on the Concord and Merrimack Rivers* became his first book. On a Sunday morning on the Concord River, Thoreau compares the waterway with "a long woodland lake bordered with willows," then focuses on a dense palisade of bulrushes, the climbing mikania, and "the balls of the button-bush." Then he zeroes in on the water willow, *Salix purshiana*, "the most graceful and ethereal of our trees":

> Its masses of light green foliage, piled one upon another to the height of twenty or thirty feet, seemed to float on the surface of the water, while the slight gray stems and the shore were hardly visible between them. No tree is so wedded to the water, and harmonizes so well with still streams. It is even more graceful than the weeping willow, or any pendulous trees, which dip their branches in the stream instead of being buoyed up by it. Its limbs curved outward over the surface as if attracted by it. It had not a New England but an Oriental character, reminding us of trim Persian gardens, of Haroun Alraschid, and the artificial lakes of the East.

Thoreau notes a "want of harmony" as he and his brother pass through a series of canals leading to the Merrimack. But, he notes:

> Nature will recover and indemnify herself, and gradually plant fit shrubs and flowers along its borders. Already the kingfisher sat upon a pine over the water, and the bream and pickerel swam below. Thus all works pass directly out of the hands of the architect into the hands of Nature, to be perfected.

More than 150 years later, in 2002, John McPhee decided to repeat the brothers' trip. He and a college roommate followed the same journey, and McPhee turned his eyes upon the landscape recorded by Thoreau. At times, McPhee's description of the Concord is as attuned to nature as is the transcendentalist's description:

> Blue herons lined it like gargoyles. Who knows what pious thoughts they were thinking. Like the Thoreaus' dory, our canoe moved through

flat-calm water that reflected the surrounding world. . . . The water we rudely broke with our paddles was clear as the air and the reflection.

Then McPhee shifts, using an entirely different palette to describe how the "hands of the architect" have transformed the riverscape. The ethereal grace of nature competes with the brand-name bounty of capitalism:

Where the brothers entered the Merrimack, whatever is left of the three locks that took them down to the river is buried beside Advance Auto Parts, 1-800-Rent-a-Car, the Tandoori Grill, and the Asian Pacific Buffet. The remains are under the sterling warehouse for North American Van Lines, and the rails of the Boston & Maine. Across Broadway from all those historic places is Hadley Field, with its baseball diamond, its skateboard park, and its low stone marker as the route of the Middlesex Canal. Coming through the park, the canal went right through the warehouse and stair-stepped down to the river.

Catechism

BERRY GOOD NOUNS: Remember Mark Twain's "potted geraniums"? And Jo Ann Beard's "pink geraniums grow[ing] like earrings on either side of the porch"? Nouns give shape to ideas, heft to sentences. It's worth taking the time to get them right. It may seem old-fashioned, or just tedious, to work with a dictionary and a thesaurus at your side, but this is part of the practice of writing. Working with word books strengthens our imaginative muscles, and in turn strengthens our own mental thesauruses, our ability to call up precise words.

Take a common noun like *fruit*. How many more specific synonyms can you come up with? Is one of them *berry*? Can you do even better than that? List as many different kinds of berries as you can, using your mental thesaurus. When you've run out, go to a literal thesaurus. How many more did you get? Now consult http://hotword.dictionary.com/berries, and prepare to be berry impressed. (It listed ninety-eight different kinds of berries the day I looked.)

SURFACE ENERGY: The first step in learning how to write evocative scenes is to increase your powers of observation. First, really look. Then start taking notes. Write down everything. Draw shapes. Note colors. Find new, more precise words. Notice the detail Thomas Pynchon squeezes into a one-paragraph description of Lt. Tyrone Slothrop's desk, early in *Gravity's Rainbow*:

> It hasn't been cleaned down to the original wood surface since 1942. Things have fallen roughly into layers, over a base of bureaucratic smegma that sifts steadily to the bottom, made up of millions of tiny red and brown curls of rubber eraser, pencil shavings, dried tea or coffee stains, traces of sugar and Household Milk, much cigarette ash, very fine black debris picked and flung from typewriter ribbons, decomposing library paste, broken aspirins ground to powder. Then comes a scatter of paperclips, Zippo flints, rubber bands, staples, cigarette butts and crumpled packs, stray matches, pins, nubs of pens, stubs of pencils of all colors including the hard-to-get heliotrope and raw umber, wooden coffee spoons, Thayer's Slippery Elm Throat Lozenges sent by Slothrop's mother, Nalline, all the way from Massachusetts, bits of tape, string, chalk . . . above that a layer of forgotten memoranda, empty buff ration books, phone numbers, unanswered letters, tattered sheets of carbon paper, the scribbled ukulele chords to a dozen songs including "Jonny Doughboy Found a Rose in Ireland."

Pynchon's description goes on for another 164 words. Your own desk might not be such a "godawful mess" (his words), but look at it closely and describe what you see. Make your description more than a mere catalog.

SEE, SEEING, SCENE: Reread the scenes early in this chapter—Paul Theroux's bus ride in Turkey, James Salter's hall at West Point, Arundhati Roy's landscape in Ayemenem. Go sit somewhere distinctive—a favorite garden, a cathedral, or even a grungy inner-city laundromat—and notice what is special or evocative about the place. Use concrete, vivid nouns to paint a picture of the scene. Carefully choose a few idea/feeling/abstraction nouns to convey what makes the place unusual. Is it a microcosm of something larger?

TRANSCENDENTAL TIME: Find a historical description of a particular place in your city, town, or county. Retrace the author's steps. Write your own description of the place as it is today, using the original as a starting point but letting John McPhee inspire you to see the essence of the place today.

CHAPTER 2

Pronouns

Bones

Pronouns are proxies for nouns. They stand in willingly when nouns don't want to hang around sounding repetitive. The noun (or noun phrase), whose bidding the pronoun does, is called the *antecedent*—because it goes (*ced-*) before (*ante-*) the pronoun in the sentence or paragraph.

Unlike nouns, a class of words that is forever morphing and mutating, the list of pronouns is finite and predictable, subdividing neatly and changed only slightly since the days of Shakespeare:

- Personal pronouns might be the subject of a sentence (*I, you, he, she, it, we, they*) or the object (*me, you, him, it, us, them*): "I come to bury Caesar, not to praise *him*." Certain personal pronouns (*my, your, his, her, its, our, their*) act as adjectives, since in indicating possession they modify nouns: "Friends, Romans, countrymen, lend me *your* ears."
- Demonstrative pronouns (*this, that, these, those*) direct attention to another word or phrase. They can be nouns: "*This* was the most unkindest cut of all." They can be adjectives: "If we do meet again, why, we shall smile; / If not, why then, *this* parting was well made."

- Relative pronouns (*that, what, whatever, which, whichever, who, whoever, whom, whomever, whose*) introduce a clause that wants to hitch itself firmly to its antecedent: "The evil *that* men do lives after them." The antecedent can be a noun, a phrase, a clause, or a sentence, as in "Let but the Commons hear this testament / *Which*, pardon me, I do not mean to read." Sometimes the antecedent is even a whole paragraph.

- Indefinite pronouns (*all, another, any, anybody, anything, both, each, either, every, everybody, everyone, everything, few, many, most, much, neither, no one, nobody, none, one, several, some, somebody, someone, something, such*) also stand in for people or things, but not necessarily ones specifically named by an antecedent: "If *any*, speak; for him have I offended." Indefinite pronouns move around sentences with abandon and can also play the role of adjectives. (Take care to see indefinite pronouns for what they are, because they make subject-verb agreement quite dicey.)

- Interrogative pronouns (*what, which, who, whom, whose*) kick off questions: "*What* withholds you then to mourn for him?" (That's a slight cheat to show you an interrogative pronoun.)

- Expletive pronouns (*it, there*) are less profane than they sound, stepping into a sentence as subject when the juice of the sentence lurks in the predicate: "*There* is no terror, Cassius, in your threats."

- Reflexive pronouns (*myself, yourself, himself, herself, itself, ourselves, yourselves, themselves*) allow a person or thing to be both the subject and the object of a sentence ("I have o'ershot *myself* to tell you of [Caesar's will]") or add emphasis (Marc Antony *himself* didn't need emphasis in his famous speech. That should tell you something).

I tweet, you tweet, we all tweet

The Tweeted Haiku Contest on National Grammar Day 2012 turned up some pretty funny 5-7-5 poems. My personal favorite, tweeted by Rachel Cooper (@RachelCooper_NS), dealt with pronouns:

First person: I love.
Second person: You love me.
Third person: Uh, oh.

Some caveats about classes of pronouns: First, though you should generally avoid reflexive pronouns, sometimes they are necessary for clarity, distinguishing, for example, in the following non-Shakespearean sentence, between two possible antecedents (May and April): "As May sashayed through the yard, April wondered whether she **herself** would ever again have the upper hand." But novices most often use reflexive pronouns when a personal pronoun would be simpler and more elegant (not to mention more correct): "Jim and **myself**, however, were holding out for June" is hardly a studly sentence; June would prefer "Jim and I."

Second, indefinite pronouns give us special trouble, since it isn't always clear which ones are singular and which are plural. *Each*, for example, is singular. *Both* is plural. *None*, though, can be either. We'll discuss this more in chapter 9, when knowing the nature of indefinite pronouns becomes key to enabling subjects and verbs to dance together as beautifully as Ginger Rogers and Fred Astaire.

WHOMDUNIT

Relative pronouns, too, can be perennially confusing. We'll punt on the difference between *that* and *which*, returning to it in chapter 11. That leaves *who* and *whom*. When faced with a two-pronged attack from these troublesome fraternal twins, most people start waving the white flag. If they toughed it out, though, they'd learn how easy it is to conquer these pronouns. Use *who* when the pronoun is acting as a subject (*Who is it?*) and *whom* when it is acting as an object (in *For Whom the Bell Tolls,* the pronoun is the object of the preposition *for*).

We'll get back to *who* and *whom* in chapter 10, but to tide you over, take these tips:

- Use *who* whenever the verb form that follows could be wrapped in parentheses without changing the sentence: "the explorer who (he believed) had been up the mountain."
- "Oprah knew he?" sounds silly; "Oprah knew who?" should, too. Replace *he* with *him* and *who* with *whom.*
- Go ahead and use *who* when the pronoun starts the sentence: "Who do you love?" sounds more natural to many people than "Whom do you love?"

That last tip is going to give strict grammarians hives. To tell the truth, I continue to use *whom* for objects, even when they are standing where we expect subjects to be (*Whom do you love?*). But *whom* can sound overly formal at the beginning of a sentence, so for a more colloquial tone, even this grammar diva will sing her tune with *who.*

Pronouns may seem puny next to their heftier noun and adjective kin, and some writers might initially view them as too homely to put much faith in. But sometimes their very simplicity is their strength. The choice of an *I* or a *you* can affect the feeling of a passage. In his 1962 cover of the bluesy standard "Corrina, Corrina," Bob Dylan tells the story of longing using the first person singular:

> **I** got a bird that whistles
> **I** got a bird that sings
> But **I** ain' a-got Corrina
> Life don't mean a thing

But when it came to the 1964 protest anthem "The Times They Are A-Changin'," Dylan relied on the second person *you*. The singer is talking to you, the listener:

Come gather 'round people
Wherever **you** roam
And admit that the waters
Around **you** have grown

(The *you* is implied in the first and third lines, in which he is basically saying "You come gather 'round" and "You admit that the waters have grown.")

In "Hurricane," written in 1975 about the controversial murder conviction of the boxer Rubin "Hurricane" Carter, Dylan uses the third person *he*:

Here comes the story of the Hurricane
The man the authorities came to blame
For somethin' that **he** never done
Put in a prison cell, but one time **he** could-a been
The champion of the world

If in the first example, the singer is crooning about himself, and in the second he is addressing the listener, in the third he is talking about someone else entirely: Hurricane.

Flesh

Pronouns keep style succinct, allowing us to skirt the needless repetition of other words. In prose as in folk songs, though, pronouns also establish the voice of the narrator. Balladeers, novelists, journalists, essayists—all must decide on a point of view for every story. The third person sets a more objective and hard-boiled tone, the first person one that is more up close and personal. The second person can slide from directly addressing the reader—even telling us what to do (as in Dylan's case)—to a hipper, more informal form used in playful advertising and jaunty journalism.

The third-person pronouns (*he, she, it, they*) allow the narrator to recede. In the most common point of view in fiction, the *third person omniscient,* the author is allowed to see into the heads of characters and to relay their thoughts to readers without necessarily being a character in the story. (Here's an example from *Bring Up the Bodies* by Hilary Mantel: "Thomas Cromwell is now about fifty years old. He has a labourer's body, stocky, useful, running to fat.") In the close third person, the narrator is inside the head of one character only, relaying his thoughts or feelings. (From the same novel: "If he had any feeling for her, he cannot find traces of it now.")

In nonfiction, the third-person point of view is not so much *omniscient* as *objective.* It's the preferred point of view for reports and research papers. It's also best for business correspondence, brochures, and letters on behalf of a group or institution. See how a slight shift in point of view creates enough of a difference to raise eyebrows over the second of these two sentences: "Victoria's Secret would like to offer you a discount on all bras and panties." (Nice, impersonal third person as subject.) "I would like to offer you a discount on all bras and panties." (Yikes, the subject shifts and lascivious fingers reach out from the page.)

Unabashed subjectivity may be fine for ever-popular memoirs on alcoholic escapades and inside-the-Beltway intrigue, but the third-person point of view remains the standard for news reporting, partly because it keeps the focus on the subject, not the writer. The following Associated Press report, dictated in 1957 by Relman Morin from a phone booth across from Little Rock's Central High School, shows how a restrained narrator can foreground the power and emotion of an event:

> The eight Negroes—the three boys and five girls—were crossing the schoolyard toward a side door at the south end of the school. The girls were in bobby socks and the boys were dressed in shirts open at the neck.
>
> They were not running, not even walking fast. They simply strolled toward the steps, went up and were inside before all but a few of the 200 people at the end of the street knew it.
>
> "They've gone in," a man roared. "Oh, God, the niggers are in the school."

The passage is also powerful for the way it shifts from focusing on individuals through nouns (eight Negroes, boys and girls) to a less personal pronoun, *they,* and the dehumanizing racist utterance.

A final third-person pronoun deserves mention: *one.* This is the most removed of all the personal pronouns, and it can work as an all-purpose replacement regardless of whether the antecedent is male or female. When I asked some writers what they thought of this sometimes starchy alternative, a colleague wrote back, "When one can keep things simple, one should do so." But then she confessed, "I grew up in England, where it's used all the time, and the culture is more formal, so it doesn't sound pretentious." And that is indeed the danger of *one*—it can sound pompous when compared with alternatives like the colloquial *you* or the inclusive *we,* as in "When we can keep things simple, we should."

YOURS, MINE, OR OURS

In certain situations, the first-person point of view comes most naturally and lets the narrator be an integral part of the story. Sometimes you need to loosen your tie and get personal. In a 1976 address at the University of California, Berkeley, called "Why I Write," Joan Didion made a persuasive case for the first person:

> Of course I stole the title for this talk from George Orwell. One reason I stole it was that I like the sound of the words: *Why I Write.* There you have three short unambiguous words that share a sound, and the sound they share is this:
>
> I
>
> I
>
> I
>
> In many ways writing is the act of saying *I,* of imposing oneself upon other people, of saying *listen to me, see it my way, change your mind.* It's an aggressive, even a hostile act. You can disguise its aggres-

siveness all you want with veils of subordinate clauses and qualifiers and tentative subjunctives, with ellipses and evasion—with the whole manner of intimating rather than claiming, of alluding rather than stating—but there's no getting around the fact that setting words on paper is the tactic of a secret bully, an invasion, an imposition of the writer's sensibility on the reader's most private space.

In her essays, Didion packs her reporting with acute—and indispensable—personal observation, and she uses the self as a mirror on the times. In the title essay of *The White Album,* Didion recalls a period—between 1966 and 1971—when, she says, she "began to doubt the premises of all the stories I had ever told myself, a common condition but one I found troubling."

Didion does not use the first person because it's easy, nor does she use it out of a rampantly narcissistic need to write about herself. She puts herself into service to explore a subject very much outside herself: the summer of 1968:

During those five years I appeared, on the face of it, a competent enough member of some community or another, a signer of contracts and Air Travel cards, a citizen: I wrote a couple of times a month for one magazine or another, published two books, worked on several motion pictures; participated in the paranoia of the time, in the raising of a small child, and in the entertainment of large numbers of people passing through my house. . . . It was a time of my life when I was frequently "named." I was named godmother to children. I was named lecturer and panelist, colloquist and conferee. I was even named, in 1968, a *Los Angeles Times* "Woman of the Year," along with Mrs. Ronald Reagan, the Olympic swimmer Debbie Meyer, and ten other California women who seemed to keep in touch and do good works. I did no good works but I tried to keep in touch. I was responsible. I recognized my name when I saw it. . . .

 I watched Robert Kennedy's funeral on a verandah at the Royal Hawaiian Hotel in Honolulu, and also the first reports from My Lai. I reread all of George Orwell on the Royal Hawaiian Beach, and I also read, in the papers that came one day late from the mainland, the story of Betty Lansdown Fouquet, a 26-year-old woman with faded blond hair who put her five-year-old daughter out to die on the center divider of Interstate 5 some miles south of the last Bakersfield exit. The child, whose fingers had to be pried loose from the Cyclone fence when she was rescued twelve hours later by the California Highway Patrol, reported that she had run after the car carrying her mother and stepfather and brother and sister for "a long time." Certain of these images did not fit into any narrative I knew.

As the essay continues, Didion includes a passage from a psychiatric report describing the results of tests administered shortly after she suffered an attack of vertigo and nausea and, she notes drily, shortly after she was named a *Los Angeles Times* "Woman of the Year." "By way of comment," she writes, "I offer only that an attack of vertigo and nausea does not now seem to me an inappropriate response to the summer of 1968." The first person in Didion's essay is not tantamount to writing as confessional; it is a way to link the schism in her own soul to the schism in society. It is an example of what Hemingway called writing "hard and clear about what hurts."

In poetry, the first-person point of view might fuel the unvarnished style of an Anne Sexton, whose poems record her battles with mental illness, or a Sharon Olds, whose most recent volume of poetry chronicles the year her husband of three decades leaves her for another woman.

The first person plural pronoun, *we,* is less aggressive than Didion's spearlike *I* and less soul-baring. After all, *we* includes the reader in the experience described. In *The Medusa and the Snail,* the physician Lewis Thomas reaches out to his reader by choosing this pronoun:

We are a spectacular, splendid manifestation of life. **We** have language. . . . **We** have affection. **We** have genes for usefulness, and usefulness is about as close to a "common goal of nature" as I can guess at. And finally, and perhaps best of all, **we** have music.

By extending his point of view from *I* (the author/physician) to *we* (all of us), Thomas broadens his subject from biology to the human condition.

It's rare to see the first person plural in fiction, but Suketu Mehta uses *we* to great effect in the short story "Gare du Nord":

> After **we** left the restaurant, **we** walked around outside the Gare du Nord. It was a Tuesday night, and **we** were the only people out, but **we** were in such good spirits that **we** were a crowd all by ourselves; **we** made the street feel inhabited. The buildings around the Gare du Nord are filled with immigrants; it is as if having come off the train from their distant homes, they were so exhausted by the journey that they put bag and baggage down in the first empty room they saw. It is not a pretty area, and the noise of trains and cars consumes the neighborhood from an early hour. But maybe what keeps the immigrants in the area is the knowledge that the first door to home is just there, in the station, two blocks away. The energy of travelers is comforting, for it makes **us** feel that the whole world, like **us**, is transient.

Mehta never actually reveals who the *we* is, though clearly it is less universal than Lewis Thomas's. At times *we* seems to refer to a couple, at times it refers to the entire expatriate community of Paris. It stands in for we and they, immigrant and traveler, those inside and those outside.

THE MORE MAJESTIC ME

The first person plural can also appear when a speaker means *I* but says *we*. The most sanctioned example of this is "the royal *we*," or *pluralis majestatis*. Don't be fooled by the Latin: the royal *we* has enjoyed popularity far beyond Rome by monarchs, popes, and even university rectors. The origin of this pronoun has been traced variously to 1169, when the English king Henry II used it to mean "God and I," and to King Richard I, whose use of the pronoun bolstered his claim to be acting in concert with the deity and to be the ruler by "divine right." A more recent example of the royal *we* would be Queen Victoria's oft-quoted "We are not amused."

It's amazing how easily politicians slide into the royal *we*, especially when they become presidential candidates, although in that case they usually mean not "God and I" but "my campaign and I." (When Margaret Thatcher went so far as to say "We have become a grandmother," though, she earned widespread guffaws.)

Editors or editorial columnists also use the royal *we* (calling it "the editorial *we*"), especially when expressing the opinion of a publication's powers that be. Science writers adopt the editorial *we* when stating a proven principal or theorem (as in Albert Einstein's "We are thus led also to a definition of 'time' in physics").

Sometimes even lowly writers can affect the authority, or the easy elegance, of the editorial *we*. Remember those "Talk of the Town" pieces in the old *New Yorker*? Lesser mortals—and writers not yet in *New Yorker* nirvana—might want to heed Mark Twain's advice, though: "Only presidents, editors, and people with tapeworms ought to have the right to use *we*."

THE COZIER YOU

The second person pronoun (*you*) lets the author hook the reader as if in conversation. Call it cozy. Call it confiding. *You* is a favorite of the Plain English folks, who view it as an antidote to the stiff impersonality of legalese and urge bureaucrats to write as if speaking to the public.

Pauline Kael, unlike most film critics of her time, frequently used the second person to enliven her reviews:

- From a review of *The French Connection*: "The panhandler in the movie who jostles the hero looks just like the one who jostles you as you leave the movie theatre."
- From a review of *Last Tango in Paris*: "It is a movie you can't get out of your system, and I think it will make some people very angry and disgust others."
- From a review of *Platoon*: "There are too many scenes where you think, It's a bit much. The movie crowds you; it doesn't give you room to have an honest emotion."

The second-person point of view gives Kael's reviews urgency and intimacy. (Fellow *New Yorker* writer Adam Gopnik called Kael's point of view the "complicitous" second person, explaining: "It wasn't her making all those judgments. It was the Pop Audience there beside her.")

The second-person point of view can also appear in literary journalism, as in Laura Fraser's *An Italian Affair*, which begins with her musing on the Italian phrase *Mi hai spaccato il cuore*:

> You're reading a fairy tale in your evening Italian class when you come across this phrase. You think you know what it means, since the sea princess says it after her one true love abandons her, but you ask the teacher anyway.
>
> "You have broken my heart," he says, and he makes a slashing motion diagonally across his dark blue sweater. "You have cloven it in two."
>
> *Mi hai spaccato il cuore.*
>
> The phrase plays over and over in your mind, and the words in front of you blur. You can see your husband's face with his dark, wild eyebrows, and you whisper the phrase to him, *Mi hai spaccato il cuore.* You say it to plead with him, to make him stay, and then you say it with heat, a wronged Sicilian fishwife with a dagger in her hand. But he doesn't understand, he doesn't speak Italian. . . .

Fraser is clearly playing with language and genre from the very first line. By using *you* instead of *I*, she includes us in her offbeat romantic escapade. (She also never names her paramour, using the archetypal *M.* instead.) A veteran journalist, Fraser says that the story came out in the second person with the quality of a fable. She was unused to writing in the first person at the time, she adds, and suspects that the second-person point of view probably helped her treat herself as a character. "I actually rewrote the entire thing in the first person," she says. "It didn't have the same feeling of being a fairy tale."

Jay McInerney used the second person in *Bright Lights, Big City*, implicating the reader (*you*) in the cocaine-fueled antics of the main character, Jamie ("**You** are not the kind of guy who would be at a place like this at this time of morning. But here **you** are, and **you** cannot say that the terrain is entirely unfamiliar, although the details are fuzzy. **You** are at a nightclub talking to a girl with a shaved head.")

But McInerney's novel points to the limits of the second person. The longer the work, the harder it is to carry off the second-person point of view. Using it might even provoke reader revolt: "Hey, dude, I have better sense than to cave to the Bolivian Marching Powder." As *Bright Lights, Big City* progresses and the novelty wears off, the reader identifies less and less with Jamie, and the second-person device comes to seem contrived and false; it's definitely Jamie, not *you,* who's self-destructing.

The second person is also capable of sliding from the informal and irreverent to the bossy, as in the imperative mood. In Henry James's *Portrait of a Lady,* the caring but consumptive Ralph Touchett is in love with his cousin, Isabel, the lady of the title. Unable to consummate his love, Ralph throws his remaining energy (and fortune) into helping her, and in a moment when Isabel is about to make a fateful decision, he resorts to the imperative·

> It's out of all reason, the number of things you think wrong. Put back your watch. Diet your fever. Spread your wings; rise above the ground. It's never wrong to do that.

Ralph is hardly an alpha type, but the imperative undergirds his command.

The bossy second person works for this character, but we're most likely to see it in ads, whether for Old Spice ("Smell like a man, man") or Levi's ("Go Forth"), or JetBlue ("Go to Jersey without the drama").

Taking advantage of pronouns as a literary device is not a light undertaking: when we choose a point of view, we must make sure it's *true*—appropriate to the story being told. Does the presence of the writer in the story add critical color, perspective, and insight? Or is *I* just evidence of a novice writer, or a little too much self-indulgence? Don't use pronouns to, in the words of the writer Jack Beatty, gratuitously drape your own attitudes over others "as if they were rhetorical tailor's dummies."

Cardinal Sins

EATING YOUR *ITS* AND *THEYS*

Remember, pronouns must agree with their antecedents in number, person, and gender. The most common pronoun-antecedent sin happens when writers use *they* instead of *it* in referring to a singular body.

Many writers defend pairing the plural *they* with a singular antecedent in the interest of gender neutrality. In our dim patriarchal past, the masculine pronoun *he* was routinely used to replace nouns like "the president," "the CEO," or "the entrepreneur." In the days of alpha businesswomen like Martha Stewart and Oprah Winfrey, *he* is a nonstarter.

But solving the problem by pasting in *they* or *them* just replaces the offensive with the objectionable—or even the inaccurate. Here are some horrible examples plucked from papers around the country:

- **He** or **she** who laughs loudest around the watercooler may not be who they say **they** are.
- Do **your child** a favor; teach **them** grammar.
- Our society has gotten to the point where **each person** does what's right in **their** own eyes.
- A **motorcyclist** has the right to decide if **they** want to wear a helmet.

No true wordsmith ever meets a sentence that can't be gracefully recast. Resist replacing *they* with *he/she*—real people don't speak in slashes. Try making the antecedent plural so that you can use *they* with impunity. Don't be afraid of an occasional *he or she,* awkward though it may be. Or take the ultimate judicious approach: some U.S. Supreme Court justices alternate between *he* and *she* when they write their decisions.

PRESIDENTIAL PRONOUNS

President Barack Obama may be a damn good rhetorician, but his use of one particular pronoun is damn bad. At a July 22, 2009, press conference, he waded into the Henry Louis Gates–Sergeant Crowley brouhaha, saying, "I think it's fair to say, number one, any of us would be pretty angry; number two, that the Cambridge police acted stupidly in arresting somebody when there was already proof that they were in their own home."

Pundits jumped on the president's case for saying the Cambridge police acted "stupidly," staying away from the thornier pronoun issue: the prez used *they* when *he* was called for.

Let's recall that *somebody* is one of those troublesome indefinite pronouns (like *anyone, anybody, everyone, everybody, someone, somebody, no one,* and *nobody*) that are always singular. This is a subject that can make word nerds—not usually prone to unbridled passions—go apoplectic. Some recite history and a seemingly infinite string of writers (everyone from Spenser to Shakespeare, Austen to Auden, Mark Twain to Rudyard Kipling) who use *they* as a singular pronoun. Others, like the lexicographers at *Merriam-Webster's Dictionary of English Usage,* argue that if this is how people use the pronoun, we should accept it. And others, like Grammar Girl, advise us to play it safe by redrafting sentences.

This isn't about either political correctness or grammatical hyper-correctness. It's about clarity. Using *their* to refer to a single person blurs meaning and introduces ambiguity.

Vice President Joe Biden has shown his sympathy with his boss in many ways, including pronoun faults. In his 2008 speech at the Democratic National Convention, he articulated what every young Democrat apparently hears from his parents: "We were told that anyone can make it if they try." *Anyone* is a singular pronoun, so Biden should have said, "Anyone can make it if he or she tries." That may not sound as smooth, but it's grammatically correct. If you don't like the sound, rework the sentence ("All of us can make it if we try" works.)

LOOSEY-GOOSEY REFERENCES

"The ladies of the church have cast off clothing of every kind, and they can be seen in the church basement Friday afternoon." This doozy, culled by Richard Lederer from a church bulletin, is an instance of "obscure pronominal reference," or, in plain English, a pronoun without a clear antecedent.

William Safire, whose "On Language" column ran for thirty years in *The New York Times Magazine*, conferred annual Bloopie Awards for unforgivable syntactic errors. Many Bloopie Awards were the results of Madison Avenue goofs in the pronoun-antecedent department:

- "**British Airways** is encouraging any passenger who can say that **their** business class isn't the most comfortable in the air to write and tell **them** why." (The admen started out right, matching *British Airways* with the singular verb *is*. But then they nosedived. A company is one entity, an *it*, not a *they*.)

- "If **the government** thinks it has a role in health reform, we've got a message for **them**." (Blue Cross blew it. Replace "the government" with "legislators," or "politicians," or "members of the administration," who think they have a role.)

- "Give **someone** a bottle of Irish Mist and you give **them** hills that roll forever, lakes that radiate light . . ." (Too much Mist: sober types know that *someone* is singular.)

- "**Anyone** who thinks a Yonex Racquet has improved **their** game, please raise **your** hand." (As Safire scores it, mixing up the indefinite singular *anyone* with the third person plural *their* and the second person singular *your* is a "double fault.")

A cousin of such errors is what the grammarians call "obscure pronomial reference," as in the spectacular example at the beginning of this section. A writer assumes the antecedent is obvious when it may be anything but to the reader or listener. Often this happens when two separate nouns precede the pronoun. In the Tom Stoppard play *Arcadia,* the character Septimus says, "Geometry, Hobbes assures us in the *Leviathan,* is the only science God has been pleased to bestow on mankind." When another character asks, "And what does he mean by it?" Septimus answers the question with his own question: "Mr. Hobbes or God?"

Don't assume the last-named object or idea is the noun the pronoun replaces. An idea or noun implied but not specifically stated can be an antecedent, but referring to it with *it* can send the wrong message: *If I said you had a beautiful body, would you hold it against me?*

MAKING THE CASE FOR CASE

When pronouns play the role of subject in a sentence or clause, they appear in the subjective, or nominative, case (*I, you, he, she, it, we, you, they*). When pronouns play the role of objects—of a verb or of a preposition—they appear in the objective case (*me, you, him, her, it, us, you, them*). Mixing the cases is common, especially in some regional dialects or street speech ("Us girls went cruising"). So it's easy to miss a confusion in cases.

It's especially easy to flub pronouns when they appear as part of a compound (i.e., two nouns or pronouns joined by *and*). Ernest Hemingway—no doubt so flummoxed by gender issues that he lost track of his cases—erred in writing to Sherwood Anderson in 1922, "Gertrude Stein and me are just like brothers." Hemingway shoulda used an *I*.

ME, NOT MYSELF, AND I

Watch your reflexive pronouns. As Patricia O'Conner writes in *Woe Is I,* "In the contest between *I* and *me,* the booby prize often goes to *myself.*" Why do people insist on *myself* when a simple *I* or *me* will do? Adding a reflexive pronoun doesn't necessarily add clarity. This classified ad, reprinted in Richard Lederer's *Anguished English,* goofed badly (even bawdily):

Tired of cleaning yourself? Let me do it.

WHOSE ON FIRST?

Some overly loyal writers cannot give up the grammar myth that the relative pronoun *whose* cannot be used for antecedents that are not human. Such folly leads to unfortunate constructions like this one:

A wonder of the ancient world, the Great Library in Alexandria was an edifice in the corridors of which resided the papyrus scrolls that amounted to the sum total of human knowledge.

That sentence might have been elegant had the writer subtly changed it:

> A wonder of the ancient world, the Great Library in Alexandria was an edifice whose corridors housed the papyrus scrolls that were the sum total of human knowledge.

Speaking of *whose*, the one truly unforgivable sin that haunts the use of pronouns is the confusion of *whose* with *who's* and *its* with *it's*. Pronouns, when they get possessive, act weird. We do not say *I's*, *you's*, *he's*, or *she's* to indicate possession, so why would we write *who's* or *it's*? Possessive pronouns are all apostropheless: *my, your, his, hers, its*. *Who's* and *it's* are contractions of *who is* and *it is* (or *who has* and *it has*).

Learn this or die.

THE WOBBLY NARRATOR

Keeping pronouns straight is to the writer what keeping a firm hand on the tiller is to sailing. If your pronouns drift away from their antecedents, your entire meaning will get lost at sea.

Most writers who jump around from *he* to *you* to *I* are novices who haven't mastered point of view, or who are afraid to pick a stance toward the material—whether the first person singular of memoir, the second person singular of colloquial writers reaching out to readers, or the third person singular of the reporter concerned with credibly and precisely observing others. The wobbly narrator is much more common in manuscripts than in published material, where copy editors have presumably helped sort things out.

It's also more common in spoken language. When the actress Jane Alexander mused about her tenure as head of the National Endowment for the Arts, she committed the Gaffe of the Shifting Pronoun: "I am sure there are always things one could have done differently," she conceded, "but I really think I did at least a couple of things right, mostly out of instinct." Notice how *one* made some missteps, yet *I* chose the instinctually correct course?

Using *one* to deflect culpability is a classic pronoun cop-out, but sometimes this pronoun leads to the snobby narrator. *One* is also brought in when people feel insecure about an opinion, or just when they want to sound pontifical: "One finds oneself unable to abide McInerney's choice of pronoun, not to mention his character's behavior." Nonacademic writers not self-confident enough to use *I* and not presumptuous enough to speak as *we* also take recourse in the neutral, neutered, and nonspecific *one*. But this is fraudulent: it's a way for people to pretend they're not being solipsistic by being stuffy.

THE AWOL NARRATOR

When the Republican speechwriter Peggy Noonan discovered that President George H. W. Bush was constitutionally unable to use the pronoun *I* and killed sentences or ideas expressed via the first person, she finessed the problem by adopting a construction more palatable to the prez: "I am one who":

- "I am one who is not a card-carrying member of the ACLU."
- "I am one who feels it is wrong to release from prison murderers who have not served enough time to be eligible for parole."
- "I am one who believes it is right for teachers to say the Pledge of Allegiance to the flag of our country."

"The speculation among his friends and staff," Noonan writes in *What I Saw at the Revolution*, "was that it was due to his doughty old mom, who used to rap his knuckles for bragging, a brag apparently being defined as any sentence with the first person singular as its subject." Noonan soon became adept at crafting pronounless sentences: *I moved to Texas and soon we joined the Republican party* became *Moved to Texas, joined the Republican party, raised a family*. On Bush, those sentences sounded natural and relaxed, though the specter of a president on the Capitol steps raising his hand and saying *Do solemnly swear, will preserve and protect* gave Noonan pause.

Sarah Palin probably did not have a mother like Dorothy Walker

Bush, but when the then governor of Alaska was the Republican vice presidential nominee in 2008, she seemed to take linguistic cues from Bush 41. Note the missing pronoun in this sentence from her unforgettable interview with Katie Couric of CBS News:

> But you know, as mayor, and then as governor and even as a vice president, if I'm so privileged to serve, wouldn't be in a position of changing those things but in supporting the law of the land as it reads today.

THE GRANDIOSE NARRATOR

There's a long history of the royal *we* in Europe, where Louis XIV declared *"L'état, c'est moi"* and where the British monarch pretends to speak for the people. But doesn't it sound strange when American politicians adopt this tic? In presidential politics, right after a candidate announces, the royal *we* starts to replace *I*. At first it means "the campaign," but then it becomes the default pronoun.

When it comes to the royal *we*, Newt Gingrich takes the cake (or the Let Them Eat Cake Award). When his top campaign staff abandoned him in 2011 during the Republican primary, Gingrich remarked:

> Philosophically, I am very different from normal politicians. We have big ideas.

And it's not just politicians who use the royal *we*. When the character Eric, in the movie *Cosmopolis,* says to his head of security, "We need a haircut," the first person plural is, as the *New York Times* film critic Manohla Dargis puts it, "preposterous, both too big for such a small desire and terribly puny for the centuries of royal prerogative that Eric evokes when he uses it." That seems to say it all, but then Dargis says more: "The first person plural also suggests that there's an identity crisis lurking behind those dark glasses, and that the man who will soon settle into the limo isn't a unified 'I' in the familiar, comfortingly coherent Cartesian sense of 'I think, therefore I am.'"

The urban *we*

For a hilarious excursion into hoi polloi varieties of the royal *we*, check out the online Urban Dictionary. Here is an edited version of some of the examples there:

- Used when a person suggests completing a task that he or she can easily accomplish to someone else, with no real intention of helping out:

  "We should clean off the sidewalk."

- Used when a person wants to say "I" and sound schizophrenic at the same time:

  —"So, we were riding our bike to school today when we ran into this old bum and this cop pulled us over, but we told the cop we were going to be late for school so he let us go."
  —"Dude, there's only one of you."
  —"We know."

- Used to say *you* in a belittling and overbearing manner:

  "Hmm . . . we seem to have left the door unlocked again, haven't we? [WHACK!] Maybe that'll teach us a lesson, hmm?"

- Used when a person has committed an embarrassing social offense:

  —"God, we got so plastered last night."
  —"The royal we. I had a vodka tonic and called it quits. You got so shitfaced you puked on my jacket."

THE NANNY NARRATOR

We could call this "the therapy *we*" (*And how are we feeling today?*), but I will lay its use first at the feet of nannies and *nonnas*, who speak baby talk to their charges: "Have we finished our Cheerios?" When adults use it instead of *you* to address someone else, *we* telegraphs that the someone else is not alone; it's code for "I am with you, we are in this together."

Of course, this *we* can smack of condescension or irony, depending on context and tone. If one hipster says to another, "Aren't we looking happy?" you can be sure that someone is down in the mouth. Finally, this patronizing *we* can also refer to a third party, as when a wife says to a sister, casting a nod in her husband's direction, "We're not in a good mood today."

Carnal Pleasures

When we are wallowing in slang or dialect, or when we are creating a rough-around-the-edges character, we might want to intentionally mash pronouns in order to convey colloquial speech. Combined with other grammatical patterns, pronoun case choices telegraph information about social background:

- I knowed it was her.
- Me and her was both late.
- If Gomer and them had not of begin kicking.
- Them dogs are us'n's.

Busted pronouns are common in the blues, the broken English often reflecting the broken souls of the singers. Bo Diddley's "Who Do You Love" would not have registered the same as "Whom Do You Love," would it? Even when songwriters are not writing in regional English, playing fast and loose with pronouns can give their songs traction—"Just Because She Made Them Goo-Goo Eyes" was a hit in the thirties, and years later Paul Simon crooned about "Me and Julio Down by the Schoolyard."

FICTION WRITERS CAN PLAY quite a bit with pronoun use to create characters or establish a narrator's voice. But playing with point of view is really the province of poets. Matthew Zapruder, my colleague at the San Francisco Writers Grotto, describes point of view as "the mechanism that makes it possible for us to talk to each other." And pronouns orient the reader. "We could paraphrase Frost," he added, "and say that if you're not at home in a pronoun, you are not at home anywhere in the world."

What does it mean for a poet to be "at home in a pronoun"? Let's take a look at Zapruder's "April Snow":

Today in El Paso all the planes are asleep on the runway. The world is in a delay. All the political consultants drinking whiskey keep their heads down, lifting them only to look at the beautiful scarred waitress who wears typewriter keys as a necklace. They jingle when she brings them drinks. Outside the giant plate glass windows the planes are completely covered in snow, it piles up on the wings. I feel like a mountain of cell phone chargers. Each of the various faiths of our various fathers keeps us only partly protected. I don't want to talk on the phone to an angel. At night before I go to sleep I am already dreaming. Of coffee, of ancient generals, of the faces of statues each of which has the eternal expression of one of my feelings. I examine my feelings without feeling anything. I ride my blue bike on the edge of the desert. I am president of this glass of water.

The passage begins almost as a piece of reportage—a third-person description that echoes a news lead, with the four W's: today (When) the planes (Who) are stranded in snow (What) in El Paso (Where). The description is matter-of-fact and concrete and might even be called "objective" until that off-kilter "they jingle," summoning at once ice in a glass of whiskey, typewriter keys on a necklace, and the "beautiful scarred" waitress herself.

Then the point of view shifts with the startling line "I feel like a mountain of cell phone chargers." The third-person voice of a ghost observer noticing the distinctive weirdnesses of air travel shifts to the lyric interiority of a very human narrator, albeit one who compares himself to a mountain of cell phone chargers and whose imagination wanders outside the plate glass window of the airport. The imagery shifts, too, from the mundane detail of frozen tarmacs and political consultants to dreams, angels, ancient generals, blue bikes in the desert. In the final line, the narrator—who stares out the window while giving us a window into his meditations about political war rooms and ancient warriors, destructive power and creative power, the quotidian and the sublime—practically winks at us: "I am president of this glass of water."

It's significant that Zapruder and so many other poets so frequently rely on the first person. (This started with Sappho, Zapruder notes.) Even sliding around between first and third is common, if a bit trickier. But Zapruder cautions against the second person. "The biggest problem, especially in beginning poetry, is *you*," he says. "Because it could mean any other pronoun (*I, we, you* singular or plural, *he, they,* or *one*). It doesn't delimit *anything*. It's a signal that the poet hasn't worked things out for himself or isn't taking responsibility for what he's saying. My poems got better the more I figured out who I was speaking to."

Catechism

THE GOURMET POINT OF VIEW: See if you can identify the point of view in these classic culinary quotes. Extra point for the ones that contain no pronouns!

> "A hungry stomach seldom scorns plain food." (Horace)
> "Eat, drink, and be merry." (The Bible)
> "A bachelor's life is a fine breakfast, a flat lunch, and a miserable dinner." (Francis Bacon)
> "First we eat, then we do everything else." (M.F.K. Fisher)
> "Probably one of the most private things in the world is an egg before it is broken." (M.F.K. Fisher)
> "A good cook is like a sorceress who dispenses happiness." (Elsa Schiaparelli)
> "I come from a family where gravy is considered a beverage." (Erma Bombeck)

Curious to see if you got these right? You'll find the answer key to this and other selected Catechisms in the Appendix.

FEED YOUR INNER CRITIC: Inspired by these examples, go to a favorite restaurant for a meal. Write three capsule reviews—no more than a paragraph in length—each from a different point of view. Notice how the point of view changes the tenor of the review, and whether a certain point of view allows you to write in a way that sounds like you—or like a different you.

CHAPTER 3

Verbs

Bones

"One day the Nouns were clustered in the street," writes Kenneth Koch in the opening line of his poem "Permanently." The next day, "a Verb drove up, and created the Sentence."

The wonderful first lines of that poem pinpoint the transformative power of verbs. They add drama to a random grouping of other words, producing an event, a happening, a moment to remember. And they kick-start sentences: without them, words would simply cluster together in suspended animation, waiting for something to click.

We often call them action words, but verbs can also carry sentiments (*love, fear, lust, disgust*), hint at cognition (*sense, know*), bend ideas together (*falsify, prove*), assert possession (*have, hold*), and conjure existence itself (*be, exist, become*).

Fundamentally, verbs fall into two classes: **static** (*is, seem, stay*) and **dynamic** (*whistle, waffle, wonder*). The ur-verb, the essential verb, *to be,* is chief among the static verbs, which either express a state of being or quietly allow nouns and adjectives to take center stage. They link starlet nouns and adjectives without demanding a lot of attention. Dynamic verbs, on the other hand, grab you by the lapels. These are the verbs we tend to think of when we define verbs as "action words."

In Hamlet's most memorable speech, Shakespeare expressed the heart of the Dane's dilemma via the ultimate static verb, before he goes on to show how verbs are central to *living*:

To **be**, or not to **be**: that is the question:
Whether '**tis** nobler in the mind to **suffer**
The slings and arrows of outrageous fortune,
Or to **take arms** against a sea of troubles
And by opposing **end** them? **To die, to sleep**;
No more; and, by a sleep **to say** we **end**
The heartache and the thousand natural shocks
That flesh **is** heir to, '**tis** a consummation
Devoutly **to be wished**. **To die, to sleep**;
To sleep: perchance **to dream**: ay, there'**s** the rub;
For in that sleep of death what dreams **may come**,
When we **have shuffled off** this mortal coil,
Must **give** us pause.

Stasis certainly has its place—whether expressed by the infinitives in *to be or not to be* or by the less anxious *is* and *'tis*. The Prince of Denmark asks "to be, or not to be" when pondering life-and-death questions. We can think of *to be* as the ultimate **existential verb**, whether in its present-tense form (*am, are, is*), its past-tense form (*was, were*), or its other, more vexing forms (*is being, had been, might have been*).

The static verbs also include what I call **wimp verbs** (*appear, seem, become*). Often, these allow a writer to hedge (on an observation, description, or opinion) rather than commit to an idea: *Hamlet appears confused. Laertes seems loyal. Gertrude remains narcissistic.*

Finally, there are the **sensing verbs** (*feel, look, taste, smell,* and *sound*), which have dual identities: they are dynamic in some sentences and static in others. If Hamlet said *I feel the wind through my coat,* that's dynamic. But if he said *I feel blue,* that's static. If he said *Claudius's feet sound clearly on the stone steps,* that's dynamic. If he said, "Ophelia *sounds* troubled," that's static.

All static verbs establish a relationship of equals between the subject of a sentence and its complement. Think of those verbs as quiet equals signs, holding the subject and the predicate in delicate equilibrium. For example, with *I feel blue,* that *I* in the subject equals *blue* in the predicate.

Remember: static verbs lack punch.

What's in a name?

Much confusion has resulted from the way that groups of verbs are named and classified. Linguists and lexicographers insist that the key bit of data to know about a verb is whether it is transitive or intransitive (that is, whether or not it takes an object). That's why you'll see that the first note provided about verbs in most dictionaries is *v.t* or *v.i.* (For more on those two categories, see chapter 10.)

Grammarians and schoolteachers often prefer the terms "passive" and "active" for verbs, sometimes calling the former "linking" or "copulative." This creates as much confusion as clarity, since verbs also can have a quality known as *voice,* which can be passive or active.

If you are interested in writing better, I believe the most important distinction to understand is how verbs function in a sentence, and how they interact with other words. So, in the interest of both clarity and style, I will stick with the terms *static* and *dynamic.* The nice thing about those terms is that they are transparent: *static* verbs indicate stasis (nothing going on, a boring state of affairs) and *dynamic* ones indicate drama (intensity, high-powered happenings.)

Dynamic verbs, on the other hand, deliver punches, jabs, and left hooks. They are the classic action words, turning the subject of a sentence into a doer in some sort of drama. They give us an instant picture of an image (*to walk, to wander, to stagger*).

Hamlet's dynamic verbs include *suffer, take, end, die, sleep, wish, dream, come, shuffle,* and *give.*

In a third, subordinate class, verbs gather around other verbs, acting as accomplices. These auxiliary or "helping" verbs—*may, might, could, should, would, have, can, must, will,* as well as *am, are, is, was, were*—are mere sidekicks, symbiotically attaching themselves to a main verb in a combo called a "verb phrase." Helping verbs exist mainly to conjugate tenses (she *was swordfighting,* she *had been swordfighting*) and to indicate volition (*will swordfight*), possibility (*can swordfight*), or obligation (*must swordfight*). They also step in to help express a negative (she *does* not *swordfight*), to transform a thought into a question (*Would* she *swordfight?*), and to emphasize (She *will swordfight, won't* she?).

THE LIST OF VERBS can seem infinite, especially since English lets us invent them so easily. Staying with Shakespeare for a second, the Bard invented all kinds of verbs, including *arouse, impede, jet, pander, petition,* and *rant.* He also took nouns like *elbow, season,* and *metamorphosis* and verbified them. (The latter became *metamorphose.*)

Shakespeare wasn't the first to turn nouns into verbs. This long-standing rhetorical tradition is called "anthimeria" by the academics and "syntactic switch-hitting" by the NPR language man Geoffrey Nunberg. In fact, Nunberg mentions a brilliant example from a novel in which the writer, Bruce Olds, describes blood that "rooster-tails" from a wound. That invention does what a verb is supposed to do: it gives an image, conveys an action.

Other especially colorful new verbs, many taken from the world of nouns, include *google, tweet, scarify, prettify, podcast, multitask,* and the slang sense of *moon.*

Flesh

More than any other part of speech, it is the verb that determines whether a writer is a wimp or a wizard. Novices tend to rely on *is* and other static verbs and lose momentum by stumbling into the passive voice (more on that in a moment). The pros make strong nouns and dynamic verbs the heart of their style; verbs make their prose quiver.

For some reason, static verbs pour out naturally when we write or speak—they are our default verbs. Even experienced writers pepper first drafts with *is* and *are, was* and *were*. There's nothing wrong with that, as long as writers indulge in many more drafts to season the prose with dynamic verbs.

This is easier than you'd think. Take a common sentence, like "The guy is on the stage." Here are some ways that that sentence might be reimagined, just by focusing on verbs:

- He **waits** onstage.
- He **lurks** onstage.
- He **stews** onstage.
- He **stalks** her.
- He **lingers**, as if standing there all day will turn him into a celebrity.
- He **pays** homage to Hamlet and **tries to shuffle** off this mortal coil.

MAKE-OR-BREAK VERBS

As the examples above show, the first key to exploiting verbs is to recast sentences. Some writers devote one entire revision to verbs, circling every *is* and *are* and trying to replace as many as possible. Eventually, dynamic verbs will start flowing from the get-go.

But just deleting *is* and *are* doesn't suffice. Don't replace static verbs with just any dynamic verb. Be inventive! Verbs like *has, does, goes, gets,* and *puts* are all dynamic, but they don't let us envision the action. Why have a character *go* when he could *gambol, shamble, lumber, lurch, sway, swagger,* and *sashay*? Why settle for a verb like *says* when *wail, whisper,* and *insist* are waiting to be heard?

Imagine the challenge of writers who cover the races. How can you write about all those horses hustling around a track in a way that makes a single one of them come alive? Laura Hillenbrand, in *Seabiscuit*, doesn't have her horse just deliver a winning sprint. Instead he "**slashed** into the hole, **disappeared** between his two larger opponents, then **burst** into the lead." Finally, Seabiscuit "**shook** free and **hurtled** into the home-stretch alone as the field fell away behind him."

If you want your writing to shake free and hurtle forward, train yourself to see differently, to watch for actions and reactions, finding rich images even if your subjects are just standing there—or squatting.

Notice how *New Yorker* writer Roger Angell relies on the verbs in this signature piece, "In the Fire." It is a paean to baseball's unseen hero, the catcher, whose many motions go unnoticed as the fans keep their eyes not on him, but on the ball:

> **Consider** the catcher. Bulky, thought-burdened, unclean, he **retrieves** his cap and mask from the ground (where he **has flung** them, moments ago, in mid-crisis) and **moves** slowly again to his workplace. He **whacks** the cap against his leg, **producing** a puff of dust, and **settles** it in place, its bill astern, with an oddly feminine gesture and then, **reversing** the movement, **pulls** on the mask and **firms** it with a soldierly downward tug. Armored, he **sinks** into his squat, **punches** his mitt, and <u>becomes</u> wary, balanced, and ominous; his bare right hand **rests** casually on his thigh while he **regards**, through the portcullis, the field and deployed fielders, the batter, the base runner, his pitcher, and the state of the world, which he now, for a waiting instant, **holds** in sway. The hand **dips** between his thighs, **semaphoring** a plan, and all of us—players and umpires and we in the stands—**lean** imperceptibly closer, **zoom-lensing** to a focus, as the pitcher **begins** his motion and the catcher half **rises** and **puts** up his thick little target, **tensing** himself **to deal** with whatever **comes** next, **to end** what he **has begun**. These motions—or most of them, anyway—**are repeated** a hundred and forty or a hundred and fifty times by each of the catchers in the course of a single game, and <u>are</u> the most familiar and the least noticed gestures in the myriad patterns of baseball. The catcher **has** more equipment and more attributes than players at the other positions. He <u>must be</u> large, brave, intelligent, alert, stolid, foresighted, resilient, fatherly, quick, efficient, intuitive, and impregnable. These scoutmaster traits **are counterbalanced**, however, by one additional entry—catching's bottom line. Most of all, the catcher <u>is</u> invisible.

Angell packs his paragraph with thirty dynamic verbs and—count 'em—four linkers. (Every writer should adopt this eight-to-one ratio.)

The verbs in "In the Fire" aren't just dynamic, they're dynamos—from *whacks* and *dips* to *sinks* and *zoom-lensing*. Angell notes all the little movements as well as the grand ones, and in his searches for the right verb drafts nouns like *semaphore*, a handheld signal flag.

Angell doesn't even let the reader remain static. "Consider," he demands, "the catcher." Using the imperative voice, he implores the reader to engage. When he resorts to the humble *to be*, Angell does so strategically. That lone *is* in "The catcher is invisible" betrays the craft in the prose: in the moment he means to convey "invisibility," Angell strips the catcher, indeed the sentence, of action.

Angell performs one other verbal sleight of hand: he lets verbs pinch-hit as adjectives. The form of an active verb ending in *-ing* or *-ed* is known as a participle; participles give you another way to load up on action. Angell's participles include *thought-burdened*, *armored*, *balanced*, *deployed*, *waiting*, *semaphoring*, *zoom-lensing*, *noticed*, and *foresighted*.

William Finnegan, in a 1992 *New Yorker* opus on surfing, uses participles to turn waves into swirls of activity. Each of these images, from "The Sporting Scene: Playing Doc's Games," depends upon a participle for its drama:

> **onrushing** water
> **punishing** waves
> **shifting** mountains of water
> twenty-foot **splitting** tubes
> the glassy, **rumbling**, pea-green wall
> the first wall of sandy, **grumbling** white water
> **pulverizing** force
> a swift, **swooping**, **surefooted** ride
> the final, **jacking** section
> the thick, **pouring**, **silver-beaded** curtain

Finnegan doesn't stop at participles. He fills his entire story with sentences that use active verbs to make inanimate things animate, like this one:

The waves seemed to be **turning themselves inside out** as they **broke**, and when they **paused** they **spat out** clouds of mist—air that **had been trapped** inside the truck-size tubes.

ANOTHER WAY TO PERK up prose is to eliminate what's known as "the passive voice." Voice refers to the form of a verb that shows the relationship between the subject and the action expressed by the verb. In the **active voice**, the subject performs the action. In the **passive voice**, the subject is acted upon.

In a classic English sentence in the active voice, the subject starts the show, followed by a dynamic verb. The subject is the *agent*, the person or thing taking the action: *She reads*. Sometimes there is a direct object: *She reads* The Odyssey. The action flows briskly from the subject, through the verb, to the object.

Let's switch to the passive voice (and to some less intimidating reading). Here, the subject is the *recipient* of the action: *Dr. Seuss is adored*. The agent may lurk elsewhere in the sentence, perhaps in a phrase that begins with *by*, as in *Dr. Seuss is adored by most children*. (The children are doing the adoring.) The agent might also be assumed, or remembered from a previous sentence: *Lucy brought* Hop on Pop *home from the library. It was read more than a dozen times*. (We remember that Lucy brought the book home, so we figure she is a voracious reader—although her siblings might have sneaked a peek at the pages.) Finally, the agent might be unknown: *The library book was found in the attic*. (Lucy might have been the finder, but it might have been Mom, Dad, or Aunt Leticia.)

Every style maven since Aristotle has urged writers to use the active voice. And for the past century the passive voice has been seriously dissed (to use the passive voice). Sir Arthur Quiller-Couch may have said it most quaintly in 1916: "Eschew the stationary passive." The linguist Arnold Zwicky found that writing handbooks of the 1930s and 1940s described the passive as weak and equated the active voice with strength and muscularity. George Orwell spread the antipassive gospel in "Politics and the English Language." Strunk and White, in *The Elements of Style*, famously tell us to "use the active voice."

Active resistance

"We've gotten used to treating the passive voice as a shady customer," wrote the *Boston Globe*'s Jan Freeman in a column headlined "Active resistance: What we get wrong about the passive voice." When we view the voice as "shifty and craven, weak and flabby," Freeman continued, "do we have any idea what we're talking about?"

Freeman noted that linguists at the blog Language Log have been tracking the use of the term "passive voice" and have found that folks who denounce the "passive" are often picking on some other kind of verb construction. Want evidence? Take the *Atlantic* post that described the sentence "[Banks] that have undergone this . . . test" as an example of the use of the passive voice. Wrong. "Have undergone" is just an example of the present perfect tense. Likewise, when the *Seattle Post-Intelligencer* found fault with the sentence "Of scenic investiture there was virtually none," the editors showed they were confusing the passive voice with a common construction using an expletive pronoun. Verbs can be passive in *nature* without being passive in *voice*.

Also, don't confuse the voice of a verb (which can be active or passive, depending on who's doing what to whom) with literary voice (which can be compelling and fierce or unassertive and limp). If you are curious to read about how the Language Loggers view the passive voice, a professor of general linguistics at the University of Edinburgh keeps a spirited watch over conceptions and misconceptions of the passive voice. Follow this link to Geoff Pullum's "Confusion over avoiding the passive": www.lel.ed.ac.uk/~gpullum/grammar/passives.html.

Writers and editors can get too literal-minded about "eschewing the stationary passive." There is certainly some merit to avoiding the passive voice; some of the flattest writing around suffers from inert verbs and the unintended use of the passive voice. Yet the passive voice remains an important arrow in the rhetorical quiver. It exists for a reason.

If you want to keep the focus on a particular person, you may want to keep that person the subject of the sentence, using the passive voice if necessary to do so. Don't let your editor fiddle with sentences like this: "Jerry Brown has never been able to settle for the Zen life. After being defeated in successive presidential campaigns, he set up camp in Oakland and reinvented himself as mayor." The passive voice (*after being defeated*) works, because the agents—in this case Carter and Clinton—are irrelevant to Brown's political resurrection.

Go back to Roger Angell's description of the catcher and note the two instances of passive voice: *are repeated* and *are counterbalanced*.

Similarly, if your intention is to emphasize a subject's very passivity, use the passive voice, as does Germaine Greer in *The Female Eunuch*:

> The married woman's significance can only be conferred by the presence of a man at her side, a man upon whom she absolutely depends.
> In return for renouncing, collaborating, adapting, identifying, she is caressed, desired, handled, influenced.

Greer underscored her point—that marriage saps a woman's power, requiring her to trade active engagement for passively standing by—by putting those final verbs into the passive voice. By using the passive voice in the first sentence, Greer also kept our focus on the married woman, the most important element of her passage, instead of the presence of the man by her side.

The passive voice can make for catchy rhythms in ads, telegrams, or other terse forms. "Made in the U.S.A." puts the emphasis on the *where*, not the *who*. And it fits on the label of a T-shirt better than "Farmers in Texas grew the cotton for this shirt, and seamstresses in a Los Angeles factory stitched it together."

When, in 1897, Mark Twain heard that his obituary had been published, he cabled the United States from London. The often-quoted version of his cable relies on the passive voice for its punch line:

THE REPORTS OF MY DEATH ARE GREATLY EXAGGERATED

NOTICE HOW THE *WIRED* writer Richard Rapaport worked his verbs to transform this description of the setting of the Sandia National Laboratories from a pedestrian catalog of nouns into a landscape shimmering with activity. An early draft of his "The Playground of Big Science" opened with a mixture of static and dynamic verbs, passive and active voice:

> It **is** nearly noon, on a cool (temperature 66°), dry (humidity 21%), high-desert day. The azurescent New Mexican sky **hangs** languidly over a flat, antediluvian landscape. It **is broken** to the East by the glowering granite of the Sandia Mountains and off to the North by the shimmering hills that **lie** past the Rio Grande River, and **mount** up to the Jemez Mountains and Los Alamos beyond.

The final, published version of the paragraph banishes the passive. In addition, Rapaport erased the opening *is*, promoted adjectives to verbs, and made the mountains move:

> At noon on a cool, high-desert day, the azure New Mexican sky **hangs** languidly over a low, antediluvian landscape. To the east the granite of the Sandia Mountains **glowers** darkly; to the north, the hills past the Rio Grande **shimmer** as they **rise** to **meet** the Jemez Mountains and Los Alamos beyond.

Going back to Shakespeare's soliloquy, when Hamlet says "a consummation devoutly to be wished," the subject, *consummation*, is *receiving* the action; who's doing the wishing remains unclear. That's the passive voice. By contrast, in the active voice, the subject of the sentence is the one *acting*: in "we end the heartache and the thousand natural shocks," it is *we* who *end*. The active voice is strong and direct.

Whether you are writing a soliloquy, a scholarly paper, a legal brief, or a brief tweet, be aware of the voice of your verbs. Try letting each sentence tell a little story, with an agent right there at the start. Set your protagonist in action. Do you want him, as Hamlet would say, "to take arms against a sea of troubles," or would you rather he be left lying flat on his back, leaving his destiny up to someone else?

Cardinal Sins

WHAT *IS* IS—AND ISN'T

In speaking and informal writing, we naturally gravitate to *to be* in all its incarnations—present tense and past, active voice and passive. But reliance on *to be* is a sure sign of a novice writer, like this high-school Mistress Malaprop, whose usages were recorded by Richard Lederer in *Anguished English*:

> The greatest writer of the Renaissance was William Shakespeare. Shakespeare never made much money and is famous only because of what he wrote. . . . Romeo and Juliet are an example of a heroic couplet. Romeo's last wish was to be laid by Juliet.

A dependence on *is* and its family screams "rough draft"—even if your piece escapes the kind of factual errors rampant in the paragraph above.

Such writing is all too common in academia. See how this description of an anthropology program at the University of East London takes the life out of studying human life:

> The programme will be of interest to graduates as well as professionals working in these areas. . . . It will be of relevance to those desirous of adding legal understandings to these perspectives. It will also be of interest to students wishing to proceed to a doctorate in the anthropology of human rights and related areas.

BE WARY

Verb phrases containing *be* verbs are often merely roundabout ways of saying something better said with a simple verb. So, for example, *be determinative of* is verbose. Just say *determine*. *Garner's Modern American Usage* lists these and other cases to be wary of:

be abusive of (abuse)
be applicable to (apply to)

be benefited by (benefit from)
be derived from (derive from)
be in attendance (attend)
be in error (err)
be influential on (influence)
be in violation of (violate)
be productive (produce)

Many such wordy constructions are more natural when they are phrased as simpler verbs in the present tense singular: *is able to (can)*, *is authorized to (may)*, *is binding upon (binds)*, *is empowered to (may)*, *is unable to (cannot)*.

THAT BAD, BAD *BEING*

A first-cousin sin of *be* is *being*. Nine times out of ten, when *being* appears, it makes for an error; the remaining time, it's probably extraneous. Try these sentences by high school composition students:

- *Being that my brother is obese, I'm embarrassed to go out with him.* This would be less shameful syntax (if an equally shameful sentiment) if written "Because my brother is obese, I'm embarrassed to go out with him."
- *My birthday, being April 6, usually falls during Easter vacation.* No need for *being*: "My birthday, April 6, usually falls during Easter vacation."
- *It is a machine which I, being one of the few, can operate.* To brag about skill, try this: "I am one of the few who can operate this machine."
- *If I could depend on myself for being aware, all of the time, then a license might add up to its expectations.* Too wordy. Go with "If I could always be more aware, my driver's license might get me somewhere."

For the record, here's *being* used correctly: "Good writers, *being* aware of the pitfalls of weak verbs, avoid *being* like the plague."

DON'T PASS THE BUCK

While the passive voice gives a writer useful flexibility, some people rely too heavily on it. When lawyers want to please the court, they follow scads of lawyers before them (*The filing deadline was unintentionally missed*). Academic writers who want to stick to convention reflexively use the passive voice (*A review of the literature has been completed*). And doctors? Just take a look at this sentence from the *British Medical Journal*:

> The use of a pencil to mark osteotomy cuts in craniofacial and maxillofacial surgery **is well established, proving superior to methylene** . . .

If those pencils come with erasers, I'd like to rub that sentence out and start over.

Entrepreneurs are, by definition, active types, so how is it that so much business writing sags with the passive voice? No letter should go out with the expression *It has come to our attention*, "We have noticed" is much stronger. Likewise, CEOs and secretaries should recast "every effort is being made" into *we are trying*. And business reporters shouldn't let this into their copy:

> Any involvement has been vigorously denied by the company; a statement will be issued shortly.

Better to say *The company denied involvement and will comment soon.*

And CEOs hide behind the passive voice after carrying out harsh actions (*The workforce has been downsized*) or to blunt criticism (*It must be said that today's economic crisis is the result of a lot of mistakes made by a lot of people*).

If you are using the passive voice to evade responsibility, start owning up. If you are using it out of habit or laziness, or because you just didn't think about it, start thinking about it.

COUCH POTATO WRITING

Drab static verbs—sure saboteurs of whatever drama lurks in a sentence—do in unsuspecting writers. The worst offenders are *seems* and *appears,* the favorites of authors unwilling to commit to a strong idea. In a profile of David Geffen, this sentence should have been re-verbed:

> Though he preferred to remain above the fray, he didn't seem to have lost his gut for pop culture.

Doesn't *he never lost his gut for pop culture* read better?

The same thing can happen with *feels, looks, smells, sounds,* and *tastes.* Why wimp out and write "my job feels rewarding"? Take a stand. Say *my job pays off.*

Look out for verbs that convey less action than other words in the sentence, and avoid them. Turn "he has a plan to" into *he plans to.* Turn "the team had ten losses" into *the team lost ten games.* Turn "an accident occurred that damaged my car" into *that teenager bashed my Ferrari.*

Often a perfectly dynamic verb lurks in a clunky prepositional phrase, and rewriting can excavate the dynamic verbs and perk up the prose. For example, why "put in an appearance" when you could just *show up?* Why write "take into consideration" instead of *consider?*

Sometimes such verbs are called "false limbs," an apt term for meaningless words that a writer grabs onto rather than searching for better pillars. Don't pass over crisp single words, such as *break, stop, spoil,* and *kill,* in favor of phrases made of a noun or adjective tacked on to some general-purpose verb:

> make contact with → write, call, text, or tweet
> exhibit a tendency to → tend to
> come to an agreement → agree
> initiate an investigation → find out
> will take steps to → will
> does not see his way clear to → will not
> is not in a position to → cannot
> is prepared to inform you → will tell you

TAKE OFF THE TUXEDOS

Avoid those bulwarks of the bad memo *utilize, prioritize,* and *implement,* which fill business writing with fuzz instead of delivering direct actions and strong statements. Many of these "tuxedo verbs" (puffed up, pompous, and self-important) rely on the Greek suffix *-ize.* Some of these cropped up long ago—*baptize,* for example, was used as early as the thirteenth century. Modern science loves this suffix and sticks it on nouns to create verbs such as *oxidize, polymerize,* and *galvanize.* When an *-ize* verb expresses something we have no better synonym for—*capsize, recognize, sterilize*—it's fine to use it. But avoid such verbs when a more succinct synonym exists—*use* is better than *utilize,* and *finish* trumps *finalize.*

This little suffix can be taken to ridiculous extremes, as in this Web description of the services offered by Sfmanchef, a caterer and personal chef in the San Francisco Bay Area:

> Hire me to cater your party or cook you a delicious meal! I'll fabulize your party with fun appetizers, then if you want, serve you up a dinner that showcases what's fresh and fun! Whatever the occasion, I'll make it groovy and delicious.

With a manchef who can fabulize, who even needs food?

Finally, don't be fooled by words like *orientate* or *commentate,* misguided back-formations from *orientation* and *commentator; orient* and *comment* do the job just fine. Don't use big words to gloss over the truth or to pump air into ideas. When you want to liven up your writing and your imagination fails you, grab a thesaurus and find a simple, strong verb.

ACTION, NOT ABSTRACTION

Linguists estimate that fully twenty percent of English verbs began life as nouns. The best of these conjure vivid actions—*to audition, to bayonet, to gel, to moralize, to pocket, to stump, to scalp,* and *to whitewash,* for example.

But this is not to say that nabbing the nearest noun beats searching for the right verb. Few public figures have engaged in this sin more than Alexander Haig. "I'll have to caveat any response, Senator, and I'll caveat that," Haig said to one politician. To another, Haig replied: "Not the way you contexted it, Senator." *Caveat* and *context* are flat-footed ideas, not fleet-footed actions. When secretary of state nominee Haig appeared at Senate confirmation hearings, a British newspaper heralded the attendant linguistic developments: "verbs were nouned, nouns verbed, adjectives adverbised," and the secretary-designate "techniqued a new way to vocabulary his thoughts so as to informationally uncertain anybody listening about what he had actually implicationed."

Haigs do it, headline writers do it, lawyers do it, managers do it. Some verb inventions work because they portray action through strong images: *stonewall* and *launder*. But what's the image conveyed by *wordsmith* as a verb—beating a word over an anvil? Here's another one: *feedback,* as in "Let me feedback later"? That sounds like the function of a machine rather than a bona fide human activity. Turning people and things, especially abstractions, into acts often invents awkward and imprecise shortcuts that reveal a lack of imagination, or a desire to sound more highfalutin than necessary. It takes only a few seconds to improve upon a verb created out of a vague noun:

> to access → to view
> to author → to write
> to finalize → to finish
> to impact → to touch
> to input → to enter
> to interface → to talk
> to prioritize → to put first

IF THE VERB DOESN'T FIT, YOU MUST ATTRIT

Verbs also enter the language through back-formation, the process that gave us *to rob* from *robber, to beg* from *beggar, to diagnose* from *diagnosis,* and *to babysit* from *babysitter.* This can make for unbridled originality, as when a senator from Utah proclaimed, "I prefer a polygamist who doesn't polyg to a monogamist who doesn't monog."

But beware of back-formations. They can range from the ugly (*burgle,* from *burglar*) to the awkward (*televise,* from *television*) to the downright dastardly, like *enthuse, liaise,* and *attrit* ("our air strike will attrit their armor"). Just because a verb descends from a legitimate noun does not mean it's got pedigree.

Carnal Pleasures

Verbs have the power to shake up sentences and shape up writing. Whether we are writing posts or poetry, love letters or longform narratives, we want verbs that dazzle, daunt, and delight, that get us beyond the clear and competent to the powerfully human. Or maybe just to the hilariously funny.

It's no coincidence that verbs sometimes take center stage in titles and headlines. Editors and copy editors, admen and Mad Men—all appreciate the way verbs can grab attention. Here are some unforgettable verb-driven titles:

- *Vex, Hex, Smash, Smooch*
    (title of the best book on verbs out there, if I may say so)
- *Break, Blow, Burn*
    (trio from a John Donne sonnet used by Camille Paglia as a title of an anthology of what she deems the "world's best poems")
- *Eat, Pray, Love*
    (title of a book by Elizabeth Gilbert and the movie based on it)
- *Divorced, Beheaded, Survived*
    (a feminist reexamination of the wives of Henry the VIII)
- "Roasted, Smashed, Dolloped, Devoured"
    (article in *The New York Times,* on the newest in crostini: mashed squash and other vegetables on toast)

- "Crash, Bang, Wallop"
  (article in *The Economist* about helicopter safety, the name of a British children's "indoor adventure wonderland," and the title of an album by Logistics)

Many of these titles put the verb front and center, doing without other parts of speech altogether. Called "the imperative mood," this form of a sentence is bracing and bold. It lets the writer address the reader directly and powerfully and asks the action word to demand our complete attention.

Advertising often goes for the all-cap effect of such verb-driven imperatives. Here's an online ad for the Killington Ski and Stay Package:

RIP. RECHARGE. REPEAT. BOOK YOUR VACATION NOW.

That ad, on the *New York Times* Web site, grabbed this reader's attention.

JetBlue Airlines uses its back-of-the-seat TV screens to get messages across to passengers before they switch to Fox News or the Travel Channel. Many of these messages use the imperative mood:

Share. Connect. Know It All.
Pack Freely.
Parents please monitor children.
Reduce what you can, offset what you can't.
Rush to Rush Street.
Snow Birds Should Fly Straight.

(Those last two examples were part of the Mr. Nonstop campaign in Boston's South Station imploring train travelers to fly direct.)

NONSTOP NAGGING

If JetBlue takes the imperative to humorous lengths, Jamaica Kincaid takes it to poignancy in a story called "Girl." She builds one long crescendoing sentence out of a lifetime of commands with which a mother tries to shape her daughter. Verbs are the heart of this poisonously poignant relationship:

> Wash the white clothes on Monday and put them on the stone heap;
> wash the color clothes on Tuesday and put them on the clothesline
> to dry; don't walk barehead in the hot sun; cook pumpkin fritters in
> very hot sweet oil; soak your little cloths right after you take them off;
> when buying cotton to make yourself a nice blouse, be sure that it
> doesn't have gum on it, because that way it won't hold up well after a
> wash; soak salt fish overnight before you cook it; is it true that you sing
> benna in Sunday school?; always eat your food in such a way that it
> won't turn someone else's stomach; on Sundays try to walk like a lady
> and not like the slut you are so bent on becoming; don't sing benna in
> Sunday school; you mustn't speak to wharf-rat boys, not even to give
> directions; don't eat fruits on the street—flies will follow you . . .

Catechism

LIFT EVERY VERB: The first step in learning to write with verbs is learning to identify them. "Lift Every Voice and Sing," also known as the Black National Anthem, was written in 1900 by James Weldon Johnson. Does Johnson rely on static or dynamic verbs? Does he use the active or passive voice?

> Lift ev'ry voice and sing
> Till earth and heaven ring,
> Ring with the harmonies of Liberty;
> Let our rejoicing rise,
> High as the list'ning skies,
> Let it resound loud as the rolling sea.
> Sing a song, full of the faith that the dark past has taught us,
> Sing a song, full of the hope that the present has brought us;
> Facing the rising sun of our new day begun,
> Let us march on till victory is won.

THESE VERBS ARE MADE FOR . . . : In the following song titles, are the verbs static or dynamic?

Blind Gary Davis	"Lord I Feel Just Like Goin' On"
Elizabeth Cotton	"Mama, Nobody's Here but the Baby"
Howlin' Wolf	"Moanin' at Midnight"
George Strait	"All My Exes Live in Texas"
Memphis Minnie	"If You See My Rooster (Please Run Him Home)"
Robert Johnson	"I Believe I'll Dust My Broom"
Lee Hazlewood	"These Boots Are Made for Walkin'"
Led Zeppelin	"The Song Remains the Same"
The Rolling Stones	"(I Can't Get No) Satisfaction"
The Seeds	"Can't Seem to Make You Mine"

CONSIDER THE CATCHER: Using Roger Angell's "In the Fire" as a model, watch one person do the same thing over and over. Perhaps it's an athlete. Perhaps it's a cashier at the grocery store. Perhaps it's a parent at the playground, pushing a swing. Perhaps it's a shoe salesman opening boxes for one shopper after another. Note the small shifts in the way the person does the action each time. Write a description of that person, capturing the smallest details of his or her movements with dynamic verbs.

CONSIDER THE PASSERSBY: In a variation of this exercise, go watch *a bunch of people* do exactly the same thing *once*. Find a way to describe each person's action differently. You might watch people getting on a bus and paying the fare, or people walking past a panhandler, or people buying beer at a baseball game. Use a thesaurus to stimulate your imagination. Can each verb you pick serve double duty, capturing an aspect of each person's character?

CHAPTER 4

Adjectives

Bones

Adjectives are consorts, never attending a party alone, preferring to hook themselves on the arm of a sturdy noun. Adjectives embellish their companions, defining the qualities of the person, place, or thing they're escorting, and sharing relevant details whenever possible.

In chapter 1, we talked about nouns that might be used in place of *house*. We can say that adjectives are the words that make the duplex, dacha, or hacienda distinctive, by suggesting the size and shape of the structure (*boxy, sprawling*), the trim around the windows and doors (*Victorian, postmodern*), the color of the siding (*cerise, celadon*), or the overall effect (*elegant, hangarlike, downright dingy*).

"Limiting" adjectives make a noun more particular. They include articles (*a* door, *the* cellar); possessive nouns and pronouns (*Benny's* bungalow, *my* favorite color); demonstrative, indefinite, and interrogative pronouns (*that* closet, *any* bathroom, *which* window?); and numbers (*three* bidets!).

The **comparative** form of an adjective is used for comparing two people or things (*she is zanier than I*), and the **superlative** is used for comparing one person or thing with every other member of its group (*she was the zaniest kid on the block*). In the comparative and superlative forms, shorter adjectives take on a suffix (*-er* or *-est*) and others hitch up with *more* (*more reliable*) or *most* (*most reliable*). And some forms are irregular: *bad* becomes *worse* in the comparative and *worst* in the superlative, *good* becomes *better* and *best*, and *much* becomes *more* and *most*.

The obituary of the philosopher and historian Isaiah Berlin, as it ran in *The Independent* of London, made it clear that he was a superlative person through superlative adjectives, calling him "the world's **greatest** talker, the century's **most inspired** reader, one of the **finest** minds of our time."

Skilled writers play with strings of adjectives to convey someone's character in the equivalent of one brushstroke (*a mustache-on-upper-lip, black-leather-jacket* type) or to explore an archetype, as in these sentences from that first salvo of sixties feminism, *The Second Sex.* Simone de Beauvoir pulls out a noun (*woman*), then explores the adjectives culture all too often uses to define the second sex:

> The term "female" is derogatory not because it emphasizes woman's animality, but because it imprisons her in her sex. . . . Females **sluggish**, **eager**, **artful**, **stupid**, **callous**, **lustful**, **ferocious**, **abased**— man projects them all at once upon woman.

So as not to ignore the full spectrum of adjectives that might apply in relationships among us, here is Cheryl Strayed, in *Tiny Beautiful Things,* using a cascade of adjectives to define *love*:

> Love is the feeling we have for those we care deeply about and hold in high regard. It can be light as the hug we give a friend or heavy as the sacrifices we make for our children. It can be *romantic, platonic, familial, fleeting, everlasting, conditional, unconditional, imbued* with sorrow, *stoked* by sex, *sullied* by abuse, *amplified* by kindness, *twisted* by betrayal, *deepened* by time, *darkened* by difficulty, *leavened* by generosity, *nourished* by humor and "*loaded* with promises and commitments" that we may or may not want or keep.

Some of those adjectives are participles—verbs that have jumped into the role of modifier. We'll come back to those in chapter 11.

OTHER PARTS OF SPEECH sometimes dress in adjective drag. Attributive nouns, for example, modify other nouns and gain a whole new life as pseudo-adjectives: *Marlboro* country, *Miller* time, *tomato* soup, *olive* bar, *wine* glass.

When modifiers double or triple up on a noun, the resulting compounds are often held together by hyphens, which help distinguish the "adjective" from the noun being modified. Bruce Sterling gave us this pileup in a *Wired* story: "Magor is the perfect model of a Czech hippie-dissident-tribal-shaman-poet heavy dude."

Generally, adjectives set the stage for the nouns they modify by preceding them, with a few notable exceptions:

- In some established terms—attorney **general**, body **politic**, notary **public**—the adjective follows the noun. This is why the plurals seem irregular: in attorneys general and notaries public, it's the first word, the noun, that gets the *s*.
- Sometimes, writers take poetic license and reverse the usual order of nouns and adjectives, as in "The loving hands of the Almighty cradled him in bliss **eternal**."
- A static verb can be wedged between the adjective and the noun it modifies (the sentence's subject): "I agree that he's **lusty**, but I never said he was **indiscriminate**."

Placement is more important than you might think. Sleep deprivation may cause us to ask for "a hot cup of coffee" when we really want "a cup of hot coffee." When a PC somnambulist asks for "an organic cup of coffee," is he being fussy about the kind of mug he wants, or does he mean "a cup of organic coffee"? This placement stuff may seem minor, but look what happened when one classified ad writer tried to save two short words, two spaces, and one letter by turning "a lover of antiques" into an "antique lover":

Four-poster bed, 101 years old. Perfect for antique lover.

That writer ended up hawking an accoutrement for a creaking Lothario!

Flesh

Remember the Jell-O commercial that built an entire sixty-second sketch around perfect adjectives? O.K., it was made by Young & Rubicam in 1969, so maybe you don't remember. Here's how it went: A lonely and somewhat dorky man in a business suit is sitting at a table in a diner. A no-nonsense waitress, in a crisp but somewhat dowdy uniform, approaches.

SHE: Dessert?

HE: Yes! I'd like something **cool**, like ice cream.

SHE: Ice cream! (*She nods and walks toward the kitchen, writing up the check.*)

HE: But not ice cream.

SHE: (*She returns.*) Not ice cream?

HE: No, I'd like something **smooth**, like pudding.

SHE (*turning back toward the kitchen*): Pudding!

HE: Not pudding. (*She returns and bends over him, her hand on the table. She's got his number now.*) Hmmm. Fresh fruit? No. Something **light**, like chiffon pie?

SHE: Uh, but not chiffon pie?

HE: Something **refreshing**, like sherbet, but . . . not sherbet. Um. (*He sits, mumbling, drumming his fingers on the table, looking desperately skyward, as she dashes off, returning a few seconds later with a bowl of Jell-O.*)

Your readers may not be as patient—or perceptive—as that waitress. Fine-tune your adjectives *before* you demand a reader's attention. Work to find the exact word that conveys your meaning. Brainstorm. Use a thesaurus. Be selective.

President George H. W. Bush's "kinder, gentler nation" is a bit of a cliché now, but that's because when speechwriter Peggy Noonan came up with the formulation in 1988, it was novel and succinct. But the words didn't just pop into Noonan's head. As she recounts in *What I Saw at the Revolution*, those two adjectives were inspired by a cascade of nouns Bush unleashed while brainstorming about the words that carry special meaning for him: "Family, kids, grandkids, love, decency, honor, pride, tolerance, hope, kindness, loyalty, freedom, caring, heart, faith, service to country, fair play, strength, healing, excellence." Out of all that effort came a phrase that worked.

That's the alchemy of adjectives: boiling down an excess of ideas to the essence of a thing. We want the words to be precise and evocative. If we pick our adjectives carefully, any description can surprise. In *Bad Land*, a book about the settling and then abandonment of the Great Plains, the travel writer Jonathan Raban describes a lightning storm moving in from the west:

> One could see it coming for an hour before it hit: the distant artillery flashes on a sky of **deep episcopal** purple.

That *deep episcopal purple* isn't just original, it carries rich associations— from the brooding skies of the American West to the velvet bands of a priest's vestments.

Travel writers like Raban trade in their ability to make a place come alive. The words must conjure the character of a place for readers who may never see it. This may seem like magic, or incomparable talent, but the inspiration starts with acute observation.

Notice how the travel writer Tim Cahill takes the care to work nouns and adjectives—together they describe the precise colors he spots along the Ferris Fork of the Bechler River, in the southwestern corner of Yellowstone National Park:

> Hot water from the pool above ran down the bank of the terrace, which was striated in several colors: **wet brown** and **garish pumpkin** and **overachieving moss**, all interspersed with running channels of steaming water and lined in **creamy beige**. The north side of the terrace was a **Day-Glo green**, overlaid with a precipitate of **flawless cream**.

This paragraph, from *Lost in My Own Backyard*, shows Cahill doubling up on his adjectives, to give us not only a precise shade but also texture ("wet" brown, "creamy" beige). There are elements of surprise, too—the "Day-Glo" green, the "overachieving" moss.

Even without the unlikely but very Cahillian "overachieving," how many of us take the time to see the striations of landscape and water, much less to name them? Think of how many times you have used the generic *yellow*? A peek in a thesaurus, a glance at the paint chips at Home Depot, or a browse in *The Pantone Book of Color* hints at the possibilities: *bamboo, butter, canary, chamois, dandelion, jonquil, lemon, maize, mimosa, mustard, ochre, old gold, popcorn, saffron, sauterne, turmeric,* and *yolk,* for starters.

Adjectives are just as important in describing people as landscapes, of course. In the profile about a North Carolina revenue agent on page 160, journalist Alec Wilkinson writes that Garland Bunting has "eyes that are clear and close-set and steel blue." Those three adjectives convey Bunting's glare and they capture his gritty personality. And notice the role of adjectives in David Kehr's portrait of Harrison Ford's face on page 18—from "comfortable, creased, familiar" to "solid, stalwart."

Adjectives can surprise and even express paradox—think of Shakespearean oxymorons like *brawling love*. It's not just the Bard who pairs nouns and adjectives together in suggestive ways; more recent inventions include Walter Winchell's *lohengrinned couple* (newlyweds), Betsey Wright's *bimbo eruptions* (Bill Clinton's ever-evolving cast of female friends), or Candace Bushnell's *toxic bachelors* (the vicious dating predators of *Sex and the City*). The Urban Dictionary adds *Microsoft Works* to that list.

Cardinal Sins

Adjectives may tart up stodgy nouns, but they can cause grammatical trouble. And they can blur meaning, taking us down blind alleys. Let's review some fine points.

LESS IS NOT FEWER

Take a stroll through the nearest grocery with its signs screaming "Less calories than ice cream" and "Express line: ten items or less." Both phrases use *less* ungrammatically. When talking about a smaller *number* of things (as you are when you're loading your arms with groceries or loading your body with calories), use *fewer*. When you are talking about a smaller *quantity* of something, use *less*. (Say, for instance, you need *less* catsup: get the smaller bottle.) You would also use *less* to refer to degree or extent. (If you have *less* patience than ever, buy fewer things and stand in the ten-items-or-fewer line.)

Wanna get more technical? *Fewer* is used with countable nouns (Are your eyes glazing over? Those would be nouns that take an *s* in the plural): *fewer* burgers, *fewer* buns. *Less* is used with uncountable, or mass, nouns: *less* mustard, *less* catsup, *less* hunger, *less* indigestion. If you use *many* with a word, use *fewer* with the same word (*many* cartons of milk, *many* shopping bags; *fewer* cartons of milk, *fewer* shopping bags). If you use *much* with a word, use *less* (*much* food, *much* hassle; *less* food, *less* hassle).

If you can count items individually, use *fewer*. If not, use *less*.

In describing Barack Obama's fiscal record at the 2008 Democratic National Convention, Joe Biden lost count of his *lesses* and *fewers*:

> Because Barack made that choice, working families in Illinois pay less taxes, and more people have moved from welfare to the dignity of work.

Here's the thing: taxes are countable. (That's what makes them so odious; we count every dollar!) "Fewer taxes" would have been more grammatical, though the best adjective might well have been "lower"—that conveys that working families paid a lower dollar amount.) Or Biden might have said that people in Illinois pay fewer types of taxes.

LESS IS MORE

"When you catch an adjective," Mark Twain once wrote to a twelve-year-old boy, "kill it. No, I don't mean utterly, but kill most of them—then the rest will be valuable." Indeed, adjectives should be used sparingly and astutely.

Novice writers goo up descriptions with lush adjectives. When Homer first imagined "rosy-fingered dawn," that was a striking description, but now it's a cliché. Pile up the adjectives, and it gets even worse: "The thin, mauve fingers of dawn reached up over the flat, charcoal-gray horizon. . . ." (Contrast that with Jonathan Raban's "episcopal purple.")

In a *New Yorker* cartoon, Michael Maslin parodies Madison Avenue's overreliance on empty adjectives. Lying on a porch swing with an iced tea nearby, a poor mensch indulging in a little summer reading hits this patch of adjective-polluted prose:

> Night fell over the land like an **L. L. Bean navy-blue summerweight one-hundred-percent-goose-down-filled** comforter covering up an **Eddie Bauer hunter-green one-hundred-percent-combed-cotton, machine-washable king-size fitted** sheet.

Using more adjectives is not more descriptive. Be selective.

When less is way more

Wall Street Journal reporters Geoffrey A. Fowler and Yukari Iwatani Kane noticed something odd when Amazon's chief executive, Jeff Bezos, sat down with Charlie Rose to discuss the Kindle. Throughout the interview, Bezos repeatedly omitted *the,* saying how "Kindle is succeeding," how "Kindle is a companion to tablet computers," and how many e-books are "available for Kindle."

Was Bezos just affecting a Russian accent? Not exactly. Fowler and Kane noted that Bezos is part of a growing cadre of marketers who avoid the tiny words like *the*, *a*, and *an* that precede most nouns.

Glenn Kaplan, creative director at Barnes & Noble, Inc., told Fowler and Kane that he winces when somebody says "the Nook." Kaplan added: "When a brand evokes something bigger than just a little object, it doesn't want to have 'the' in front of it."

Apple, they noted, approaches articles as it does buttons on its gadgets. A person familiar with the article-free computing brand said that Apple tries to simplify language out of "a desire for white space."

"In Silicon Valley especially, dropping 'the' before product names has become an article of faith," they wrote, perhaps intending the pun. "Branding gurus defend the 'the' omission," they added, quoting an adman who argued that dropping the article gives a brand "a more iconic feel."

The marketing blogger and business book author Seth Godin took the idea of an article of faith one step further. Removing articles, he said, "is an artifact of the desire of some brand professionals to turn brands into religions or cults."

DESCRIPTIVE DOUBLERS

Back in 1783, Hugh Blair admonished his students at Edinburgh to "Beware of imagining that we render style strong or expressive, by a constant and multiplied use of epithets. Epithets have often great beauty and force. But if we introduce them into every Sentence, and string many of them together to one object . . . we clog and enfeeble Style; in place of illustrating the image, we render it confused and indistinct."

Updating Blair just a bit, let's put his advice this way: a few well-chosen descriptors trump a pileup of adjectives. A *luau of fruits and fishes* is better than "a delicious, inviting, attractive spread of food."

Then there is redundancy—saying twice what needs to be said only once. Sometimes the redundancy is just lame, as in this line from the song "I Will Buy You a New Life" by the nineties band Everclear:

I will buy you a new car, perfect, shiny and new.

How many ways, or times, do you need to say *new* in order for your meaning to be everclear?

Lest you think that redundancy is as passé as that Portland rock band, look no farther than your nearest legal contract. Take this boilerplate clause from a loan agreement generated at Lendingkarma.com:

If one or more of the provisions of this Promissory Note shall be declared or held to be **invalid, illegal, or unenforceable** in any respect

in any jurisdiction, the validity, legality, and enforceability of the remaining provisions hereof shall not in any way be affected or impaired
thereby and any such declaration or holding shall not invalidate or
render unenforceable such provision in any other jurisdiction.

Many books would also be full of redundancies—or just verbosity—
if not for editors and copy editors. Here are some redundancies plucked
from real manuscripts:

- Administering the many partnerships and acquisitions stretched
  employees already stressed by the **rapid** and **numerous** Internet
  projects. (Try replacing these two words with *proliferating*.)
- The AOL deal positioned Intuit as one of the **leading** and **most
  aggressive** players in the online financial services industry. (Can
  those two adjectives be replaced by one? How about *dominant*?)

Sometimes redundancy can be eliminated by just striking one of
the two adjectives, as in these examples, also from manuscripts:

- Sara had brought her ~~many and~~ considerable natural talents to
  bear.
- It was the beginning of a ~~solid and~~ stable financial recovery.
- The market for goods from China remains ~~large and~~ robust.

Finally, there's the trick of analyzing the meaning of a sentence and
recasting it using a dynamic verb. This sentence suffers from several
failures:

- The game "Monopoly" was seen as unique and promising.

This sentence could be recast using a verb: *"Monopoly" intrigued armchair capitalists.*

DON'T SLAP ON AN adjective that merely repeats what a noun makes obvious. In "the first vote we'll start with," *first* is extraneous. So are the ad-

jectives clinging to these nouns: *free gift, future plans, personal opinion, general consensus, little baby,* and *afternoon matinee.* (Of course, those who know French might argue that *matinee* has the word "morning" embedded in it; nevertheless, most of us attend matinees in the afternoon.)

Sometimes the redundancy seems part of a failed effort to hype up reporting or to give a news story a false urgency, as in *true facts, convicted felon, vast majority, wide range, acute crisis,* or *grave danger* (Is there any other kind?).

In an odd twist, sometimes we pair an adjective with a noun coined to mean the opposite. We're so habituated to these clichés that we miss the ridiculous—and confusing—image they summon: *new tradition, original copy, partial cease-fire, limited lifetime guarantee,* and (a personal favorite) *tight slacks.*

And let's not forget the pet peeves of mid-twentieth-century humorist James Thurber: *pretty ugly* and *a little big.*

SHOW, DON'T TELL

The most common criticism many writers hear from editors is "show, don't tell." The dictum is often invoked reflexively, and it can seem opaque. But take it as a warning against frothy adjectives that fail to convey an experience to a reader. "It's no use *telling* us that something was 'mysterious' or 'loathsome' or 'awe-inspiring' or 'voluptuous,'" writes C. S. Lewis, echoing the editor's standard lecture to the newsroom novice. "By direct description, by metaphor and simile, by secretly evoking powerful associations, by offering the right stimuli to our nerves (in the right degree and the right order), and by the very beat and vowel-melody and length and brevity of your sentences, you must bring it about that we, we readers, not you, exclaim 'how mysterious!' or 'loathsome' or whatever it is. Let me taste for myself, and you'll have no need to *tell* me how I should react."

Certain adjectives should be avoided altogether if you want to "show." Beware adjectives favored by politicians and pundits trying to gin up the importance of legislative efforts, like *epic* or *historic.* Resist the adjectives of mediocre critics, like *unforgettable, triumphant, age-old.* Don't be seduced by *inevitable, inexorable,* or *veritable.*

Then there are the staples of the high school English paper, which stick around to clutter our prose long after we've stopped analyzing *The Great Gatsby* and *Romeo and Juliet*. These lightweights describe the reaction of the observer rather than the qualities of the thing observed: *unique, interesting, boring, good, bad, important*. Ban these snoozers from your prose, lest you end up sounding as silly and insipid as this restaurant critic:

> Hillary's, a singularly distinctive and unique restaurant, has made a well-planned and suspicious début, bringing a special new flavor and excitement to the North Jersey scene.

Add *singularly distinctive* and *special* to that list of no-brainers. (Oh, and don't you have a suspicion that Hillary's début was more auspicious than sneaky?)

MARKETING MADNESS

In a misguided effort to be "fresh," some writers of marketing copy verge on the ridiculous. Have you ever studied the syntax of women's clothing catalogs? O.K., I got it that "aubergine" stockings are gonna make my legs look like eggplants, but will "mist" stockings make them disappear? What, exactly, does Spanish Flesh look like? Or Cold Morn, Pearly Gates, Kitten's Ear, or Folly?

The wine industry may have even textiles beat. With all sympathy for oenophiles trying to describe sensations on the palate, does anyone think these blurbs from a wine magazine help us figure out what a wine will *taste* like? The Chablis Grand Cru Vaudésir, we're told, is "fat, rich, quite heavy, overdone . . . full-bodied and quite mature, as evidenced by its yellow color." The Albert Boxler Riesling Alsace Grand Cru Sommerberg is "as fresh and clean as a mountain stream. Aromas of wet stones and herbs make way for a racy palate of grapefruit and lime. Light but intense, it's a lively match for food." If you're not racy enough to drink wet stones, you might try the J.-B. Adam Tokay Pinot Gris Alsace: "Thick, almost viscous, yet dry, with herbal and pear flavors. Big but inarticulate."

Who wouldn't love a wine that doesn't talk back?

Carnal Pleasures

They can be empty, they can be redundant, they can be fuzzy, they can be silly. But the right adjective can speak mountains. Or rain forests. The poet and nature writer Diane Ackerman, in *The Rarest of the Rare*, described the golden lion tamarin as "a sunset-and-corn-silk-colored creature." Elsewhere she describes one male of the species as having "sweet-potato-colored legs, a reddish beard and arms, and a chest and belly the tawny gold of an autumn cornfield."

And Ackerman describes a Brazilian rain forest as populated by "shy, quick-footed, promiscuous" plants, "swelling purple bougainvillea," and an "aphrodisiac brew" of pollen. Here vines are "clutching" and "slime-coated," flowers are "gaudy," and the soundtrack is a "Saran Wrap–like crinkling of leaves."

Adjectives can also turn a brand into a cultural icon. Given a brand name that was, effectively, an adjective, TBWA Advertising (now TBWA Chiat Day) conceived an ad campaign for a brand of vodka with endless memorable permutations. Since 1981 the ad agency has treated us to Absolut Perfection, Absolut Proof, Absolut Larceny, Absolut Wonderland, Absolut Joy, Absolut Brooklyn, Absolut Citron, Absolut au Kurant, Absolut Warhol, Absolut Avedon, and a host of other absolutes.

SINCE WE'VE MADE FUN of oenophiles enamored of adjectives, let's remember that some grape-squishers *do* get it right. The winemakers at California's Bonny Doon Vineyards know how to mix a little wit with their words. Tongue firmly in palate, the scribes at Bonny Doon carom between metaphoric parody and over-the-top gushiness in these bits of bottle copy:

> Vin Gris de Cigare: "the thinking person's pink wine"
> Pacific Rim Gewürztraminer: "neither too tannic nor Teutonic"
> Big House Red: "full-bodied eclectic pan-Mediterranean blend"
> Monterey Refosco: "rich, plummy with a haunting almond
>   fragrance . . . enriches the world with its unique
>   strangeness"

Barbera: "alarmingly rich, dense brambleberry fruit . . . the
  perfect accompaniment to grilled *qualcosa*"

As for that grilled *qualcosa,* when your adjectives are working for
you, who needs nouns?

Catechism

ADJECTIVE ALERT: Articles, common adjectives, proper adjectives, mul-
tiword adjectives, nouns as adjectives, and verbs as adjectives—that's a
lot to keep track of! To practice, try to identify all the adjectives in the
following character description (extra credit for articles and possessive
pronouns):

Met Johnny while at the gate in Honolulu: 20, mixed-race (black,
American Indian, and some sort of white), beanpole-like. He's
naive and streetsmart at the same time, a fetching combination of
wide-eyed curiosity and hard-luck stories. Raised in Berkeley, he went
to Malcolm X Elementary, worked at Johnson's Barbershop on Sacramento, went to Hawaii to cut hair with his uncle, had his brand-new
equipment robbed. He's headed home to get his old equipment and
see his three-day-old brother. He wants to go back to Honolulu, where
he and his uncle cut hair "off of Likelike." I sensed something truly
sweet about him, answered his funny questions about Hawaiian history ("is it true they had warriors, but the white man had guns?"),
gave him a brief history of Queen Lili'uokalani, told him to visit 'Iolani
Palace when he goes back. Took a gamble and offered him a ride
home. Bruce was dubious, but then as taken in as I had been. We
left him at his mother's house, where a pink Karmann-Ghia and a VW
bus painted with flowers were standing guard. He put Bruce's number
into one of his two iPhones—the work phone—and told Bruce he'd
give him a haircut anytime—cheaper than SuperCuts, and better.

START SKETCHING: Adjectives always work in concert with nouns, and
when we pick killer nouns we need fewer (not *less*) adjectives. But

those adjectives still need to be killer. In character sketches, adjectives do double duty, painting both physical and psychological detail. To develop your powers of description, start a journal just for character sketches. Much as a painter might draw a compelling face on a napkin or in a sketchbook, the writer needs to take the time to stop, to watch, and to find words to describe people. (That description of Johnny comes right out of my character journal.)

COCK YOUR GIMLET EYE: In personal essays or memoirs, the ability to deftly sketch character must be turned inward. Write down three adjectives to describe yourself. Consult a dictionary or thesaurus to refine them. These adjectives probably get at your personality. Next, write three adjectives to describe yourself to someone *who has never seen you before*. Imagine that that person is going to use your three words to pick you out from the crowd at a café. Is the second set of adjectives different from the first? Less interior, perhaps? Ideally, you will avoid adjectives that are vague (*short* or *male*), or that miss the chance to say two things instead of one (*statuesque*, for example, gets at physicality and personality); *soccer dad* tells more than *male*).

LOCAL COLOR: Noting Tim Cahill's use of color in his description of the Ferris Fork trail, take a hike along a beach, down a path in the woods, or through an urban alleyway plastered with signs. Force yourself to look closely at the colors around you and write a description using them as a starting point.

THE SKY IS THE LIMIT: One of the hardest things to describe is the sky—whether at dawn, at dusk, or before a storm. Remember Jonathan Raban's sentence? "One could see it coming for an hour before it hit: the distant artillery flashes on a sky of deep episcopal purple." Taking inspiration from that snapshot of Montana, watch a turbulent sky and paint a picture using nouns and adjectives.

CHAPTER 5

Adverbs

Bones

Adverbs are more promiscuous than adjectives. They partner loosely, modifying verbs, adjectives, or other adverbs. Sometimes, adverbs even modify an entire sentence, as in the case of *sometimes* in this sentence.

You probably thought adverbs modify verbs, because that is what your grade-school teacher made you memorize. And it's true, especially for all those adverbs ending in *-ly*: *sleep soundly*, *walk humbly*, or, quoting the King James Bible, *weep bitterly*. Those adverbs express Manner. But other perfectly good adverbs express Time (*immediately, now, soon*), Place (*here, there,* and *everywhere*), and Degree (*absolutely, quite, very*).

Another way to think of adverbs is in terms of the questions they answer:

- **When?** (In "Yesterday, all my troubles seemed so far away" the adverb *yesterday* situates Paul McCartney's troubles in time.)
- **Where?** (In the title of the 1956 John Osborne play *Look Back in Anger,* the adverb *back* describes where the disaffected protagonist directed his attention.)
- **How?** (In the *Star Trek* preamble, "To boldly go where no one has gone before," the adverb *boldly* tells How to go.)
- **How much?** (In an entry from *Pudd'nhead Wilson's Calendar*—

"When angry, count a hundred; when *very* angry, swear"—Mark Twain uses the adverb *very* to up the ante on an adjective.)

Three classes of adverbs demand a little extra attention. First we have the **conjunctive adverbs**, hybrids that share the DNA of both adverbs and conjunctions, like *however, thus, nevertheless,* and *indeed.* These juxtapose fully formed ideas, linking muscular independent clauses that might stand alone. Mark Twain used the conjunctive adverb *whereas* in this line: "War talk by men who have been in a war is always interesting; *whereas,* moon talk by a poet who has not been in the moon is likely to be dull."

Then there are the mysterious adverbs that do not identify themselves with a loud *-ly.* Many of these are **flat adverbs,** which can also work as adjectives: In *hold fast,* the *fast* is an adverb because it modifies a verb, but in *fast car, fast* is an adjective. The word *hard* exhibits a similar dual identity—in *hit hard,* it's an adverb, and in *hard currency,* it's an adjective. Verbs of motion often take such adverbs: *go slow, drive fast, stop short,* with the unfortunate result that those adjectives are creeping into spots where an adverb is called for: "Cook it slow, and taste often."

Finally, some adverbs, like *clearly, seriously, mercifully,* and *regrettably,* announce themselves at the beginning of a sentence and are followed by a throat-clearing comma. These **sentence adverbs** qualify the whole shebang before the period and stand in for longer, clumsier collections of words. Telegraphing something along the lines of "let me speak without one iota of delicacy," Rhett Butler was as brutally suave with a sentence adverb as he was with Scarlett: "*Frankly,* my dear, I don't give a damn."

(It's not just adverbs, by the way, that can modify entire sentences. Adverbial prepositional phrases can, too. So, for example, I can use the sentence adverb *additionally* to say "*Additionally,* we sent chocolate," or I could use an adverbial phrase to say "*In addition,* we sent chocolate.")

Innocent though they may seem, sentence adverbs can stir wild passions in grammarians. By far the likeliest to raise hackles is *hopefully,* which can indeed modify verbs. ("'It's my birthday, you're flush, and I'm hungry,' she hinted hopefully"; *hopefully* tells How she said it, in a hopeful manner.) But everyone seems to prefer *hopefully* as a sentence adverb ("*Hopefully,* you'll get the hint and take me out to dinner").

Some grammatical sticklers disparage *hopefully* as a sentence adverb, considering it one of the ugliest changes in grammar in the twentieth century. (And it's true that in some instances it can lead to ambiguity; for example, who's hoping in this sentence, me or my squeeze: "*Hopefully*, my paramour will ask me what my favorite restaurant is.") Others see in the demise of "I hope that" a thoroughly modern failure to take responsibility, and even worse, a contemporary spiritual *crisis*, in which we have ceded even our ability to hope.

The New York Times is sticking to the more restrictive use, but the Associated Press, a long holdout, recently declared (in April 2012) that its reporters could use *hopefully* at the start of a sentence.

Traditionalists, get a grip.

Flesh

Adverbs are crashers in the syntax house party. More often than not, they should be deleted when they sneak in the back door. Brilliant raconteurs don't recount in adverbs, and glorious passages tend to pass on them.

Adverbs do manage, though, to steal the show every now and then. In the 1970s, London Weekend Television produced two series (both featuring Pauline Collins) that depended on adverbs in the title: *Upstairs, Downstairs* and *No, Honestly*. Then, in 1990, came the film *Truly, Madly, Deeply*. Trust the British—the only people who manage to turn *actually, absolutely,* and *indubitably* into upper-crust guests—to name things with nothing but adverbs. The title of the film about a love that survives death when a boyfriend returns as a ghost comes from a snippet of dialogue in which the two main characters play a game of adverbial one-upmanship:

> Nina: I love you.
> Jamie: I love you.
> Nina: I really love you.
> Jamie: I really truly love you.

Nina: I really truly madly love you.

Jamie: I really truly madly deeply love you.

Nina: I really truly madly deeply passionately love you.

Jamie: I really truly madly deeply passionately remarkably love you.

Nina: I really truly madly deeply passionately remarkably deliciously love you.

Jamie: I really truly madly passionately remarkably deliciously juicily love you.

(Jamie skipped "deeply," and Nina won the game.)

Let's face it, adverbs are not the stuff of great literature, but some clever writers find ways to elevate them. Take this Six-Word Memoir by C. C. Keiser, which turns on the adverbs:

Unexpectedly,
However belatedly,
Love came gracefully.

Some copywriters pull out a good adverb when it counts. A smart ad for Porsche by the agency Goodby, Silverstein & Partners let the adverb *fast* carry as much weight as the noun: "Kills bugs fast." *Fast* is the key word in the phrase, leaving no doubt about what makes this sports car soooo different from a blast of Raid.

Cardinal Sins

You may truly, madly, deeply love adverbs, but don't ever drag one in to help out a wimpy verb. Why waste time with "He ran very quickly" when you can say *He dashed* or *She hightailed it outta there*? Don't use adverbs to bolster shopworn adjectives either; doesn't "She's a knockout" knock you out more than *She's very pretty*?

When you're conducting your adverb audit, beware of the most common ways adverbs clutter prose.

IT'S THE VERB, STUPID

Many adverbs—especially the *how?* variety—merely prop up a limp verb. Strike "speaks softly" and insert *whispers*. Erase "eats hungrily" in favor of *devours*.

Other adverbs are hauled in just to add emphasis—*very, definitely, really, quite*. But, oddly enough, in writing these actually subtract power. In lieu of "very pretty," write *fetching*. Forget "extremely good"; favor *delicious*. Rather than "really nervous," go with *trembling*.

Then there are redundant adverbs, which merely repeat the meaning of the verb:

rudely insult
voice **aloud**
stumble **awkwardly**
meld **together**
mentally recall
caper **antically**
gasp **theatrically**

In each of these cases, the verb is visual and concrete. We may feel that the adverb adds emphasis, but actually it competes with the verb and drains energy from it.

Unlike the examples above, some redundancies occur because the verb was no great shakes to begin with:

see **visually**
verbally tell
manually place
search **physically**
think **personally**

William Safire once called such redundant words "adverbial lapel-grabbers" forced upon us by speakers "who worry about being considered too unimportant to be listened to—or who think their listeners are too preoccupied to understand." Such redundancy may be a signal to pick better verbs to start with—like *spot, regale, set down, scour,* and *believe.*

At the other end of the bad-adverb scale are those that contradict the meaning of the verb they are modifying. When President Reagan confessed that he was "not fully informed" about the diversion to the Nicaraguan contras of money raised illegally by selling arms to Iran, he was using an adverb as an escape route. He wasn't alone: Admiral John M. Poindexter was "not directly involved," and Don Regan was not "thoroughly briefed." Such claims are no less convincing, William Safire pointed out, than the admission of the nonbureaucrat who says she's "a little bit pregnant."

TOO TOO SULLIED PROSE

Hamlet got away with "this too too sullied flesh," but the rest of us should shun adverbs expressing degree. (A footnote: no modern editions delete the second *too,* but some print "sallied" or "solid" instead of "sullied.") Knee-jerk attempts to add oomph drain a phrase of whatever energy it might have had. Rather than using an adverb to bolster a weak adjective or verb, search harder for another word. Say *inexpensive* instead of "pretty reasonably priced," *thrilled* instead of "quite happy," *lethargic* or *wiped out* instead of "very tired," and *touched* instead of "truly moved." "Very unique" should of course be dropped altogether.

Degree adverbs betray authorial laziness—the habit of piling on the first flabby words that come to mind rather than finding one supple, strong one. But something more egregious can also be at work: authorial insecurity. Putting words on the page means having the courage of your convictions. "Don't hedge your prose with little timidities," writes William Zinsser in *On Writing Well.* "Good writing is lean and confident. . . . Every little qualifier whittles away some fraction of trust on the part of the reader. Readers want a writer who believes in himself and in what he is saying. Don't diminish that belief. Don't be kind of bold. Be bold."

But not so bold that you lose control of tone. Stephen King, in *On Writing,* admonishes those writers who evade the no-adverb rule by "shooting the attribution verb full of steroids":

"Put down the gun, Utterson!" Jekyll grated.

"Never stop kissing me!" Shayna gasped.

"You damned tease!" Bill jerked out.

Those verbs, King rightly says, should stay in pulp fiction.

THE VALLEY GIRL *VERYS*

Certain trash adverbs—*really, very, too, pretty much, extremely, definitely, totally*—reflect the mindless banter of surfers, Valley Girls, and adolescent mallmouths. Take, for example, these tidbits from the movie *Clueless*:

"I, like, **totally** choked."

"That's Ren & Stimpy. They are **way** existential."

"Christian is **brutally** hot."

"Those shoes are **so** last season."

Unless you want to sound like a lightweight, stay away from them.

Even some "grown-ups" stay stuck in linguistic adolescence. Casino kaiser Donald Trump publicly turned on Governor Christine Todd Whitman of New Jersey during her reelection campaign, whining, "I was totally a good friend to her, and she showed totally no loyalty."

Unfortunately, adults who eschew adolescent fluff often replace it with pomposity, using adverbs like *arguably, basically, certainly, clearly, eminently, entirely, essentially, highly, fully, rather, quite, virtually, veritably,* and *wholly*. One English rhetorician calls these "adverbial dressing gowns"; Sir Alistair Cooke calls them "tics." Whatever you call 'em, it's eminently preferable to stay away from them in prose.

One of today's worst adverbial offenders is *literally*—an adverb most often used when its exact opposite, *figuratively,* is meant: You say "His eloquence literally swept the audience off its feet," and I'm seeing a hall full of felled bodies. You write "Mario literally exploded during the argument," and I see prose blown to smithereens.

ADVERBS SHOULD ALWAYS BE USED AS ADJECTIVES. NOT.

In her book *English As She Is Taught: Being Genuine Answers to Examination Questions in Our Public Schools*, the nineteenth-century teacher Caroline Bigelow Le Row compiled students' fumbling replies to questions about grammar, among other subjects. One young citizen offered this bizarre twist: "Adverbs should always be used as adjectives and adjectives as adverbs."

Schoolchildren aren't the only ones to conflate adjectives and adverbs. The two pairs that are most confusing are *good/well* and *bad/badly*. But, listen, this doesn't require an advanced degree in linguistics. *Good* and *bad* are adjectives, and they modify nouns. (She's a *good* dancer, but a *bad* cook.) *Well* and *badly* are adverbs, and they modify verbs. (She dances *well* but cooks *badly*.)

If you're trying to convey the street rather than a bourgeois dining room, go ahead and write *She cooks good*. But know that *She cooks well* is unimpeachable.

Carnal Pleasures

Finding writers who devote their energies to making mischief with adverbs takes a little scrounging around, but they're out there. Gertrude Stein, ever the linguistic contortionist, subverted the adverb *there* in her famous line about Oakland: "There is no there there." The sentence is often misconstrued as a put-down of that fabulous California city, home to occupiers, artists, and, um, yours truly. But actually Stein was describing what it was like to see her childhood home no longer standing on the street. *"There is no there, there."* The Steinian repetition turns the first *there* into an explicative pronoun, the subject of the sentence. It turns the second *there* into a noun complement. And, finally, the third one is an adverb.

A sculpture on the borderline between Oakland and Berkeley makes more subversive fun with Stein's adverb. Titled "HERETHERE" and part of the "Gateway Series" designed by artist Steve Gillman, the piece of public art was commissioned by the City of Berkeley and completed in 2005.

Not far from Berkeley and Oakland, the Bonny Doon winery has been doing a little subverting—or perverting—of its own. The label of its Bloody Good Red parodies the overuse of adverbs and the over-the-top, flushed tone they produce:

> ". . . **astonishingly** full-bodied, w/ good, firm backbone yet still **rather** fleshy, **esp.** about the middle . . . great legs and a huge and **utterly** complete nose . . . **excruciatingly** long & dramatic finish . . . all in all, I must admit that it **really** was **bloody** good . . ."

Apple Computer's "Think Different" campaign also subverts the adverb, lopping off the final syllable of "Differently." That skimpy tagline should read *Think differently,* since *differently* tells us How we should think. But by swapping in the adjective *different*, Apple creates a double—or even a triple—entendre: We are encouraged to think differently, to make our thinking "iconoclastic" and "out-of-the-box." We are also encouraged to think of an Apple computer as *different* from all the others. (The sentence reads as if it contained a colon—Think: Different.) Finally, *think* reads as a synonym for visualize, daring the reader to imagine revolutionary things.

Catechism

GRAB THESE ADVERBS BY THE LAPELS AND SHAKE THEM OFF: In the examples below, verbs are propped up by adverbs. Replace both with more precise verbs that need no adverbs.

My waitress's face lights up brightly at their arrival.

My waitress hooks a loose strand of baby-fine dark blond hair behind her ear, jots down my order briefly, and snatches the menu from the table.

Soon the kitchen door swings open and the waitress briskly ambles toward me, her stride long and deliberate. She carefully deposits my plate before me, then somewhat mechanically inquires if I need anything else. She disappears, swiftly maneuvering through the room with a sixth sense, negotiating tables, chair legs, customer, other waiters, and pocketbooks protruding into the aisles.

As he looks closely at each item, he discovers one he likes.

GET THOSE VALLEY GIRL *VERYS* OUT OF YOUR SYSTEM: In a short paragraph, write about one of your favorite possessions, using as many lame "degree" adverbs as you can. (These include not just *very, really, so, totally,* and *definitely,* but also *truly, exceedingly, extremely, largely, completely, absolutely, wholly, suddenly, gradually,* and the like.) Notice in what direction these adverbs push your writing.

CHAPTER 6

Prepositions

Bones

Let's compare crafting prose to building a house. The foundation and framing would be constructed of nouns (and pronouns) and verbs. Adjectives and adverbs would give us the frills—the *clapboard* siding, the *sage green* of the paint, the *modestly Victorian* trim. Prepositions would be like our house's closet doors—features essential to the house's functioning, but hardly meriting mention on the MLS.

From the Latin for "to put before," a preposition appears before a noun, called its *object*. These objects can be as small as a linen closet or as grand as a dressing room.

Now, some people might buy a house for its walk-ins, but the closets could never be called a house's defining feature. Likewise, prepositional phrases exist not to express the core of a sentence, but to modify something within it. The preposition and its object (a noun or pronoun together with any adjectives and articles that modify it) make up a prepositional phrase. That entire phrase acts as an adjective or adverb in the larger sentence.

Adjectival prepositional phrases modify a noun or pronoun: *Women on the verge of a nervous breakdown* contains two adjectival prepositional phrases—*on the verge* tells us which women we're talking about (the ones on the verge) and *of a nervous breakdown* tells us the kind of verge they're on. Adverbial prepositional phrases modify a verb, adjective, or adverb, or a whole sentence: *In 2004, that woman wowed the boy next door* contains the adverbial prepositional phrase *in 2004,* which tells us *when* she wowed the boy next door.

Clog the log?

Prepositions often convey spatial relationships, telling us where X is in relation to Y. With this property in mind, inventive schoolteachers came up with a useful mnemonic for students struggling with prepositions. To test whether a word is a preposition, try putting it in front of "the log." If the phrase makes sense, you've got a preposition:

> *before* the log (Yes)
> *outside* the log (Yes)
> *to* the log (Yes)
> *under* the log (Yes)
> *within* the log (Yes)
> *frog* the log (No)
> *bog* the log (No)
> *clog* the log (No)

Prepositions come solo (*in, on*) as well as in clusters (*as well as*). Sometimes, lone prepositions (lacking objects) can attach themselves to verbs, in which case they are called "particles" and form part of a verb phrase. Some of the favorite phrases of gurus and geeks rely on these two-stroke engines. Timothy Leary's indelible "Turn *on,* tune *in,* drop *out*" used three particles. The prophets of high tech tune in to particles, too: boot *up,* dial *in,* log *on.*

No one, though, knows prepositional ins and outs like poet and professor Morris Bishop. He wrote a ditty in 1947 called "The Naughty Preposition," in which the speaker laments that he has lost one:

It hid, I thought, **beneath** my chair
And angrily I cried "Perdition!
Up from out of in under there."

Perhaps inspired by that last line, ending with seven prepositional nits, many word lovers cite a charming story whose punch line concludes with eight of them:

A father of a little boy goes upstairs after supper to read to his son but he brings the wrong book. The boy says, "What did you bring that book that I don't want to be read **to out of about down under up for**?"

(This is a story attributed to various beloved wordsmiths, including E. B. White. *Caveat lector.*)

And we can't end this discussion without remembering one more joke that turns on prepositions. The *New Yorker* humorist James Thurber included this bit of dialogue in his 1957 book, *Alarms and Diversions*:

"It's a bad city to get something in your eye in," the nurse said.

"Yes," the interne agreed, "but there isn't a better place to get something in your eye out in."

Flesh

In an 1840 letter to his eight-year-old son and namesake (later known as Lewis Carroll), Charles Dodgson, Sr., availed himself of a passel of prepositions. Is it a surprise that the son grew up to launch the title of his most famous book, *Through the Looking-Glass*, with one? Prepositions must have been in the blood:

My dearest Charles,

. . . As soon as I get **to** Leeds I shall scream **out in** the middle **of** the street, *Ironmongers, Ironmongers.* Six hundred men will rush **out**

of the street, **in** a moment—fly, fly **in** all directions—ring the bells, call the constables, set the Town **on** fire. I will have a file and a screw driver, and a ring, and if they are not brought directly, **in** forty seconds, I will leave nothing **but** one small cat alive **in** the whole town **of** Leeds, and I shall only leave that, because I am afraid I shall not have time to kill it. Then what a bawling and a tearing **of** hair there will be! Pigs and babies, camels and butterflies, rolling **in** the gutter together—old women rushing **up** the chimneys and cows **after** them—ducks hiding themselves **in** coffee-cups, and fat geese trying to squeeze themselves **into** pencil cases. At last the mayor **of** Leeds will be found **in** a soup plate covered **up with** custard, and stuck full **of** almonds to make him look **like** sponge cake that he may escape the dreadful destruction **of** the Town. . . . Then comes a man hid **in** a teapot crying and roaring, "Oh, I have dropped my donkey. I put it **up** my nostril, and it has fallen **out of** the spout **of** the teapot **into** an old woman's thimble and she will squeeze it **to** death when she puts her thimble **on**. . . ."

In the hands of Charles Dodgson, Sr., prepositions create mischief, what with cows rushing up chimneys and mayors in soup plates and men in teapots and donkeys in thimbles. Most writers, though, are content to use prepositions to ground their material, to tie nouns and pronouns logically to other parts of speech. In this regard, prepositions are indispensable.

"EVERY SINGLE PHRASE IS a string of perfect gems, of purest ray serene, strung together on a loose golden thread." So wrote George du Maurier, in a reworking of an earlier quote by Thomas Gray. Indeed, prepositional phrases can also make passages glitter—especially when each gem is discriminately picked and carefully strung. Prepositional phrases not only impart information about their objects, but they allow us to play with nuance, sound, and rhythm.

Let's take, for example, the opening of *Swann's Way*, the first volume of Marcel Proust's *Remembrance of Things Past*:

"For a long time, I went to bed early."

That is an adverbial prepositional phrase, telling us *when* the narrator used to fall asleep.

CASCADING PHRASES

Ideas expressed through prepositional phrases must be crafted into parallel pieces, as in this clause from the Bible: "Though I speak with the tongues **of** men and **of** angels." Those two prepositional phrases (**of** men and **of** angels) are nice and symmetrical, adding rhythmic value to the sentence.

In a list, it is especially helpful to conceive phrases so that they are parallel in structure. Parallel phrases flow logically and help readers follow the drift. They can even lift an idea into eloquence. Take the phrases in the last clause of Abraham Lincoln's Gettysburg Address:

> Government **of** the people, **by** the people, and **for** the people, shall not perish from the earth.

Parallelism etched those three neat prepositional phrases into the national consciousness.

A century later, in his first inaugural address, John F. Kennedy used a string of adjectival phrases, each with a prepositional phrase nestled within it, to issue his own clarion call:

> The torch has been passed to a new generation of Americans—**born in this century, tempered by war, disciplined by a hard and bitter peace, proud of our ancient heritage**. . . .

The phrases form a rhetorical cascade, each one building on the one before.

Using parallel phrases can also make ideas catchy. Parallelism is at the soul of Republican Herman Cain's wit. Voters could wrap their minds (or at least their tongues) around his neat (if ultimately unsuccessful) "9-9-9" plan. When he bowed out of the 2012 presidential race because of rumors of womanizing, he left us with this parallel phrasing:

I am **at peace with my God.** I am **at peace with my wife.** And she is **at peace with me.**

The skilled use of prepositional phrases doesn't necessarily lead to soaring rhetoric or biblical phrasing. An orator might intentionally soften a startling statement with multiple phrases, as did Barack Obama in the 2012 presidential campaign, when he explained on ABC News his shift in position on marriage:

At a certain point, I've just concluded that **for me personally** it is important **for me to go ahead** and affirm that I think same-sex couples should be able to get married.

"I believe in gay marriage" would have gotten straight to the point, but that formulation would not have reflected the start-and-stop evolution of the president's position.

Cardinal Sins

Prepositional phrases can help give a sentence depth, detail, and movement, but they can also make it muddy. So when do they enhance a sentence and when do they not?

Remember that nouns and verbs are the foundation stones of a sentence. Lodge your ideas in those strong words. The murkiest abstractions and the greatest circumlocutions, when not caused by adjectives, tend to be expressed as prepositional phrases (or pileups of them).

CLEAR THE CLUTTER

The most frequent prepositional sin is to replace one terse word with a stack of prepositional phrases. If we say, for example, "Let's go to the store on the corner of my street," we've used two prepositional phrases: *on the corner* tells us which store, and *of my street* tells us which corner. But isn't it cleaner just to say *the corner store*?

Sometimes prepositional phrases clutter up sentences, taking four or five words to accomplish what might be done in one or two. And they can lead to endless abstraction. The worst prepositional train wrecks crop up in legal writing, with its *hereinafters*, *with respect theretos*, and *thereins*. But lawyers are hardly the only offenders. Have you ever counted the number of ways windy writers and speakers avoid the adverb *now*?

> as of now
> at present
> at this point in time
> for the time being
> in this day and age
> in the not too distant future

Of course, none of these beats Alexander Haig's all-time worst way not to say *now*: "at this juncture of maturization."

When a sentence is larded with both abstract nouns and prepositional phrases that are in turn larded with *more* abstract nouns, ideas become not just cluttered but impenetrable. Here's an example from *Africa & Global Economic Trends Quarterly Review*:

> Recent data indicate a deceleration in world trade volumes since mid-2010. In particular, imports by developing economies appear to have moderated, in conjunction with slower growth . . .

I think that means that *some African countries are importing less coffee, and that the volume of the coffee trade generally has gone down since mid-2010.* But give me a strong cup of coffee and I might see it differently.

ANYTIME YOU CAN REPLACE a cluster of words with one elegant one, do it. Use *before* instead of "prior to" or "in advance of." Use *because* instead of "due to the fact that" or "in light of the fact that." Use *imagination* rather than "the eye of the mind" and *I'm thinking* instead of "I'm inclining in the direction of." Scour your writing for prepositional barnacles and scrape them away, replacing them with simpler words:

in regard to → *about*
the approximate amount of → *about*
for the purpose of → *for*
in order to → *to*
in the event that → *if*
a great number of → *many*
the reason is because → *because*
neat in appearance → *neat*

Beware the parasitic *of,* which sucks blood from the following phrases and can often be deleted without sacrificing meaning:

- How big of a deal was her departure?
- She wasn't that good of an editor.
- He gave all of his property.
- Outside of the office, he was a real card.
- Get down off of that table if you expect me to come home with you.

"OUT" ALL VERBS

Some prepositional phrases are more dungeons than closets; trapped within are much worthier verbs, yearning to burst out. In *David Copperfield,* Mr. Micawber corrects his own circumlocution by replacing a prepositional phrase with a simple verb: "It is not an avocation of a remunerative description—in other words, it does *not* pay."

Follow the lead of Charles Dickens—get the action front and center:

to be of the opinion that → *to believe*
to be indicative of → *to indicate* (or *to show*)
to put in an appearance → *to appear*
to raise some doubts about → *to question*
to set out certain of its characteristics → *to expose*
to perform an analysis of → *to analyze*
to study in depth → *to examine*
for the purpose of providing → *to provide*

Piles of prepositional phrases can drain even a dynamic verb of its energy. In "her dark Dominican eyes brighten with excitement," excise *with excitement* for a more vivid description of those wondrous eyes.

LOST IN PREPOSITIONAL NOWHERE

Prepositional phrases can act like little tangents. Or we might say they slow the forward momentum of a sentence the way tow lines drag down a boat. Professional obfuscators may purposely spin out sentences no one can follow or hold them accountable for, but over-use of prepositional phrases often just reveals unfocused thought. In 1998, Senate Judiciary Chairman Orrin Hatch, on NBC's *Meet the Press*, got lost in prepositional nowhere when discussing the vast Clinton-Whitewater-Filegate-Lewinsky scandal:

> I don't think the First Lady's going to be indicted, no matter how much her fingerprints are **on** almost everything **from** Whitewater **up to** now **in** the eyes **of** many who are looking **at** this objectively.

The point of Hatch's commentary gets lost among his meandering phrases. Trimming the prepositional phrases would make his point clearer: "Any objective observer can see that the First Lady's finger-prints are on almost every White House screwup since Whitewater. But I doubt she'll be indicted."

PREPOSITIONS ARE NOT ADVERBS

The best headline writers create the journalistic equivalent of haiku—fitting words into tight spaces, breaking their lines just right, and con-veying the gist of an entire story in a few picas. But boner headlines result when copy editors forget that the best way to state an idea is with a strong subject and a dramatic verb. When they "save space" by relying on teeny prepositions, the ideas shrink to nothingness. Take this head-line that ran in *The New York Times*:

KILLER TO DIE FOR SOLE MURDER
OF HIS 10 THAT IS IN DOUBT

What's with that headline? Did someone hack up a fish? Rewrite the thing. Since it's a headline, you have to keep within the same amount of space, which is possible with an active verb and fewer prepositional phrases:

TEXAS KILLER'S EXECUTION HINGES
ON HIS ONE UNPROVEN CRIME

Not only is the new headline clearer, but it adds information and avoids the horrible phrase "That is in doubt," which, though technically correct, is downright dowdy.

Sometimes prepositions are called upon to do the work of verbs, as in "he's into soccer." If you want to sound super-colloquial, go ahead and talk or write this way. But don't hijack a preposition when a verb would allow you to say more: "He'll watch soccer at home, in a bar, or at Best Buy while his kids wander the mall."

THE MICHELE BACHMANN *AT*

Every politician has a rhetorical Achilles' heel. For Minnesota congresswoman Michele Bachmann, it's a preposition. Take this statement of hers from one of the many Republican primary debates during the 2012 presidential race:

> We didn't know who the rebel forces were in Libya. Take a look at where we're at in Libya today.

Tacking *at* onto a form of *to be* is a common American tic, but it's not elegant. When you can leave off a preposition without changing meaning, leave it off.

OBJECTION!

The most common prepositional error is forgetting that the noun or pronoun in a prepositional phrase is the *object* of the preposition. The object of the preposition must be expressed in the objective case.

Who can forget Jane Russell's line, in a 1970s Playtex ad, for a bra "for we full-figured gals." The preposition *for* mandates the pronoun *us*. But, then, Russell never was known for her pronouns.

Grammatical errors are probably as common as fielding errors in the wide world of sports. In April 2012, a story ran about Gregg Williams (the former defensive coordinator for the New Orleans Saints) and an infamous tape made by the filmmaker Sean Pamphilon. In a pregame speech, Williams encouraged players to injure opponents. (He was later suspended by the NFL for overseeing a bounty program.) Pamphilon filmed the speech as part of an agreement to document former Saints safety Steve Gleason's struggle with amyotrophic lateral sclerosis (ALS). That's a lot of setup, but it's necessary before we scrutinize the pronouns in this sentence from an espn.com story:

> Pamphilon told Yahoo! Sports on Friday he did not violate a contractual agreement between he and Gleason.

To anyone who knows his grammar, that sentence registers like a body blow. The agreement would be between *him* and Gleason.

The problem of the case of the pronoun after *between* is common—and controversial. On the one hand, you have the inimitable Henry Watson Fowler, who despised as "regrettable" the phrase *between you and I.* "Anyone who uses that phrase," he growled, "lives in a grammarless cavern."

On the other hand, you have linguists and some usage gurus who argue that we should stop worrying about this grammatical infelicity. They cite writers like Mark Twain: he regularly employed *between you and I,* as in a letter written toward the end of the *Innocents Abroad* voyage:

> Between you and I . . . this pleasure party of ours is composed of the rustiest, ignorant, vulgar, slimy, psalm-singing cattle that could be scraped up in seventeen States.

Whichever camp you put yourself in, notice how compound subjects throw us off—and not only when there's a *between* in the mix. Few of us would say "Me went to the store," but many of us would say "Jan and me went to the store." The compound disguises the subject.

It disguises an object, too. We wouldn't say "if it's up to I," but we might very well say "if it's up to Jan and I."

> ## Just between *between* and *among*
>
> Even those who understand the objective case become befuddled over when to use *between* and when to use *among*. The key is etymological: *between* derives from the Old English word *twain,* or "two." While many style mavens argue that *between* should be used only when there are two alternatives, and *among* should be used for three or more, linguists point out that many words have changed their meaning in the past millennium, and that *between* has been used to refer to more than two since Middle English. *The American Heritage Dictionary* advises that the choice of *between* or *among* depends on the sense intended: *between* is best when the entities are being considered as distinct individuals, *among* when they are considered as a group. For example, "a series of scrimmages between the teams" suggests that each team was an independent force; on the other hand, "a series of scrimmages among the teams" allows for the possibility that the teams were part of a larger entity—like a league or conference. That's pretty techie for football, but there you have it.

BAD GRAMMAR, GOOD SONG

It's not just sportswriters and Jane Russell's copywriters who forget that pronouns after prepositions must be in the objective case. One especially troubled pair is "you and I," which appears in the Irish drinking song "Boozing":

Boozing, boozing, when you are dry
Boozing, boozing, suits you and I
Some do it open, but more on the sly
Still all of us likes to go boozing

It's hard to fuss over pronouns in a drinking song, but "suits you and me" would be above reproach.

This particular pronoun error suits rockers, too. The band Queen, in "Good Old Fashioned Lover Boy," included this line:

I'd like for you and I to go romancing.

O.K., maybe good grammar isn't what *you* associate with romance. Unless you're as smitten by Mr. Darcy types as I am.

Let's correct a bit of lore

The line "the rich are different from you and I" is frequently attributed to F. Scott Fitzgerald. But the literate Princeton grad actually got his grammar right in the 1926 story "The Rich Boy." "Let me tell you about the very rich," Fitzgerald wrote. "They are different from you and me." The story appeared in the collection *All the Sad Young Men*. They may have been sad, but they knew their syntax.

THE LAST WORD ON PREPOSITIONS

In a sorrowful little drama linguists call "preposition stranding," sometimes the two lovebirds in a prepositional phrase drift away from each other—or are wedged apart by selfish other parties (aka other words). The preposition is then left abandoned, often at the end of a sentence.

Starting in 1672, with the poet and playwright John Dryden, some language sticklers have lamented the stranding of prepositions. (Dryden in particular objected to Ben Jonson's phrase *the bodies that those souls were frighted from,* but he never explained why he would have preferred *the bodies from which those souls were frighted.* Dryden's preference was set down as a rule in prestigious grammar textbooks at the end of the eighteenth century.)

Preposition, remember, means "to stand before," and yes, prepositions generally stand before the nouns they govern (their objects). Since we hate to force prepositions apart from their objects, the most graceful sentences don't end with prepositions. But prepositions and their objects should not be unnaturally forced together, either.

An apocryphal story has Winston Churchill making fun of pedants who refuse to allow terminal prepositions. "This is the sort of arrant pedantry up with which I will not put," he is said to have written in the margin of a report after a civil servant had convoluted a sentence so as not to end it with a preposition. (That story, after having made the rounds for half a century, was debunked in 2004 by linguist Ben Zimmer. But the point is well taken: that rule is pure pedantry.)

Grammar Girl calls the prejudice against prepositions at the tail end of sentences one of today's top ten grammar myths, and usage manuals have been trying for years to set the sticklers straight. In fact, there are cases when it is folly not to end a sentence on a preposition, as when prepositions and verbs are joined at the hip. (These are called phrasal verbs, and include everything from *wake up* to *turn in.*) In "Use *eggnog* as a password when you want to log in," the preposition *in* must follow the verb *log,* whether or not it ends the sentence.

WHATEVER YOU DO, DON'T try to have it both ways. One neurologist interviewed on TV decided to cover his bets, using his preposition twice: "the HMOs to which they go to." This is a common overcompensation by professionals who have lost track of their phrases.

Similarly, a lawyer at a technology conference in Minneapolis warned an audience nervous about using credit cards on the Internet, "You have to have a reasonable comfort level with whom you're working with." That's one lawyer who needs a reasonable comfort level with prepositions.

And a San Francisco judge refused to give one convict probation, arguing, "It's not the type of crime of which you get a second chance with." That judge doesn't deserve probation, either.

Carnal Pleasures

HONEY, I SHRANK THE PREPOSITIONAL PHRASE

Online denizens, masters of economy in phrasing (in the interest of easy typing), grasped early on that prepositions are a drag. Starting with the belletrists at the Well, a precursor to today's social media world, keyboard caperers developed a host of initialisms to cut prepositional phrases down to size: BTW replaces *by the way,* IMHO replaces *in my humble opinion,* IRL replaces *in real life,* and OTOH replaces *on the other hand.*

People who speak Pidgin English often do away with prepositions altogether, preferring to take the most direct tack possible. In Sierra Leone, *wait for water small small* means "wait for the water for a little while"; a preposition is also pared in *all dem plenty* ("plenty of them"). Go to Hawaii and listen to the island creole, and you'll hear blunt sentences like "He go school," "She make plenty money," and "Try look da sunset" (in place of "Take a look at the sunset").

WHILE SOME WRITERS CHOOSE to drop prepositions, others embrace evocative ones that stretch the grammatical frontier. Steve Simpson at Goodby, Silverstein & Partners created an ad for Norwegian Cruise Line that amounted to one long riff on a preposition. Here, *beyond* transcends its syntactic identity, becoming not just a closet door, a means to an end, but the end itself:

Beyond the horizon
Beyond heavy woollens
Beyond hurry
Beyond the Nightly News
Beyond snow
Beyond the dayindayout
Beyond the salt spray (and the idea beneath)
Beyond the gossip of seagulls
Beyond your regular stock of adjectives

Beyond work
Beyond the routine spasm . . .
Beyond the northern front of cold Canadian air
Beyond the idea you have of a fish and a fish has of you
Beyond the equator
Beyond speech
Beyond the trigonometry of the most meticulous mapmaker
Beyond the grottoes of the sea
Beyond the gull's flight lanes
Beyond the wind
Beyond tomorrow and today and yesterday . . .
Beyond the ordinary everyday vocabulary of 400 words
Beyond talk show hosts who hate you
Beyond See America First
Beyond the wave flipping its hair forward to dry
Beyond your property line
Beyond the molecules normally thought to compose you
Beyond any hope you are still reading this . . .
Beyond beyond
Beyond the advertised attractions
Beyond the identity you put on with your good clothes
Beyond the laws of the land
Beyond a decent rate of return in the mutual fund of Memory
Beyond ambition
Beyond anything the present 353 words can say
Beyond all that.
It's different out here.

Catechism

NAUGHTY PREPOSITIONS: Before we set about getting rid of unnecessary phrases, let's make sure we can find them. Each of the following opening lines of a great novel uses a prepositional phrase or four. Can you spot the prepositions? Can you tell what the phrases are modifying?

It is a truth universally acknowledged, that a single man **in possession of a good fortune**, must be **in want of a wife**. —Jane Austen, *Pride and Prejudice* (1813)

Once an angry man dragged his father **along the ground through his own orchard**. —Gertrude Stein, *The Making of Americans* (1925)

It was a bright cold day **in April**, and the clocks were striking thirteen. —George Orwell, *1984* (1949)

Vaughan died yesterday **in his last car-crash**. —J. G. Ballard, *Crash* (1973)

SALOONSPEAK: In the following tale, many of the prepositional phrases should be pared back. Try your hand at making these sentences leaner.

Madame Maybelle was speaking to the piano player **in regard to the rules** of the house.

With reference to your pay, she said, I have many thoughts.

The approximate amount of your retainer will be $20.

She said she'd be willing to increase that **in the interest of keeping him.**

So **for the purpose of making him happy,** she upped his wage.

He said that **in order to please him** she'd have to feed him dinner, too.

She agreed she would **in the event that** patrons started praising his music.

He started to play **a lot of popular tunes.**

A great number of patrons were happy, and said so.

But their pleasure varied **according as to whether** they were drunk.

Nevertheless, Madame Maybelle showed integrity **in her word.**

BEYOND BEYOND: Try writing a poem or a poetic ad mimicking Goodby, Silverstein's ad for Norwegian Cruise Line. Pick a common preposition (through? beside? before?) and tell a story with it.

CHAPTER 7

Conjunctions

Bones

In our grammatical house, conjunctions are the archways between adjoining rooms, the hallways that connect the bedrooms, the staircases leading from floor to floor. Conveniently, the term comes from the Latin for "join with." Conjunctions bring things together, they "conjoin" other words.

Bob Dorough, the Schoolhouse Rocker who unleashed "Conjunction Junction" on kids in 1973, settled on the perfect title for his mnemonic number, since conjunctions place themselves at critical *junctions* in a sentence, where they connect words and link ideas (by "hookin' up words and phrases and clauses").

Different kinds of conjunctions, of course, conjoin things in different ways.

COORDINATING CONJUNCTIONS hold equivalent things in balance. A coordinating conjunction might hold together grammatically parallel words (naughty *but* nice) or parts of a list (X, Y, *and* Z). It might also conjoin two phrases playing parallel roles in a sentence ("I'm so broke, I'll have a garage sale *and* hawk all my heirlooms"), or keep distinct clauses together ("I'll have the sale soon *so* I won't get too desperate").

The term FANBOYS works as a mnemonic device to help keep these guys straight; it stands for *For, And, Nor, But, Or, Yet, So.*

Coordinating conjunctions pull pieces together into graceful sentences, as in this example from Genesis:

> And she came down to the spring and filled her jug and came back up.

CORRELATIVE CONJUNCTIONS (*both . . . and, either . . . or, if . . . then, neither . . . nor,* and *not only . . . but also*) create equilibrium, too, between separate though grammatically equal elements. But they operate differently from the FANBOYS: they come in pairs, and they are separated by the words they bring into relation ("If you buy my stuff, I'm *neither* bound to give change *nor* able to demand it").

Correlative conjunctions can also correlate a fluid stream of items, as in this sentence from the Bible using *neither . . . nor:*

> **Neither** death, **nor** life, **nor** angels, **nor** principalities, **nor** powers, **nor** things present, **nor** things to come, **nor** height, **nor** depth, **nor** any other creature shall be able to separate us from the love of God.

SUBORDINATING CONJUNCTIONS attach themselves to the beginning of a full-blown clause (a string of words that could stand alone as a sentence) and, by doing so, make that clause dependent on another clause. For example, the clause "I hear snap, crackle, and pop" can stand on its own. But when you add *until,* that clause must now attach itself to an independent clause to make sense: "*Until* I hear snap, crackle, and pop, my tears will not stop." Subordinate conjunctions—*after, although, as, as if, as long as, as though, because, before, even though, if, in order that, once, since, so that, though, unless, until, when, whenever, where, whereas, wherever, whether,* and *while,* to name a few—can come at the beginning of a sentence or smack-dab in the middle.

The opening passage of I Corinthians 13 uses a series of echoing subordinate clauses to prove that of the three things "that last for ever"—faith, hope, and love—"the greatest of them is love":

I may speak in tongues of men or of angels, but **if** I am without love, I am a sounding gong or a clanging cymbal. I may have the gift of prophecy, and know every hidden truth; I may have faith strong enough to move mountains; but **if** I have no love, I am nothing. I may dole out all I possess, or even give my body to be burnt, but **if** I have no love, I am none the better.

Half a century later, the brothers Gibb used subordinate conjunctions when they riffed on love in slightly less lofty terms:

If I can't have you, I don't want nobody baby
If I can't have you, ah, ah,
If I can't have you, I don't want nobody baby
If I can't have you, ah, ah.

Now we must pause to pay respects to those strange hybrids, the **conjunctive adverbs**—*accordingly, afterward, also, besides, consequently, earlier, finally, first, for example, furthermore, hence, however, indeed, instead, later, likewise, moreover, nevertheless, nonetheless, on the other hand, otherwise, second, similarly, still, then, therefore, thus.*

Conjunctive adverbs have two major roles. First, they help to juxtapose fully formed ideas, linking strong independent clauses that could just as easily stand alone: "I think; *therefore* I am." Second, they act as "transitional expressions," momentary bits of commentary that break into the flow of the clause, adding a little kink. These are surrounded by commas: "Quoting Descartes is cool. Subverting him, *however,* is better. Just ask Apple. (I think; therefore iMac.)"

Conjunctive adverbs can be especially helpful for handling complicated subjects and formulating complex sentences. Notice how Steve Jobs's obituary in *The Wall Street Journal* relies on them:

Although Mr. Jobs officially handed over the reins of the company to Mr. Cook, his death **nevertheless** raises a question for Apple of how it will sustain its success without his vision and guidance.

Flesh

At first blush, conjunctions seem to offer little in the way of literary flash. But they help to smooth prose, link ideas, and telegraph contradiction. Coordinate conjunctions put ideas in relation to each other: *and* likens them, *or* separates them, and *but* throws them into opposition.

The deceptively simple coordinating conjunctions can give a passage at once an almost liturgical cadence and a very twentieth-century stream-of-consciousness aspect. Take this passage, from Cormac McCarthy's masterpiece, *The Road*:

> Out on the roads the pilgrims sank down **and** fell over **and** died **and** the bleak **and** shrouded earth went trundling past the sun **and** returned again as trackless **and** as unremarked as the path of any nameless sisterworld in the ancient dark beyond.

There are echoes in McCarthy of Ernest Hemingway, who is often remembered as a writer of short, simple sentences and clipped rhythms. But in fact Hemingway's sentences showed a lot more sophistication than he is often given credit for. Those crisp parallel clauses butting up against each other often contained *parataxis*, the placing of clauses side by side. Parataxis holds disparate ideas in a kind of equilibrium. Sometimes it bluntly juxtaposes them, using a piece of punctuation—a comma, a semicolon, a full stop—to force the juxtaposition. Sometimes parataxis uses *and* and *but* and *or* to smooth the jump from one idea to the next and to lend elegant rhythms to the entire formulation. Here's an example of parataxis, from "Hills Like White Elephants":

> The woman brought two glasses of beer **and** two felt pads. She put the felt pads **and** the beer glass on the table **and** looked at the man **and** the girl. The girl was looking off at the line of hills. They were white in the sun **and** the country was brown **and** dry.

Those sentences are what we think of as classic Hemingway, but the author was equally fond of long and seemingly endless ones. In

Green Hills of Africa, Hemingway describes reading a passage of Tolstoy's *Sevastopol* and being thrown into a reverie about the Boulevard de Sébastopol in Paris. He uses *and* to link elements of his long sentence into a dreamlike description:

> Riding a bicycle down it in the rain on the way home from Strassburg **and** the slipperiness of the rails of the tram cars **and** the feeling of riding on greasy, slippery asphalt and cobble stones in traffic in the rain, **and** how we had nearly lived on the Boulevard du Temple that time, **and** I remembered the look of that apartment, how it was arranged, **and** the wall paper, **and** instead we had taken the upstairs of the pavilion in Notre Dame des Champs in the courtyard with the sawmill (*and the sudden whine of the saw, the smell of sawdust and the chestnut tree over the roof with a mad woman downstairs*), **and** the year worrying about money (*all of the stories back in the post that came in through a slit in the saw-mill door, with notes of rejection that would never call them stories, but always anecdotes, sketches, contes, etc. They did not want them,* **and** *we lived on poireaux* **and** *drank cahors* **and** *water*), **and** how fine the fountains were at the Place de L'Observatoire. . . .

Parataxis or paradoxis?

I first heard the word *parataxis* when sitting in on a lecture at Harvard (long after I'd graduated from college) and listening to a discussion of Cormac McCarthy's *The Road.* Para-*what*? I understood from the lecture that parataxis had something to do with biblical rhythms.

So I started with my standard source for all words unknown to me, *The American Heritage Dictionary.* The big book defined *parataxis* as "the juxtaposition of clauses or phrases without the use of a coordinating or subordinating conjunction, as *It was cold; the snows came.*"

Parataxis, in fact, comes from the Greek for "a placing side by side." (The Greek term corresponds to the Latin term *coordinate.*) The term was coined around 1842.

A Web site devoted to the study of the Old Testament conceded that conjunctions *do* play a role in parataxis: elements are placed in a sequence of simple phrases linked together by the conjunction *and* or *but*. The Web site mentioned another biblical way to express relationships between successive ideas: *hypotaxis*. In hypotaxis, the site continued, clauses are joined by subordinating conjunctions such as *when, although,* and *after*.

Hypotaxis emerged as a term in 1883, from the Greek for "subjection" or "arranging under." In sentences it refers to "the dependent or subordinate relationship of clauses with connectives."

In writing or speaking, parataxis appears in short, simple sentences that may or may not use coordinating conjunctions. Parataxis allows us to say "here's this and now here's that." In poetry, parataxis allows a writer to juxtapose two starkly independent images or fragments that work off each other in ways that the reader is left to figure out. Hypotaxis, on the other hand, doesn't just juxtapose disparate ideas; it forces them into a hierarchical relationship with each other, and it's the subordinating conjunctions that express the hierarchy. "First this, then that."

When it comes to building texture and complexity into writing, nothing beats subordinate conjunctions and conjunctive adverbs. These words set up contradiction—and paradox is, after all, the root of almost everything interesting. They take fully formed, well-spun ideas and knot them into macramé.

Although we think of E. B. White, as we do of Hemingway, as a master of clear, simple sentences, he certainly pulled out a subordinating conjunction, from time to time. Take these sentences from "The Ring of Time":

> **After** the lions had returned to their cages, creeping angrily through the chutes, a little bunch of us drifted away and into an open doorway nearby, **where** we stood for a while in semi-darkness watching a big brown circus horse go harumphing around the practice ring.

It's the words *after* and *where* that put crimps into this sentence.

Although we can find examples of hypotaxis in poetry and literary essays, the idea of subordination really comes into play in compelling arguments—whether on a debate team, in a thesis paper, or on the op-ed pages. Go on a hunt for subordinating conjunctions or conjunctive adverbs in prose meant to persuade. In this effective thesis contrasting two Hemingway stories, "The Short Happy Life of Francis Macomber" and "The Snows of Kilimanjaro," the writer telegraphs paradox through the conjunctions *but* and *while*:

> In both stories the hero confronts the African wild, Death, and his unhappy wife, **but** the two men respond oppositely: **while** Francis struggles to live, Harry struggles to die. [*But* can be either a coordinating conjunction or a subordinating one, as in this example.]

Conjunctions, though seemingly inconspicuous, can alter the tone and voice of a paragraph. The least inspired writers just spit out straightforward sentences without any effort to link ideas and frame the prose; they produce stories that may be precise but lack panache. An abundance of *and*s can make prose so fluid it's downright goopy. On the flip side, too many subordinating conjunctions can so ratchet up the tension that readers'll need a stiff drink to stay with you.

Start by commanding your tone. Do you want to link phrases or clauses with short pauses, creating a steady drum of ideas, and sometimes a seamless flow of one idea into the other? Or do you want to create not just strong pauses, but maybe twists and turns, between or within sentences?

Words like *plus* can seem too breezy and informal; words like *indeed* can make you sound prissy and antiquated. Unless you *want* to sound like a pontificating professor, stay away from *moreover, nevertheless,* and *thus*. Nobody talks like that.

Cardinal Sins

DICK AND JANE

The principal sins with conjunctions are sins of omission—pasting choppy pieces of prose together without any artful seaming. Hacks unable to weave ideas with conjunctions end up sounding as if they ought to go back to grade school.

Beware too many simple sentences in a row.

"See the toys," said Sally.
"Horses and cows and pigs!
And a funny red duck!
I want that funny red duck."

Clearly, it's not enough just to plug in innocent coordinate conjunctions; *and*s and *or*s and *for*s can lead to Dick-and-Jane-and-Sally repetitiveness and declarativeness.

Also, beware too many *but*s, *yet*s, and *however*s. A paragraph can stand only so many changes in tack. Keep your contradictions under control lest your reader get dizzy: "I want that funny red duck, **but** not if it comes at too high a price. **However**, if Mom and Dad would pay for it, I might change my mind. **Yet**, if Mom and Dad are willing to pay, do you think they might spring for a funny red truck, **however** different it is from a duck?"

Make my day—start a sentence with a conjunction

A-student types who memorized everything their English teachers said insist that coordinating conjunctions cannot begin sentences. If editors ever try to feed you such wrongheadedness, throw these gems their way:

And God said, Let there be light; and there was light. (Courtesy the Old Testament)

Man is the only animal that blushes. Or needs to. (Courtesy Mark Twain)

And after all the weather was ideal. They could not have had a more perfect day for a garden-party if they had ordered it. (Courtesy Katherine Mansfield)

THE *THAN* CHRONICLES

Let's take a peek at the longstanding debate over the conjunction *than* and what pronouns should follow it. (Tip: if you can't remember the difference between subjective and objective case, go back to page 51.)

William Safire, reflecting on his years as Spiro Agnew's speechwriter, once wrote, "Nobody was angrier at Agnew than me." Safire then braced himself for the salvos. "Sure enough," he later wrote in his "On Language" column, "the Concerned Conjunctionites turned out in force." He continued:

"As all Bronx Science graduates should know," harrumphed Edward Silberfarb of New York, "the conjunction *than* should be followed by the nominative *I,* which is the subject of *was angry.*" . . .

When it comes to *than,* I am a preppy. That is, I treat *than* as a preposition taking the object *me,* and not—as great parsing of English teachers and great squeezing of editors do—as a conjunction taking the subject *I.*

Yes, it's illogical. The meaning is "angrier than I was," which is why those hordes of careful writers hurling missives into my "U-ofallpeople" file stick with the *I* when they chop off the *was.* You are good, rule-abiding grammarians, you Conjunctionites, and like a card-carrying empathetic, I feel your pain. But the language, it is a changin'.

. . . The hard-line Conjunctionists have been fighting this battle a long time. Give them credit: they had to go up against the poet Milton's treatment of *than* as a preposition—*than whom* in "Paradise Lost"—and against Shakespeare's "a man no mightier than thyself or me." in *Julius Caesar.*

Safire ran the question past Dennis Baron, a rhetoric professor and the author of *Guide to Home Language Repair*. Baron, wrote Safire, "copped a straddle." Both interpretations are right, the prof replied. "*Than* is both a conjunction and a preposition; it's a floor wax and a dessert topping." Like—I mean *as*—Safire said, the language, it is a changin'.

That may be true, but if you pride yourself on clean grammar, be aware that others may notice—and accord you a certain respect—when you know your pronoun cases.

LIKE YOU LIKE IT

Although each part of speech has a distinct function, and although putting the right parts in their right places always makes for more graceful writing and eloquent speech, some errors are so persistent that many grammarians just give up and go descriptive—that is, they stop *prescribing* "correct" usage and start *describing* common usage. The swapping of *like*, a preposition, for *as* or *as if*, both conjunctions, is one case that only the grittiest grammarians continue to oppose. Believe me, *like* wants to be followed by a good noun; it is longing to make a nice, tight prepositional phrase: *He looks like Woody Allen. As* is used correctly when it introduces a clause (a subject and a verb): *Do as I say, not as I do*.

This is not rocket science. It's easy to rephrase a thought through either a subordinate clause or a prepositional phrase. So there's no reason to write "You can learn this little lesson, *like* I have" when these options are available: "You can absorb this little lesson, *as* I have" or "*Like* me, you can learn this little lesson."

But people still use *like* loosely all the time: "Looks like he'll get the job, lucky sucker." Or "She piled up her hair like she was Marie Antoinette." Even Graham Greene wrote about girls who "change their lovers like they change their winter clothes."

Greene's compatriot Evelyn Waugh once disparaged this use of *like* as "proletarian grammar." If you wanna be a prole, go ahead, use *like* instead of *as*. But if you wanna be a pro, don't act as if you don't know what you're doing.

Carnal Pleasures

SUBVERSIVE SUBORDINATION

The most memorable conjunction scandal happened in the early 1960s when R. J. Reynolds launched an ad campaign with this infamous tagline: "Winston tastes good like a cigarette should."

The grammar queens ignited. (And wouldn't you, too, now that you've learned the little lesson of *like*?) They were right: the lowly preposition *like* is just not up to the task of linking the two clauses "Winston tastes good" and "a cigarette should" ("taste good" is implied). What was needed, the pedants proclaimed, was the subordinating conjunction *as*. The tag should have read "Winston tastes good as a cigarette should."

Sure, sure. A preposition is not a conjunction. But guess what? The sentence works. Winston, unbowed, came back with a follow-up series of ads asking, "What do you want—good grammar or good taste?" The exquisite choice is expressed by—what else?—the conjunction *or*.

SUBLIME SUBORDINATION

Oliver Wendell Holmes, Jr., may be best known as a legal writer, and surely he had occasion to use *if*s and *where*s and *wherefore*s and *whereas*es. But in an 1895 Memorial Day speech at Harvard (well before he was appointed to the Supreme Court), he used his *if*s, in addition to an *as* or two, in a speech on "The Soldier's Faith":

> If you have advanced in line and have seen ahead of you the spot you must pass where the rifle bullets are striking; if you have ridden at night at a walk toward the blue line of fire at the dead angle of Spottsylvania, where for twenty-four hours the soldiers were fighting on the two sides of an earthwork, and in the morning the dead and dying lay piled in a row six deep, and as you rode you heard the bullets splashing in the mud and earth about you; if you have been in the picket-line at night in a black and unknown wood, have heard the splat of the bullets upon the trees, and as you moved have felt your foot slip upon a dead man's body; if you have had a blind fierce gallop

against the enemy, with your blood up and a pace that left no time for fear—if, in short, as some, I hope many, who hear me, have known, you have known the vicissitudes of terror and triumph in war; you know that there is such a thing as the faith I spoke of.

Holmes uses *if* to build a complex chain of ideas that culminates in a final point, "you know that there is such a thing as the faith I spoke of." (The speech was not just a stirring evocation of his Civil War experiences, but an argument that men are eternally idealists, willing to give their lives in obedience to a blindly accepted duty.) Holmes's hypotaxis is made especially powerful through repetition, which we'll return to in chapter 14. But the subordinating conjunction allows him to lay out each component of his argument, to hold us in suspension, as we wait for a conclusion to emerge at the end of a passage. *Hypotaxis* ranks ideas through a passage, building individual bits into a transformative end.

CONJUNCTIONS CAN SIMULATE THE immediacy of thought, putting ideas side by side without pauses or full stops. So a passage can lull like quiet surf or startle like successive claps of thunder.

Let's look at a few sentences on the very first page of *The Namesake* by Jhumpa Lahiri:

Tasting from a cupped palm, she frowns; as usual, there's something missing. She stares blankly at the pegboard behind the countertop where her cooking utensils hang, all slightly coated with grease. She wipes sweat from her face with the free end of her sari. Her swollen feet ache against speckled gray linoleum. Her pelvis aches from the baby's weight. She opens a cupboard, the shelves lined with a grimy yellow-and-white checkered paper she's been meaning to replace, and reaches for another onion, frowning again as she pulls at its crisp magenta skin.

Within these few lines the reader learns so many things: the character is from India, she's cooking, she's unsatisfied, she's uncomfortable, she's pregnant, her kitchen is grimy. The structure of the sentences makes all these ideas weigh nearly equally, and readers have a complete picture of the scene. The parataxis contributes an accumulation of detail rather than a step-by-step argument.

Catechism

CONJUNCTION JUNCTION

Identify the conjunctions in the following passages. Then, for a gold star, identify whether the writer is using parataxis or hypotaxis:

From John Milton, *The Tenure of Kings and Magistrates*:

If men within themselves would be governed by reason and not generally give up their understanding to a double tyranny of custom from without and blind affections within, they would discern better what it is to favor and uphold the tyrant of a nation.

From Ernest Hemingway, *A Moveable Feast*:

You got very hungry when you did not eat enough in Paris because all the bakery shops had such good things in the windows and people ate outside at tables on the sidewalk so that you saw and smelled the food. When you had given up journalism and were writing nothing that anyone in America would buy, explaining at home that you were lunching out with someone, the best place to go was the Luxembourg gardens where you saw and smelled nothing to eat all the way from the Place de l'Observatoire to the rue de Vaugirard. There you could always go into the Luxembourg museum and all the paintings were sharpened and clearer and more beautiful if you were belly-empty, hollow-hungry. I learned to understand Cezanne much better and to see truly how he made landscapes when I was hungry. I used to wonder if he were hungry too when he painted; but I thought possibly it was only that he had forgotten to eat. It was one of those unsound but illuminating thoughts you have when you have been sleepless or hungry.

From Joan Didion, "Goodbye to All That," in *Slouching Towards Bethlehem*:

I remember walking across 62nd Street one twilight that first spring, or the second spring, they were all alike for a while. I was late to meet someone but I stopped at Lexington Avenue and bought a peach and stood on the corner eating it and knew that I had come out of the West and reached the mirage. I could taste the peach and feel the soft air blowing from a subway grating on my legs and I could smell lilac and garbage and expensive perfume and I knew that it would cost something sooner or later. . . .

NEWS *IF*S, *AND*S, OR *BUT*S: Think of a recent news event covered widely in the press. Find the article covering the event that appeared in either Reuters or the Associated Press. Then find the article that appeared in *The New York Times*. Scan each story, circling all the conjunctions you can find. Do the different sources rely on different kinds of conjunctions and therefore on different kinds of sentences? How do the conjunctions affect the style of the story?

SAVORING SUBORDINATES: Compose a few sentences—nothing fancy, just stream of consciousness—about your last meal. After you've written them, analyze the sentences for your use of conjunctions. If you write short, crisp sentences without any *since*s or *when*s or *although*s, try stringing varied sentences together by using subordinate conjunctions. If you already rely on subordinate conjunctions, try rebalancing your sentences with *and*s and *but*s and *for*s and *so*s. Does the change of conjunctions change your style?

CHAPTER 8

Interjections

Bones

To the house constructed of the parts of speech, we must finally add interjections—the banging windows and bursting pipes that add excitement to the story inside. And maybe also the bits of detritus that randomly clutter shelves, or the dust bunnies that collect in stray corners. Meaning something "thrown between or among" other things, an interjection is a cry, cluck, or sudden outburst: *wow!, goddammit, oh, jeesh . . . , hey!, tsk! tsk!* Whether single words or short phrases, interjections don't function structurally in sentences. But, boy, are they fun, expressing as they do bursts of passion, disbelief, or awe. And sometimes even speechlessness.

You'll most likely find interjections at the beginning of a sentence, followed by a comma or an exclamation point: **Ahem!** *Wake up—this is the last chapter on parts of speech.* Typically, when an interjection pops up in the middle of a sentence, it is surrounded by commas: *I am awake. You're telling me,* **alas**, *that this is the last word on words?*

Some interjections, like *er, uh,* and *um,* are often dismissed as "discourse markers"—the equivalent on the page of a throat clearing or a tentative pause or a stammering to buy a little time while the mind and the mouth get into sync. These are sometimes thrown into prose to make it a little less starchy, a little more conversational.

Sometimes these little bits express a huge bite of meaning. Throw something like *Aha!* after a sentence and you get an implied "I thought that was the case all along!" Some interjections even made people famous, like Steve Irwin's "Crikey!," Homer Simpson's "D'oh!," and Howard Dean's "BYAH!" from his 2004 presidential primary campaign speech.

Vestiges of our preverbal past

Are you a grammar freak if you get off on interjections? If so, I plead guilty as charged. I had always wondered why interjections were considered a part of speech at all, since, unlike all other kinds of words, they exist sort of outside of grammar. We throw them into speech but they don't really relate grammatically to the other words in a sentence. Take them out and sentences will be syntactically unchanged. Like chocolate chips in trail mix, or the plastic baby Jesus hidden in a Mardi Gras cake. If you're the lucky one to bite into either, you are likely to yell an interjection.

So I was excited to learn of the research of two linguists, Derek Bickerton and Ray Jackendoff. Bickerton suggests a two-stage process in which we spoke a "protolanguage" before we started using the strings of words we recognize in modern language. Building on this idea, Jackendoff has used what he calls a kind of "reverse engineering" to map out our first words.

First, Jackendoff explains, we might have just formed certain clusters of sound that we used in random situations. Things like "uh" or "bah"—more grunts than pieces of syntax. Then we may have started to use expressions for specific situations; these might have been sounds like *ssh, psst,* and *hey*. Slowly, we might have become more intentional in the sounds we put together, using specific sounds for greetings as well as ideas like *yes* and *no*. Imitation and pointing may have followed. Then we may have started using acoustical bits with particular meaning—perhaps even entire syllables. Once we started combining these, we were on our way to developing words and an ever-expanding vocabulary.

Interjections like *dammit!* and *wow!* and *oboy!* may be the vestiges of those early, preverbal expressions.

DESPITE THEIR RANK AS possible precursors to full words, interjections have had trouble getting any respect. When the Greek grammarian Thrax divided language into parts of speech in about 100 B.C., he excluded them. And in the eighteenth century, when English grammar was being created out of whole cloth, figures like the politician and philologist John Horne Tooke were downright disparaging. As Ben Yagoda tells us in *Slate*, Tooke decried "the brutish, inarticulate *Interjection*, which has nothing to do with speech, and is only the miserable refuge of the speechless."

Modern lexicographers, too, have all but ignored interjections, because the dictionary makers tend to concentrate on the *written* word. See, interjections dominate *speech*, not *writing*; in fact, they are usually scrubbed from written texts by copy editors, if writers have even left them in. You'd be hard-pressed to find interjections in a favorites list, such as in Merriam-Webster's top ten words of the year. No interjection has ever appeared. On the other hand, the American Dialect Society named an interjection—*not!*—its Word of the Year in 1992. In 2009, *fail*—as a noun or interjection ("used when something is egregiously unsuccessful and usually written as 'FAIL!'")—was deemed the "most useful" word of the year, and in 2010 the runner-up for Word of the Year was *nom*, the onomatopoeic form that "can be used as an interjection or noun to refer to delicious food." It might have been yummy, but that interjection was thrown out of English almost as quickly as it was thrown in.

Flesh

But some philologists—those, like this writer, who simply love words of all kinds—take this part of speech seriously. And for writers there is much to appreciate in sentence jetsam.

Here's what William Mathews, in *Words: Their Use and Abuse*, had to say back in 1876 about the interjection: "These little words, so expressive of joy, of hope, of doubt, of fear, which leap from the heart like fiery jets from volcanic isles,—these surviving particles of the ante-Babel tongues, which spring with the flush or blanching of the face to all lips, and are understood by all men,—these 'silver fragments of a broken voice' . . . are emphatically and preëminently language."

Interjections sit perhaps most naturally in writing such as Lewis Carroll's *Jabberwocky*—because they carry about as much weight as their nonsense neighbors:

> **One, two! One, two!** And through and through
> The vorpal blade went snicker-snack!
> He left it dead, and with its head
> He went galumphing back.

> "And hast thou slain the Jabberwock?
> Come to my arms, my beamish boy!
> **Oh** frabjous day! **Callooh, Callay!**"

But interjections pop up in serious writing as well. One nineteenth-century critic claimed that the interjection *indeed,* in the following passage from *Othello,* contains "the gist of the chief action of the play, and it implies all that the plot develops":

IAGO: I did not think he had been acquainted with her.
OTHELLO: **O** yes, and went between us very oft.
IAGO: **INDEED!**
OTHELLO: Indeed? **ay. Indeed**. Discern'st thou aught in that? Is he not honest?
IAGO: Honest, my lord?
OTHELLO: Honest! **ay**, honest!

In the dialogue of plays or novels, interjections convey colloquial verve, as in this example from Tennessee Williams's *The Glass Menagerie*:

> Knowledge—**Zzzzzp!** Money—**Zzzzzp!** Power! That's the cycle democracy is built on!

Zzzzzp is hardly Standard Written English, but it's the kind of word we throw into speech all the time. It fits perfectly in Williams's script.

Since speech tics reveal as much individuality as conventional syntax, interjections can help impart character. While editors and copy editors may strike any interjection they see, reporters who care about conveying the salt of the people they've interviewed should fight to keep them in. That's what David Kline did for his 1994 interview with John Malone, the head of cable TV giant TCI. Known as telecom's Darth Vader, the bad boy of the cable industry, Malone peppers his speech with expletives and earthy metaphors. Kline left his interjections in, as they reflected the personality of the "Infobahn Warrior":

> **Look**, if you could really get the RBOCs to tell the truth, they'd tell you that the plain old telephone business is huge—**I mean,** look at their revenues—and that's what they're primarily going after. And the interactive video business is a lucky strike extra, **OK?** US West's attitude, when we started seeing the penetrations we were getting in the UK . . . **I mean,** they just said, "**Geez,** if you project these numbers to the US—**wow!** This is a terrific business!

Leaving in so many interjections is not typical in profiles of corporate CEOs. But then, Malone is no typical CEO.

Finally, consider interjections in your own narratives. Injected—er, interjected—strategically, these clumps of consonants make phrasing less formal. Use 'em when you're ready to loosen the old rhetorical tie, when you want to sound like *you,* talking.

Cardinal Sins

Some would argue that every interjection is a sin. "Brutish and inarticulate," critics have called them. "Beautiful and gaudy," say some; "the miserable refuge of the speechless," say others. Interjections aren't evil, but it's good to watch for certain bad habits.

NOW HEAR THIS

Listen to jittery broadcast reporters, and you'll hear them filling their patter with a relentless series of *uh*s and *yeah*s and *well*s. One TV reporter in the San Francisco Bay Area begins almost every sentence with the interjection *now:* "Now, you may be wondering . . . Now, officials say . . . Now, the parade starts at . . ."

Don't let your writing be as thoughtless as a breathless broadcast. Don't do impromptu prose. If you want to use interjections, don't merely repeat them ad infinitum. Make sure they add something.

THERE WAS, LIKE, THIS INTERJECTION . . .

As you know from reading chapter 7, the preposition *like* often gets hijacked and carried off into conjunctionland. Even worse, sometimes it gets enslaved as an interjection.

Like can properly be used as a verb (I *like* Mike), a preposition or "simile marker" (he acted *like* my BFF), and a synonym for *such as* (with friends *like* Mike, who needs enemies?). And even as an adverb, although it carries a whiff of dialect, meaning *about to* (Mike was *like* to tell a story when I said I'd had enough).

It can, in colloquial contexts, appear as a conjunction (he seemed *like* he would be loyal).

It can also be used as a hedge, a stand-in for *approximately,* a way to indicate that the words coming next may not be quite right but are close enough (I called *like* twelve guys before I got a date). And before quoted material it signals a guess or a lone example of a set of similar statements: I said something **like** "I know this is not the best time in the world, but will you marry me?"

This is when *like* starts to slide into the lazy zone.

Sometimes it's just filler, or, as the linguists are wont to say, a "discourse particle" ("I have, *like*, no BFFs anymore," or "I, like, don't know what to do"). This is smack in the middle of the lazy zone, and while it is common, it's not eloquent.

But this use of *like* is as old as the hills. Or at least the highlands. In Scotland, it was used at least as early as the nineteenth century, appearing in Robert Louis Stevenson's 1886 novel *Kidnapped* ("'What's, like, wrong with him?' said she at last"). It's common on this side of the pond, too. It found a place in a *New Yorker* cartoon of 1928, in which two young ladies are discussing a man's workplace:

—What's he got—an awfice?

—No, he's got like a loft.

Loose uses picked up in the 1950s, especially in beat and jazz culture, when *like* joined *cat* as a sign of cool ("Like, let's hear that horn, man"), and by 1962 it sprang from the mouths of teenagers in *A Clockwork Orange* ("I, *like*, didn't say anything").

The folksinger Loudon Wainwright III, in his 1995 composition "Cobwebs," wonders aloud whether using *like* instead of *as if* started "back with Jack Kerouac." But whenever it started, he notes, *like* has become "an audible pause," or "just an ugly little four-letter word."

Well it stumbles and it falls off of almost every tongue . . .

Give a listen and you will hear . . .

It's an assault to my mind's ear

The empty *like* has become ubiquitous. In speech, *like* buys you a little time when your mind can't keep up with your mouth. But in prose it has the effect of whittling your words down to whimpering, simpering sissyspeak.

THE LIL WAYNE *LIKE*

While we're on the subject, one more use of *like* deserves mention. The linguists call it "the quotative *like*," one of those absurd academic labels that is about as nononomatopoeic as they come. What is being described is very nonacademic language like this, from Lil Wayne's "Damn Damn" chorus:

Like whoa whoa whoa whoa whoa whoa

I was like whoa whoa whoa whoa whoa oh ohhh

She was like damn damn damn damn damn damn damn

And we was like damn

(The chorus itself basically repeats "Like, baby, baby, baby noo.")

The quotative *like* is associated, variously, with Valley Girls, Britney

Spears, and college students. It can be used to introduce a demonstration of someone's speech, as when teen celebrity Miley Cyrus told *Seventeen* magazine about her ex-boyfriend Nick Jonas:

> We became boyfriend and girlfriend the day we met. He was on a quest to meet me, and he was like, "I think you're beautiful and I really like you." And I was like, "Oh, my gosh, I like you so much." Nick and I loved each other. We still do, but we were in love with each other."

As you can see, this *like* often introduces a quotation, but it signals that what follows is not a verbatim quote but rather a suggestion of the general feel or spirit for what was said. *Like* often appears with a form of *to be*. This *like* takes the place of more traditional quotatives, like *say* and *ask* and *tell*, but doesn't imply the same literalness implied by those verbs. The loosey-goosey *goes* started appearing as a quotative around the 1940s, with its fraternal twin *like* coming on the scene in the 1960s or 1970s.

Carnal Pleasures

Political impersonators hang entire caricatures of Ronald Reagan on the Great Communicator's predilection for the interjection *well*. Rich Little said a presidential aide's advice to start everything with *well* gave him the hook he needed to mimic Reagan. Comedians couldn't get enough of Reagan's put-down of Jimmy Carter ("Well, there you go again"), and *Saturday Night Live*'s Jim Morris was still doing the Reagan *well* in 1998: "Well, am I still president? No? Well, I'll have you know . . ."

Across the pond, British comedian Catherine Tate does Little one better, managing to craft an entire monologue out of a Valley Girl's one-word interjections. It's best if you watch it on YouTube, but the first fifteen seconds of Tate's skit go basically like this:

> I'm like "Ooh," and he's like "Wow!" and I'm like "Dude—" and he's like "Cool!" and I'm like "So?" and he's like "Well. . ." and I'm

like "Fine," and he's like "Great," and I'm like "Duh!" and he's like "What?!" and I'm like "NO!" and he's like "Yes," and I'm like "Bye," and he's like "Oh!"

The quotative *like* is disdained as a symptom of laziness, carelessness, bad habits, or just bad rhetorical manners. But linguists argue that it encourages a narrator to embody various participants in a conversation. The speaker vocalizes what various participants say, while at the same time expressing her own *attitudes* toward those utterances. She can dramatize multiple viewpoints, one after another, telegraphing which views she sympathizes with and which she does not. It's much better than a he-said, she-said recitation, the single syllable allowing the expression of moral indignation, sarcasm, or slapstick humor.

Lest you think this kind of language is merely the province of lightweight teenagers, here is Pulitzer Prize–winning playwright August Wilson as quoted in *The New Yorker*: "When they said no one could figure out the Holy Trinity, I was **like**, 'Why not?'" Wilson uses *like* to express an "inner monologue"; he expresses an idea or sentiment he thought to himself but waited to say aloud.

The quotative *like* can also be tantamount to a virtuoso impersonation, a pantomime of facial expressions, hand gestures, gestures, sounds, and random noises:

- I was like [speaker puts hands up in surrender, puts up peace sign, points finger down throat, or something similarly dramatic]
- The announcer was like, "GOOOOOOOOOOOAL!"
- I ran into my ex and was like [speaker makes a face of horror]

And here's what's cool: None of these sentences would work if *say* were substituted for *like*.

As Jessica Love writes in *The American Scholar*, *like*, especially when followed by words like *well* or *dude, is* "much like a mask or good make-up or the right dialect coaching." Call them Bernhardt *like*s, Britney *like*s, or quotative *like*s, "these words further distinguish the current speaker from the person (or earlier self) being quoted. They give the performance a bit of flair."

INTERJECTIONS ARE SUCH FUN to play with because they allow us to capture the world of the spoken. Or the merely uttered. In an article on *Slate*, Ben Yagoda mentions *meh* as a personal favorite of recently popular interjections. *Meh* has no definition in the *OED,* but at this writing it had 284 definitions on urbandictionary.com. (Those include "A random word when people either don't know what to say, don't care, can't answer a question or are too drunk to form a coherent english phrase.") Yagoda noted that *meh* was used as an adjective meaning "indifferent" (as in "I felt kind of *meh* about the whole thing") in a *Simpsons* exchange:

> **Homer** *(after watching Blockoland commercial):* All right, kids . . . who wants to go . . . to . . . Blockoland?
> **Bart and Lisa:** Meh.
> **Homer:** But the commercial gave me the impression that . . .
> **Bart:** We said *meh.*
> **Lisa:** M-E-H. Meh.

Segueing from comedy to comics, we can find the true home of interjections. In comics, these "throwaways" hold their own against nouns and verbs and are styled bold for extra intonation and emphasis. *Beetlejuice #1,* by Harvey Comics, is packed with 'em:

> Smek!
> Thoom!
> Skathrak!
> Bwaaaah!
> Puff! Gasp! Wheeze!
> Eeyew! Glub! Gasp!
> Umm . . . Thank you!

Some interjections—"?!?," for example, or "#@%*!"—go completely off the deep end. Leaving letters in the dust, they let us depart the world of words altogether.

Catechism

PICK OUT THE DUST BUNNIES: In the *Schoolhouse Rock!* song "Interjections!" the character Reginald, home with the flu, gets "one small injection" from the doctor and responds with a surfeit of interjections. Find them:

> Hey! That smarts! Ouch! That hurts! Yow! That's not fair, givin' a guy a shot down there!

MAKE A MONOLOGUE: Write a soliloquy like Catherine Tate's in which one person is recounting a conversation whose content is conveyed mostly with interjections. Let the monologue tell a story—let the choice and sequence of interjections tell the reader who the characters are, what their relationship is, and what the tone or mood of the conversation was.

REMAKE A DIALOGUE: Take a scene with dialogue, either one of yours or one from a book, and rewrite it, condensing utterance and attitude by using the quotative *like* and other interjections.

PARSE THIS! There is no better way to test your grasp of the various parts of speech than by parsing sentences. Parsing—that is, going word by word through the sentence and naming which part of speech each word is—used to be a standard feature of English classes. As creativity became foregrounded in "language arts" classes, though, grammar was backgrounded, and parsing fell out of favor.

But as a way of reviewing what we've done so far, take the elegant paragraph below, from an essay called "A Report in Spring" by E. B. White, and see if you can figure out which part of speech each word is. (N = noun, P = pronoun, V = verb, Aj = adjective, Av = adverb, Pp = preposition, C = conjunction, I = interjection.)

> On Tuesday, in broad daylight, the coon arrived, heavy with young, to take possession of the hole in the tree, but she found another coon

in possession, and there was a grim fight high in the branches. The new tenant won, or so it appeared to me, and our old coon came down the tree in defeat and hustled off into the woods, to examine her wounds and make other plans for her confinement. I was sorry for her, as I am for any who are evicted from their haunts by the younger and stronger—always a sad occasion for man or beast.

PART 2

Sentences

I like to imagine a sentence as a boat. Each sentence, after all, has a distinct shape, and it comes with something that makes it move forward or stay still—whether a sail, a motor, or a pair of oars. There are as many kinds of sentences as there are seaworthy vessels: canoes and sloops, barges and battleships, Mississippi riverboats and dinghies all too prone to leaks. And then there are the impostors, flotsam and jetsam—a log heading downstream, say, or a coconut bobbing in the waves without a particular destination.

Much more than "everything between the capital letter and the period," the sentence tells who did what to whom. It has shape (a beginning, an end, and a dramatic arc), and it has either levity or gravity. If it's well made, it also has energy.

To craft a sentence that makes heads turn with its sleekness and grace, we need to bring various elements together so that—even when the sentence boat is rather outrageously tricked out—the whole thing has unity as well as purpose.

RELISH EVERY WORD

Sentences should vary as much as our objects of desire—sometimes we want them brawny, sometimes we want them brainy, sometimes silken, sometimes brutal. We *don't* want them to stay the same, day after day.

Yet we're so used to sound bites, to tweeting, to teenagers bypassing whole paragraphs with "duh" or "whatever," that we are tempted, in sentences, to the short and quick. But, remember, the imagination courses in unpredictable waves. As writers, we must become intimate with the ferocity of simple sentences as well as the gentle tumbling of phrases and clauses.

AIM DEEP, BUT BE SIMPLE

In high school, many of us were assigned term papers that seemed impossibly long. (*How do I fill fifteen pages?!?*) We learned to stretch them out, to write windy, to "state, restate, and summarize," to say what you plan to say, then to say it, then to say what you just said. We must unlearn such tricks as we refine our writing skills. The best sentences are models of economy, getting to the point (well, the period) quickly.

"*Mangia!*" cries the Italian *mamma*, and her single-word sentence speaks worlds. You'd be surprised how little you need to get your points across. Strip sentences down to the essentials. Clear out the clutter.

Henry David Thoreau worked tirelessly in this vein, peeling off unnecessary phrases until he reached the pith. In a first draft of *Walden*, he crafted this sentence:

> Over the south shore of the pond which was a low hill covered with shrub oaks & scattered pines which seemed to rise to an illimitable tableland—I seemed to look toward the country of a new ideal race of Tartars, where tribes of men dwelt in tents.

By the sixth version, Thoreau was able to make the same sentence much more elemental:

> The low shrub oak plateau to which the opposite shore arose stretched away toward the prairies of the West & the steppes of Tartary, affording ample room for all the roving families of men.

Thoreau simplified his sentence structure, keeping to one main clause and restricting himself to one *which*.

Sentences can meander—but they should have reason to do so. Virginia Woolf used wordathons to explore the labyrinthine interiors of her characters. Jamaica Kincaid created one breathless outpouring as a fitting response to a lifetime of commandments forced on a girl by her mother. William Faulkner spun out vast Southern sagas in sentences that include a thirteen-hundred-word doozy beginning "They both bore it as though in deliberate flagellant exaltation of physical misery transmogrified into the spirits' travail of the two young men during that time fifty years ago. . . ."

Before *you* go spinning out a thirteen-hundred-word opus, heed Hugh Blair, a very emeritus Edinburgh professor whose advice from 1783 has stood the test of more than two centuries: "Remember . . . every Audience is ready to tire; and the moment they begin to tire, all our Eloquence goes for nothing. A loose and verbose manner never fails to create disgust . . . better [to say] too little, than too much."

TAKE RISKS

Tame savage sentences, combing through them until every hair falls in place. Then muss them up and see how you like the look.

Experiment. Be dangerous. Play with words, mixing the curt with the lofty. Play with chains of words. Play with phrases and clauses and dashes and full stops. Mix short and long, neat and nasty.

Such experimentation was the province of David Foster Wallace, who took risks with length and lexicon in his novels and in these sentences from his 1993 essay "E Unibus Pluram: Television and U.S. Fiction":

The next real literary "rebels" in this country might well emerge as some weird bunch of anti-rebels, born oglers who dare somehow to back away from ironic watching, who have the childish gall actually to endorse and instantiate single-entendre principles. Who treat of plain old untrendy human troubles and emotions in U.S. life with reverence and conviction. Who eschew self-consciousness and hip fatigue. These anti-rebels would be outdated, of course, before they

even started. Dead on the page. Too sincere. Clearly repressed. Back-
ward, quaint, naive, anachronistic. . . . Real rebels, as far as I can see,
risk disapproval. The old postmodern insurgents risked the gasp and
squeal: shock, disgust, outrage, censorship, accusations of socialism,
anarchism, nihilism. Today's risks are different. The new rebels might
be artists willing to risk the yawn, the rolled eyes, the cool smile, the
nudged ribs, the parody of gifted ironists, the "Oh how banal."

Wallace may have been rebelling against the pat, self-conscious irony
of contemporary fiction, but he was also taking arms against pat sentences, wasn't he?

Entire sentences can play off one another just as solo words do.
Consider the patterns. Which best suits your story: lots of staccato? a
powerful crescendo? a long, slow diminuendo? pure cacophony?

SEEK BEAUTY

How do you keep sentences lively and lovely? Listen to the way the
words combine—the cadences, the blending of vowels, the balances
and imbalances. The nineteenth-century critic George Saintsbury once
noted how "shrift ought to be sooth" was identical in meaning to "con-
fession ought to be truthful" but very different in music. Saintsbury's
descendants, Strunk and White, mused similarly about Thomas Paine's
"These are the times that try men's souls." They noted how changes in
phrasing muck up Paine's elegant pentameter:

Times like these try men's souls.
How trying it is to live in these times!
These are trying times for men's souls.
Soulwise, these are trying times.

All the alternatives lack the original's noble spirit.

Whether you call it "turning a phrase" or "line editing," the simple
reordering of words can add ineffable beauty to a sentence. Notice the
subtle difference between these two examples:

- Many of the veterans knew more about the soldiers he was describing than the president *did*.
- Many of the veterans knew more about the soldiers he was describing than *did* the president.

The ever-so-slight change makes the second more elegant and memorable.

In *What I Saw at the Revolution,* the speechwriter Peggy Noonan recalls a line she wrote for Ronald Reagan about the Democrats:

They've gone so far left, they left America behind.

Fearing that the sentence gave Democrats credit for moving forward while the rest of the country was stuck in place, Noonan's White House boss, Richard Darman, changed two beats and transformed the sentence:

They're so far left, they've left America.

FIND THE RIGHT PITCH

Why do so many of us, when we sit down to write, sound like word processors rather than wordsmiths? Why do we spew the slogans of the consumer culture we work for, rather than sounding like the bards we want to be?

Let's face it, we're surrounded by chatter, clatter, clutter, and cloudiness. We read less and watch more, which leaves us swimming in unrefined language, unedited sentences, ill-considered commentary. Our litigious times lead us to words full of ominous legality but empty of humanity.

Our sense of language is also blunted by the speech around us: We give microphones to inarticulate sports heroes. We read tweets about celebrities ("Kim Kardashian's baby is so lucky. On the one side it's got hip-hop pop star genes and on the other it's got, um . . . Hold on. Uh . . . nope"). We tolerate the sanitized statements of political candidates. (Check out David Letterman's 2008 "Mitt Romney Cliché Count.")

Some public servants, though, manage to craft simple sentences that are also humble and real. Go back and review the strong words delivered to Lt. Col. Oliver North by senators George Mitchell and Warren Rudman at the end of the Iran-contra hearings in 1987, for great examples. Rudman's crisp sentences convey all the blunt rhythms of his New Hampshire roots, while Mitchell's softer cadences and grander sentences reflect his judicious temperament.

President Barack Obama, after the 2012 shooting of twenty-six children at the Sandy Hook school, spoke as a parent to the families of Newtown, Connecticut. His clauses were pared down, softened by sympathy, cadenced in the comforting rhythms of a sermon, and pitched at the audience in the room and around the world:

> I come to offer the love and prayers of a nation. I am very mindful that mere words cannot match the depths of your sorrow, nor can they heal your wounded hearts. I can only hope it helps for you to know that you're not alone in your grief; that our world too has been torn apart; that all across this land of ours, we have wept with you, we've pulled our children tight. And you must know that whatever measure of comfort we can provide, we will provide; whatever portion of sadness that we can share with you to ease this heavy load, we will gladly bear it. Newtown—you are not alone.

Crafting sentences that are *true* is a struggle, but such craft offers an opportunity. Writing, after all, affords us a luxury we lack in conversation: we can go back to recast our sentences, paying attention to syntax and sensuality in a way that's impossible when we're being extemporaneous—in speaking or in writing. And, paradoxically, when rewriting works, the prose sounds natural. It echoes the true voice.

CHAPTER 9

The Subject, the Predicate

Bones

At some point in our lives, maybe in grade school, teachers give us a pat definition for a sentence: "It begins with a capital letter, ends with a period, and expresses a complete thought." We learn, eventually, that that period might be replaced by another strong stop, like a question mark or an exclamation point. But that expanded definition misses the essence of sentencehood.

If a sentence is a boat, its outline, its meaning, is given form by nouns and verbs. Nouns give us sentence subjects: our boat hulls. Verbs give us predicates: the forward momentum, the twists and turns, the abrupt stops.

Another way of thinking about this is to say that a sentence needs a What (the subject) and a So What (the predicate). The subject is the person, place, thing, or idea we want to express something about; the predicate expresses the action, condition, or effect of that subject. The predicate expresses a *predicament*—the situation the subject is in.

So we can imagine the whole sentence as a mini-narrative. It features a protagonist (the subject) and some sort of drama (the predicate): *Kimo lowers his machete. The coconut cracks open.* The drama makes us pay attention.

Let's look at some opening lines of great novels to see how this sentence drama plays out. Notice the subject, in bold, in each of the following sentences. It might be a simple noun or pronoun, a noun modified by an adjective or two, or something even more complicated:

> "**They** shoot the white girl first." —Toni Morrison, *Paradise*

> "**The Miss Lonelyhearts of the New York Post-Dispatch (Are-you-in-trouble?-Do-you-need-advice?-Write-to-Miss-Lonelyhearts-and-she-will-help-you)** sat at his desk and stared at a piece of white cardboard." —Nathanael West, *Miss Lonelyhearts*

The predicate, remember, includes everything that is not the subject. In addition to the verb, it can contain direct objects, indirect objects, adverbs, and various kinds of phrases. More important, the predicate names the predicament of the subject.

> "Elmer Gantry <u>was drunk</u>." —Sinclair Lewis, *Elmer Gantry*

> "Every summer Lin Kong <u>returned to Goose Village to divorce his wife, Shuyu</u>." —Ha Jin, *Waiting*

And sometimes there is more than one subject-predicate pairing within a sentence:

> "We <u>started dying before the snow</u>, and like the snow, we <u>continued to fall</u>." —Louise Erdrich, *Tracks*

MISSING IN ACTION

No sentence is complete until you know what the subject *did*. The verb is usually explicit, but not always. The subject, though, is frequently implied, almost embedded in the verb. One of the strongest opening lines in American literature—"Call me Ishmael"—seems to possess no subject. But Herman Melville merely exploits the imperative voice, in which the subject—*you*—is implied.

The imperative mood can be used to convey immediacy, by co-opting the reader, or it can be used as a command, to convey authority: *Be there or be square,* for example, or *Readme.* First person pronouns can also make implied subjects: *Been there. Done that.* (*I* is the subject.)

We don't need no stinkin' verbs

Sometimes groups of words make perfect sense without a verb. Readers of the *New York Times* Opinionator series "Draft" posted numerous comments in response to the idea that a sentence must have a subject and a verb.

"Verbs? We don't need no stinkin' verbs," wrote a reader with the handle "aattlee." This haiku, aattlee wrote, provides an example:

grasshopper on leaf
hungry bird on branch above
lunch in paradise

(But then many nonnarrative forms—poetry, song lyrics, ads—forgo sentences.)

Greg Shenaut commented: "The human mind creates the dynamism of language, not the words or the types of words we use." To prove that we can create dynamic images without verbs, Shenaut sent this sentence:

Horse in a race, jockey out of saddle, big collision, ambulances and sirens.

The problem is, that reads more like a telegram, or a tweet, than the opening line of a great work.

"In English, can a sentence have a subject and predicate without a verb?" asked John Tallman, answering his own question with an example:

John drinks coffee for breakfast; Alice, tea.

John's got a point, but the verb *drinks* is implied in the clause describing what Alice imbibes.

VISUALIZING SENTENCES

Remember how to diagram a sentence? I know, I know, memories of grammar school make you groan, but diagramming sentences really puts things into perspective. Why? Because diagramming casts the sentence as an elegant line, as a boat with a stern and a pointy prow, or as a forward-moving story with a start (the subject) and a finish (the predicate):

$$\rightarrow \text{Subject} \mid \text{Predicate} \rightarrow$$

Caesar's "I came," for example, would be diagrammed:

$$\rightarrow \text{I} \mid \text{came} \rightarrow$$

Diagramming shows that every sentence, no matter how complicated, derives energy, clear direction, and momentum from its subject and predicate.

Here's the diagram of a less simple sentence—"The waterway flowed sombre under an overcast sky"—from the end of *Heart of Darkness:*

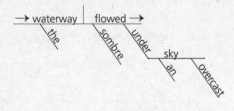

Diagramming sentences also exposes a brutal truth about pileups of modifiers and phrases: they do not advance the message; they dangle off the hull of a sentence like tow lines. The more a sentence drags extraneous words and phrases, the more it slows from schooner to barge.

Here's a less elegant sentence, courtesy of the Bulwer-Lytton Fiction Contest, which invites authors to craft the opening sentence to the worst of all possible novels: "Like an overripe beefsteak tomato rimmed with cottage cheese, the corpulent remains of Santa Claus lay dead on the hotel floor." The sentence diagram shows why that sentence is such a brilliant boner:

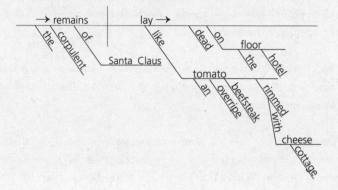

As you can see, the stuff of this sentence does not follow the through-line, but rather drags it down.

Flesh

To tell a story in few words, think strong subject, strong predicate. No one knows this better than the headline writers of the world, who, when they pull it off, manage to convey the news and the blues with a minimum of words and a maximum of wit.

The winner in the subject-predicate category would have to be this headline from the *New York Post* announcing that Elizabeth Taylor tied the knot in 1991 for the eighth (count 'em) time:

I DO . . . I DO . . . I DO . . . I DO . . . I DO, I DO . . . I DO . . . I DO!

(That double "I do, I do" in the middle stands for the two separate weddings of Liz and Richard Burton.)

Like headline writers, the best reporters stand back, squint like painters taking in landscapes, and sketch out the bold outlines of their stories through strong subjects and predicates. Their stories distill the drama into a few select sentences.

The classic news lead is Subject-Predicate City, collapsing a story into a thirty-five-words-or-fewer sentence that tells Who, What, When, Where, and maybe even Why. When an American caused a royal stir in London, Jason Bennetto, of the *London Independent*, nailed all five W's in the opening of his story:

> Buckingham Palace came under aerial assault Saturday for the first time since World War II, when a half-naked American paraglider landed on the roof.

In case you missed 'em all, here are the five W's: Who—a half-naked American. What—landed on the palace roof. When—Saturday. Where—London. Why—Don't you want to read on to find out?

Even when reporters at the best metropolitan dailies defy the five-W formula with abandon, they hardly abandon simple subjects and predicates. Take Beth Hughes's opener for a story on the California tofu business, which ran in the *San Francisco Examiner*:

> It's white. It's weird. It wiggles on a plate.

Whether you write short, punchy sentences or long, flowing ones, keeping track of your subjects and predicates can prevent your prose from shifting and drifting.

IN A *NEW YORKER* profile of the North Carolina IRS agent Garland Bunting, Alec Wilkinson tracks his subject without ever losing him. It is a collection of taut sentences whose focus never wanders: almost every sentence features as its subject *Garland, Garland Bunting,* or *he:*

> For more than thirty years, **Garland Bunting** has been engaged in capturing and prosecuting men and women in North Carolina who make and sell liquor illegally. To do this, **he** has driven taxis, delivered sermons, peddled fish, buckdanced, worked carnivals as a barker, operated bulldozers, loaded carriages and hauled logs at sawmills, feigned drunkenness, and pretended to be an idiot. In the mind of

many people, **he** is the most successful revenue agent in the history of a state that has always been enormously productive of moonshine.

Garland is fifty-nine. **He** is of medium height and portly. **He** has a small mouth, thin lips, a nose that is slightly hooked, and eyes that are clear and close-set and steel blue. What hair he has is bristly and gray. A billed cap bearing the emblem of a fertilizer company or a trucking concern or an outfit that makes farm equipment customarily adorns his head. **He** has a splayfooted walk and a paunch like a feed sack. **He** possesses what he calls "that sweet-potato shape—small at both ends and big in the middle," and **he** says, "It's hard to keep pants up on a thing like that." A few years ago, **he** walked into a clothing store to buy a suit, spread his jacket wide for a salesman, and said, "I'd like to see something to fit this," and the salesman said, "I would, too."

In only a couple of sentences of those first fifteen does Wilkinson let his subject stray: "[What] hair . . . is" and "A billed cap . . . customarily adorns his head."

Notice how nicely the subjects and predicates work in these sentences from Cormac McCarthy's *All the Pretty Horses*:

They <u>rode</u> out along the fenceline and across the open pastureland. **The leather** <u>creaked</u> in the morning cold. **They** <u>pushed</u> the horses into a lope. **The lights** <u>fell away</u> behind them. They rode out on the high prairie where **they** <u>slowed</u> the horses to a walk and **the stars** <u>swarmed</u> around them out of the blackness. **They** <u>heard</u> somewhere in that tenantless night a bell that tolled and ceased where no bell was and **they** <u>rode</u> out on the round dais of the earth which alone was dark and no light to it and which carried their figures and bore them up into the swarming stars so that **they** <u>rode</u> not under but among them and **they** <u>rode</u> at once jaunty and circumspect, like thieves newly loosed in that dark electric, like young thieves in a glowing orchard, loosely jacketed against the cold and ten thousand worlds for the choosing.

Like the pace of the mounts they're describing, McCarthy's sentences start at a controlled clip before stretching out into a graceful canter as horses and riders reach the Texas high prairie. Finally, they gallop wildly, trusting their fate to the infinite night sky. Did you notice the repetition of that subject-predicate combo "they rode"? It keeps us grounded as the sentences get more and more wild.

Cardinal Sins

Remember, every sentence is a mini-narrative. Stop for a second and think before you write. What is your subject? Will every sentence pertain to your subject? Can you keep your sentences from wandering off on tangents?

FLOTSAM

When a sentence lacks one of its two essential parts, it is called a *sentence fragment*. Fragments drift unmoored, without clear direction or purpose. They may start with a capital letter and end with a period, but they are shards of thought, shadows of ideas. Fragments usually make prose halting and choppy, and they often come off as phony—gratuitous attempts at edgy informality.

A letter offering a credit card from Chase Manhattan Bank starts off with a bona fide sentence but then veers into bonehead fragments:

> As someone with a good credit history, you know the importance of having a flexible financial tool. <u>One that enables you to pay for all your major expenses, yet still allows you to make low monthly payments. A credit option that gives you greater cash flow, without stretching the limits of your credit cards or using your home as collateral. A flexible tool like Chase Advantage Credit®.</u> It's the line of credit you access simply by writing a check.

Despite the periods, none of the underlined statements is a complete sentence ("that" makes two of them dependent clauses). That last line qualifies as a sentence, but—really—*access* as a verb?

Playing with sentence fragments can be fun—the best copywriters use them for advertising slogans (Alka-Seltzer's "Plop plop, fizz fizz").

But there are plenty of competing Madison Avenue slogans to convince you that a full sentence registers equally well—from Esso's "Put a tiger in your tank" to the Heublein Company's "Pardon me, would you have any Grey Poupon?" While sentence fragments can be witty, they are hard to do well, and better suited to hawking antacids than to transforming inchoate thoughts into indelible words.

JETSAM

If sentence fragments are like flotsam, a profusion of subjects is like jetsam. Too many subjects thrown in can cause a passage to herk and jerk like a cigarette boat whose gears have jammed. Take these off-the-cuff remarks by President George H. W. Bush at a 1988 Milwaukee campaign stop around Halloween:

> We had last night, last night we had a couple of our grandchildren with us in Kansas City—six-year-old twins, one of them went as a package of Juicy Fruit, arms sticking out of the pack, the other was Dracula. A big rally there. And Dracula's wig fell off in the middle of my speech and I got to thinking, watching those kids, and I said if I could look back and I had been president for four years: What would you like to do? Those young kids here. And I'd love to be able to say that working with our allies, working with the Soviets, I'd found a way to ban chemical and biological weapons from the face of the earth.

As the subjects in those sentences keep shifting—from *we* to *twins, one of them, the other, we* (implied), *wig, I, I, I, I, you, kids, I,* and *I*—Bush's message keeps shifting, too.

Vice President Joseph R. Biden, Jr., may not share Mr. Bush's aversion to *I*, but a sentence from his 2008 vice presidential debate shows how he, too, could lose track of his subjects:

> If you need any more proof positive of how bad the economic theories have been, this excessive deregulation, the failure to oversee what was going on, letting Wall Street run wild, I don't think you needed any more evidence than what you see now.

Biden not only shifts from *you* to *I* and back to *you* again, he throws three fragments into the middle of his sentence, each featuring a different subject.

Syntax gets a lot more complicated than subjects and predicates, but understanding the relationship between the hull and the sail, the What and the So What, is the first step in mastering the dynamics of a sentence.

SENTENCES AS NONNARRATIVES

Subjects and predicates—especially if they're not strong—can get lost in a mass of fluffy words. This line from a *Times of London* editorial on July 25, 1815, announced that the defeated Napoleon had arrived in England—well, sort of:

> He is, therefore, what we may call, here.

That sentence, in all its softness, equivocation, and absence of action, may have worked to describe a broken and imprisoned ex-emperor, but that doesn't mean *you* should surrender when it comes to subjects and predicates.

If subjects and predicates drift too far apart in sentences, separated by endless intervening clauses, the reader may give up. The second sentence in this paragraph from the *San Francisco Chronicle* needed a copy editor:

> The baby was delivered Tuesday by Caesarean section. With the approval of the infant's family, the respirator that had kept the mother's heart and lungs functioning for 64 days so the baby could live in her womb was turned off.

Here's how that sentence might have been tamed:

> The baby was delivered Tuesday by Caesarean section. With the approval of the infant's family, the doctors then turned off the respirator

that had kept the mother's heart and lungs functioning for 64 days so the baby could mature in her womb.

On the other hand, sometimes statements get so condensed, so squished together, that subjects and predicates become indistinguishable. Can you figure out what story this headline in the *Toronto Star* is trying to tell?

Fire put woman in coma highrise inquest told

Maybe some punctuation would have helped (*Fire put woman in coma, highrise inquest told*), but that headline writer was thinking comas, not commas.

Richard Lederer, in *Anguished English,* has collected what he calls "two-headed headlines," in which the blurring of subject and predicate makes for syntactical mayhem:

WILLIAM KELLY, 87, WAS FED SECRETARY
How did she taste?

HERSHEY BARS PROTEST
Are candy bars going on strike?

STUD TIRES OUT
Did the hunk lose his edge? Or were the tires just not cool anymore?

BRITISH LEFT WAFFLES ON FALKLAND ISLANDS
And the Argentineans ask, *Donde están los* waffles?

TEACHER STRIKES IDLE KIDS
Ouch!

THE SUBJECT-VERB TANGO

Some sentences do contain a clear subject and a clear predicate, but the poor things aren't dancing in unison. Just as pronouns must agree with their antecedents, verbs must agree with their subjects. A singular subject requires a singular verb; a plural subject requires—guess what?—a plural verb.

Here's a description of a nineteenth-century lady whose subject and verb are improper, despite her very proper kid gloves:

> A horse car. Enter an elaborately dressed lady, diamond solitaires, eight-button kids, etc. Car crowded. At first no one moves. Soon a gentleman offers his seat. "Thank you; you are the only gentleman here. The rest is hogs."

Since the "lady" is referring to all the other men on the car, she of course should have said "The rest *are* hogs." Appearances can be deceiving. Anyone can buy good clothes, but it's harder to acquire good grammar.

Collective nouns—words like *band, troupe, group,* or even *government*—present a subject-verb minefield. Those nouns embrace a number of members, people, or bodies, but the nouns themselves are generally singular and require the singular form of the verb. Can you spot the trouble in this sentence, from a *Newsweek* article about mischief at a 2004 Republican gathering?

> A group of politically active "hacktivists" are plotting to disrupt the convention electronically.

The subject of that sentence is *group*, and it's singular. So the verb should have been *is*, not *are*. That plural neologism (*hacktivists*) right before the verb surely confuses things. (And the copy editor's bible, *The Chicago Manual of Style*, is less absolutist than this editor on the subject of collective nouns.)

Disagreement between the subject and verb is common in song lyrics, which are often in colloquial rather than standard English.

Take this example from "Every Little Thing She Does Is Magic" by the Police:

Everything she do just turns me on.

Sting might be keeping in line with the whole reggae/ska feel of the Police's early music, but unless you have a similarly good excuse, use "does" at a time like this.

Timbaland went so far as to abandon sense in the title of the song "The Way I Are." It got uglier in this line:

Can you handle me the way I are?

Does anyone really talk like this?

Let's agree not to disagree

Here's a simplified, slimmed-down list of tricky subject-verb agreements:

- When two nouns are joined by *and,* that compound subject is plural and needs a plural verb: "**The green eggs and the yellow eggs** are in the Easter basket; the blue egg is still hidden in the yard."
- When two nouns are joined by *and* but act as one entity, the verb must agree with the single subject: "**Green eggs and ham** is not my favorite breakfast (much as I love Dr. Seuss)."
- When two nouns are linked by prepositions like *with, in addition to,* and *as well as,* beware—the verb must agree with the first noun, the true subject: "***Green Eggs and Ham,*** together with ***The Cat in the Hat,*** keeps the kids from horsing around."
- When an indefinite pronoun is the subject, take special care. Pronouns like *anybody, each, everyone, much,* and *nobody* take singular verbs: "**Everyone** remembers that cold, cold wet day." But other indefinite pronouns, like *both, few, most,* and *some,* take plural verbs: "**Few**, though, ever face Thing One and Thing Two."

- Collective nouns (*government, corporation, band, group*) are generally singular, and so take the singular verb: "**The company** decides whether or not its chef can serve green eggs and ham." (If you want to unpack that "generally," see *The Chicago Manual of Style,* 16th edition, §5.8.)
- Certain plural quantities act as singular entities when they are the subject of a sentence: "**Twelve months** is a long time to wait for a change of menu."
- Some nouns that might seem plural—partly because they end in *s,* like *the United States* or *mathematics*—are actually singular: "**Mathematics** always makes me want to seek refuge in green eggs and ham."
- Certain words (*alumnus/alumni, datum/data, medium/media, memorandum/memoranda*) live in a weird limbo between Latin and English. Latin telegraphs a word's number via its ending: *-us* and *-um* are *singularis.* So if you want to sound hypercorrect, observe the Latin: "This new **medium**, this World Wide Web, is no place for Dr. Seuss." If you want to sound hypercurrent, forget the Latin: "This **data** on green eggs and ham is taxing my hard drive."

FALSE STARTS

Beware of sentences that get off on the wrong foot by starting with "I think," "There was," or "It is." Strike those beginnings and start right in with your true subject:

~~I think that~~ This book will set you straight.
~~There are~~ Writers out there ~~who~~ are desperate for pithy advice.
~~It is my opinion that~~ Everyone needs grammar.

If you are a reporter taking care to get down verbatim everything a source says, you're on the right track. But you don't have to report every "I think" a subject utters. Make the cut in quotes like this:

"~~I think~~ The biggest problem in American schools has been the search for one right way," says Chris Whittle, founder of the Edison Project.

Part of rewriting and editing is taking the slack out of sentences, eliminating the false starts and fitfulnesses. Here, for example, is how the *Wired* writer Po Bronson tightened a graf in a story on Silicon Valley headhunters:

If I show up at 3Com with a knockout candidate, you think they're going to slam the door in my face? Every time a startup backs off from an IPO, ~~there's~~ disappointed employees there ~~who~~ will take my call. Every time a new manager takes over an ongoing project, ~~there are~~ employees who are supposed to work under him ~~who~~ won't get along with the new boss, and they'll take my call.

Carnal Pleasures

In the hands of skillful writers, sentence fragments can perk up prose, making it less stiff and formal. They can also help punctuate long sentences. Call it pause and effect, the fragment brightening the narrative with a dash of staccato.

Email subject headers—the words you see when you check your daily torrent of messages—must pack a terse and enticing thought into a small field. How's this one, from an editor at work to her lover:

>Subject: go ahead and call—coast is clear. m

That got two sentences, a signature, and a sense of urgency into a few bits.

Sometimes the subject and predicate are artfully embedded in a few keystrokes. In the following subject header, the mini-narrative lurks not in a subject and predicate but in the punctuation itself:

>Subject: dinner?

A one-word narrative. In the crook of the question mark is the crux of the sentence ("Would you like to join me for . . .").

Sometimes headers are flat-out teases, catching your interest by keeping the subject and predicate a mystery:

>Subject: airsex

Is *airsex* the subject? Is *airsex* the verb? You can bet a lot of cooped-up office workers opened the email, which contained a newswire story on "a trend toward more brazen consensual sex" on all commercial flights. ("Formerly rare seat and lavatory couplings are now reported as commonplace by flight crews worldwide. Flight attendant consultants' advice on how to deal with in-seat trysters: address passengers by name, crouch down to eye-to-eye level with them, and don't threaten.")

SENTENCE FRAGMENTS MAY BE the stuff of headlines, but they don't appear often in news copy. Narrative nonfiction, though? That's another story. Gay Talese plays with narrative voice in his *New Yorker* story "Travels with a Diva," about the opera singer Marina Poplavskaya:

> The first thing I saw when I entered the living room with Poplavskaya and her mother was a large poster of the singer, advertising a performance at Covent Garden. It bore the caption "Turbocharged. Marina can do 0–60 in one second. Decibels that is. One voice. Complete control. Total power. Va va voom."

Of course, Talese is quoting a poster. The sentence fragments work in paragraph form, too. Sort of like the timpani in the orchestra pit.

Novelists have even more latitude than journalists. In *The God of Small Things,* Arundhati Roy uses sentence fragments to often comic effect. In the following paragraphs, she mixes long and lyrical sentences with some pipsqueaks:

> From the dining-room window where she stood, with the wind in her hair, Rahel could see the rain drum down on the rusted tin roof of what used to be their grandmother's pickle factory.

Paradise Pickles & Preserves.

It lay between the house and the river.

They used to make pickles, squashes, jams, curry powders and canned pineapples. And banana jam (illegally) after the FPO (Food Products Organization) banned it because according to their specifications it was neither jam nor jelly. Too thin for jelly and too thick for jam. An ambiguous, unclassifiable consistency, they said.

As per their books.

The sentence fragments add punch to the pathos of a family's failed enterprises.

The first sentence of David Foster Wallace's *The Pale King* is practically a noun symphony, without a subject or verb to be found anywhere:

Past the flannel plains and blacktop graphs and skylines of canted rust, and past the tobacco-brown river overhung with weeping trees and coins of sunlight through them on the water downriver, to the place beyond the windbreak, where untilled fields simmer shrilly in the a.m. heat: shattercane, lamb's quarter, cutgrass, sawbrier, nutgrass, jimsonweed, wild mint, dandelion, foxtail, muscadine, spinecabbage, goldenrod, creeping charlie, butter-print, nightshade, ragweed, wild oat, vetch, butcher grass, invaginate volunteer beans, all heads gently nodding in a morning breeze like a mother's soft hand on your cheek.

Don't even try to diagram that. Just float on the current, enjoying the flotsam and jetsam.

Catechism

OPEN ME: Whether or not they technically contain a subject and a predicate, the best email subject headers convey everything a sentence conveys. Take a look at the following subject headers. Are they sentences or sentence fragments? If the latter, do they contain a subject only, a predicate only, or neither?

>Subject: Oh, Mexico . . .
>Subject: woe
>Subject: RSVP to Soiree 98 by 1/18!!
>Subject: the official word
>Subject: point blank pie
>Subject: Prepare to Be Overwhelmed
>Subject: last chance
>Subject: my mother
>Subject: writer threatening suicide
>Subject: peep

That last one is especially enigmatic. Is *peep* the plaintive cry of someone badly in need of attention? Is it the promise of a risqué glimpse?
Or is it an imperative (Look here or you will forever face regret . . .)? It
works because it could be all three.

SIX-WORD MEMOIRS: In 2006, Rachel Fershleiser and Larry Smith, editors of the Web-based *Smith Magazine,* reminded readers that Ernest
Hemingway had told an entire story in six words: "For sale. Baby shoes.
Never worn." They dared readers to top him by writing personal stories,
and they published the best of the enthusiastic responses. Here are
two Six-Word Memoirs that do the subject-predicate tango:

"Googled what he called me. Ouch." (Emily L.)
"My parents should've kept their receipt." (SarahBeth)

Using those as models, write your own mini-memoir—either seriously
or in jest.

CHAPTER 10

Simple Sentences

Bones

Writers dream of sentences that sail through the waters of thought. We carefully design their build and girth, and we struggle at the helm to keep them gliding rather than thrashing at sea. We can think of the subject of a sentence, crafted mainly from nouns, as the hull of a boat. And we can think of the predicate, whose key component is a verb, as the sail or motor, the part that makes the boat move.

All it takes is a simple sentence to get a What and a So What, a protagonist and a story. What is a simple sentence? A mini-narrative that contains one and only one subject-predicate pair. In the example *Animals swerve,* the subject is *animals,* the verb is *swerve*. Simple.

But a sentence can be simple without being stark. The subject and the predicate can contain multitudes—adjectives, adverbs, and all kinds of phrases. Or the subject can be a compound, containing two nouns of equal weight, as with *Moths and mammals swerve through the night air*. The predicate can be a compound, too: *Animals swerve and flutter through dense walls of green*. These are still simple sentences.

The simple sentence comes in five basic patterns. The following sentences that illustrate those patterns, like the one in the preceding paragraph, are based on lines from Diane Ackerman's description of the Brazilian rain forest in *The Rarest of the Rare*.

S + V

In the first pattern, the subject is paired with an intransitive verb, as in *Cicadas buzz* or *Mosquitoes whine*. Intransitive verbs, remember, do not need objects to complete an action, so the minimum requirement for an S + V sentence is merely a subject and a verb. Of course, any number of adjectives and adverbs or prepositional phrases may join the fray. In *Gemlike hummingbirds swoop among bird-of-paradise flowers,* the single subject-predicate pair (*hummingbirds swoop*) keeps it a simple sentence:

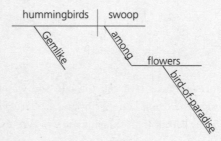

S + V + DO

In the second pattern, the subject is paired with a transitive verb. Transitive verbs require direct objects—the noun or pronoun that receives the action—so the complete sentence pattern includes the subject, the transitive verb, and the direct object: *The meek inherit nothing.*

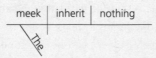

S + V + IO + DO

In the third pattern, the subject is paired with a ditransitive verb, which may take an indirect object as well as a direct object. Ditransitives include *give, send, cook, make, prepare,* and *tell.* Indirect objects identify the person or thing to whom or for whom something is being done. So here the complete sentence pattern includes the subject, the verb, the indirect object, and the direct object, usually in that order: *The scientists give the monkeys bananas and crickets.*

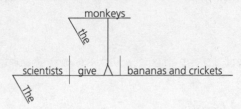

(This sentence pattern, common though it is, can befuddle grammar novices. Perhaps the best mnemonic example is Patrick Henry's "Give me liberty or give me death.")

Objects of our affection

One way to think of the direct object is as the answer to the question *Whom?* or *What?* With *The meek inherit nothing,* when you ask the question "The meek inherit *what*?" the answer, the direct object, is "nothing." With *Slime-coated vines may send golden lion tamarins skidding,* the question becomes "The slime-coated vines may send *whom* skidding?" The answer, the direct object, is "golden lion tamarins." (For our purposes, *who* and *whom* extend to the animal kingdom.)

The indirect object answers the question *To (or For) whom* is the action committed? or *To (For) what?* In *The scientists give the monkeys bananas and crickets,* when you ask the question "To *whom* do the scientists give bananas and crickets?" the answer, the indirect object, is "the monkeys."

S + SV + C

In the fourth simple sentence pattern, the subject is paired with a static verb, which is followed by a noun or an adjective called a *complement*. (Complements are also called *predicate nouns* and *predicate adjectives*.) The static verb sets up a kind of "relationship of equals" between the subject and the complement. The complement may re-identify the subject if it is a noun: in "Jungle plants have become incredible tricksters and manipulators, conning others into performing sex acts with them," *plants* are reidentified as *tricksters* and *manipulators*.

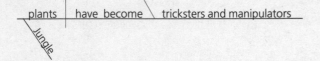

The complement can also do the usual modifier thing and describe the subject: in "Plants are promiscuous," *promiscuous* is a straight-up adjective:

Plants | are \ promiscuous

Remember, static verbs include state-of-being verbs like *to be* or *to become;* the "senses" verbs *to look, to sound, to feel, to smell,* and *to taste;* and that group of verbs including *to appear, to prove, to remain,* and *to seem.* Occasionally the complement is an adverbial prepositional phrase: "Suzy's graduation bash will be <u>at the beach house</u>."

S + V + DO + OC

In addition to the subjective complement, certain sentences contain an *objective complement*. This is a noun or adjective that follows the direct object, modifying it (and not the subject). Let's take the sentence *Some orchids, with their splashy color or blossoms, make unsuspecting bees pollinators*.

| orchids | make | bees | pollinators |

The thing is, only a certain class of verbs, known as *factitives*, can set up this kind of sentence pattern. In addition to the verb *make*, as in the sentence above, other factitive verbs include *choose, judge, elect, select, name*, and *found*. (For practice, let's try another sentence: *The male tachinid fly found one particular orchid irresistible*. (He tried to mate with it and ended up dusted with pollen.) Can you spot the objective complement?

Flesh

In a journalistic rite of passage, new beat reporters with Faulknerian delusions are hauled into the city editor's office for an upbraiding. "Remember, kid," begins the salty veteran, "you get paid by the period."

For power and punch, nothing beats the simple sentence. The best journalists know it cold, and nowhere do they use the simple sentence better than in opening paragraphs, known in newspaper parlance as "ledes."

The crime reporter Gene Miller, who became an editor at the *Miami Herald*, got so good at launching stories with a couple of longish sentences followed by one short one that his brand of news lede earned its own name: the Miller Chop. The *Miami Herald* crime beat veteran Edna Buchanan, one of his disciples, crafted this lede with Miller for a story on the murder of a high-living Miami lawyer:

> . . . He had his golf clubs in the trunk of his Cadillac. Wednesday
> looked like an easy day. He figured he might pick up a game later with
> Eddie Arcaro, the jockey. He didn't.

Buchanan, author of *The Corpse Had a Familiar Face,* has improvised on the Miller Chop, crafting what Calvin Trillin calls in a profile "the simple, matter-of-fact statement that registers with a jolt." On the killing of a rowdy ex-con who lurched into a Church's outlet, demanded fried chicken, and started a fatal brawl when offered chicken nuggets instead, Buchanan led with this simple sentence:

Gary Robinson died hungry.

Then there is Buchanan's lede in a story about a lovers' spat, which alternates between simple and not-so-simple sentences before stopping short:

The man she loved slapped her face. Furious, she says she told him never, ever to do that again. "What are you going to do, kill me?" he asked, and handed her a gun. "Here, kill me," he challenged. She did.

SIMPLE SENTENCES CAN TELL eloquent stories, too. After a bomb killed four girls on September 15, 1963, at the Sixteenth Street Baptist Church in Birmingham, Alabama, Eugene Patterson (then editor of the *Atlanta Constitution*), wrote his most famous column, "A Flower for the Graves." Its opening lines turn four simple sentences, made rich by rhythmic prepositional phrases, into a dirge:

A Negro mother wept in the street Sunday morning in front of a Baptist Church in Birmingham. In her hand she held a shoe, one shoe, from the foot of her dead child. We hold that shoe with her.
Every one of us in the white South holds that small shoe in his hand.

The simple sentence is not solely the province of the Fourth Estate. Charlotte Brontë made music out of the S + V + DO sentence (punctuated with semicolons rather than periods) in the following passage from *Villette*. The narrator awaits reunion with her beloved, and her sentences bristle with anticipation:

The sun passes the equinox; the days shorten; the leaves grow sere; but—he is coming.

Frosts appear at night. November has sent his fogs in advance; the wind takes its autumn moan; but—he is coming.

The skies hang full and dark; a rack sails from the west; the clouds case themselves into strange forms—arches and broad radiations; there rise resplendent mornings—glorious, royal, purple as monarch in his state; the heavens are one flame; so wild are they, they rival battle at its thickest—so bloody, they shame victory in her pride. I know some signs of the sky, I have noted them ever since childhood. God watch that sail! Oh, guard it!

Muhammad Ali makes a wholly different kind of poetry out of the simple sentence. While in Zaire in 1974 preparing for his "Rumble in the Jungle" against heavyweight champion George Foreman, Ali forged this unforgettable S + V + DO rap:

Only last week, I murdered a rock. Injured a stone. Hospitalized a brick. I'm so mean, I make *medicine* sick.

Much of Ali's humor turned on his jabbing sentences. "I am the astronaut of boxing," he once said, reflecting on his place in the history of the sport. "Joe Louis and Dempsey were just jet pilots. I'm in a world of my own."

Simple sentences can pack a punch, and they can deliver a punch line. Groucho Marx depended on simple sentences ("Alimony is like buying hay for a dead horse"). And Jon Stewart tweets them: "Obama just lost the Civil War reenactment vote." (That tweet requires some backstory: after Mitt Romney lamented the shrinking size of the military in a 2012 presidential debate, President Barack Obama laughed it off, asserting that while the United States has fewer ships than at any time since 1916, "we also have fewer horses and bayonets.")

In ads and adages, simple sentences can be straightforward ("A diamond is forever"), authoritative ("Don't change horses in midstream"), didactic ("A penny saved is a penny earned"), or cheeky ("I'd walk a mile for a Camel").

Cardinal Sins

PURPLE PROSE

By one account, Samuel Johnson suffered when he picked up a revised version of the New Testament at the country house of a friend. There, in the eleventh chapter of John, he found the simple, touching words "Jesus wept" unceremoniously replaced with "Jesus, the Saviour of the world, overcome with grief, burst into a flood of tears." Dr. Sam blew a gasket.

So should you when you find purple prose ruining a good read. But what, exactly, is purple prose? Mark Twain, in "A Double-Barreled Detective Story," a tale about California's gold mining country, engaged in all kinds of satire, including naming a character "Ham Sandwich." Twain parodies a romantic description of nature written for its euphony rather than its content:

> It was a crisp and spicy morning in early October. The lilacs and laburnums, lit with the glory-fires of autumn, hung burning and flashing in the upper air, a fairy bridge provided by kind Nature for the wingless wild things that have their homes in the tree-tops and would visit together; the larch and the pomegranate flung their purple and yellow flames in brilliant broad splashes along the slanting sweep of the woodland; the sensuous fragrance of innumerable deciduous flowers rose upon the swooning atmosphere; far in the empty sky a solitary esophagus slept upon motionless wing; everywhere brooded stillness, serenity, and the peace of God.

That prose is literally purple!

Remember the Bulwer-Lytton Fiction Contest? It crowns writers who intentionally craft horrid opening lines of hypothetical novels. You may not recognize Edward George Bulwer-Lytton's name, but you know his words (from the opening of *Paul Clifford*): "It was a dark and stormy night." The litterateurs who ranked high in the competition created doozies like this:

> With a curvaceous figure that Venus would have envied, a tanned, unblemished oval face framed with lustrous thick brown hair, deep

azure-blue eyes fringed with long black lashes, perfect teeth that vied for competition, and a small straight nose, Marilee had a beauty that defied description.

Marilee's beauty may have defied description, but it inspired purple prose. Unless you're competing in spoof writing contests, tame sentences like these. Break them up. And while you're at it, could you trim a few adjectives?

UNPLAIN ENGLISH

The Plain English Campaign, based in London, officially began in 1979 when its founder publicly shredded hundreds of official documents in Parliament Square. For a fee, the group will take a document from you, clean it up, and sell you a "Crystal Mark" you can display on the document—a kind of Good Housekeeping Seal of Good Language.

The Plain English Campaign also gives mock awards, including the Golden Bull awards, "for the worst examples of written tripe." In 2010, the honoree was the Web site of the Northern Ireland Civil Service, which offered these instructions on how to take a half-day's holiday:

If the annual leave request that you are entering is less than a full day on the First Day or the Last Day, then please select Hours from the drop down list of values in the Part Days Unit of Measure field. Then select the amount of hours absent on the first day in the Fraction of Start Date field or the last day in the Fraction of End Date field. If the absence is only for one day, use the Fraction of Start Date field to record the hours absent.

Wouldn't it be easier just to go to work, put your feet up on your desk, and lean back in your chair for a few hours?

WHO KNOWS GRAMMAR BETTER THAN WHOM?

In many languages, prefixes or suffixes on nouns telegraph the role that noun is playing in a sentence. For example, in Latin, the nouns for man and dog, *homo* and *canis*, change their endings depending on who is biting whom:

> *Canis hominem mordet.* (Dog bites man.)
> *Homo canem mordet.* (Man bites dog.)

These cases help us sort out the interconnected thoughts that make up a sentence, especially because words don't always tumble out in a strict S-V-O order. In English, the process of giving case to pronouns is called "agreement." (The linguist Steven Pinker, who supplied those Latin examples in *The Language Instinct,* calls agreement an engineering solution that, along with the structure of the sentence itself, solves "the problem of encoding a tangle of interconnected thoughts into strings of words that appear one after the other.")

Centuries ago, English, like Latin, had suffixes that marked case overtly. But over time the suffixes eroded. Today overt case survives mostly in personal pronouns—*I, he, she, we, they* are used in the subject role; *my, his, her, our, their* are used in the possessor role; *me, him, her, us, them* are used in all other roles.

Fortunately, sentence syntax makes the distinction between *who* and *whom* super easy. Just think *subjects* and *objects. Who* is the subject of a sentence or of a clause: **Who** is calling? *Whom* is the object of a verb or of a preposition: You are calling <u>whom</u>? or <u>To whom</u> shall I direct your call?

If you're ever in any doubt about whether to use *who* or *whom,* substitute *he* and *him* in the same sentence. If *he* (a pronoun in the subjective case) sounds right, stick to *who* (another pronoun in the subjective case). If *him* sounds right (a pronoun in the objective case), go with *whom* (another pronoun in the objective case).

Sometimes, especially in sentences containing an internal clause, it takes a bit of parsing to figure out whether a pronoun is a subject or an object: With "Who/Whom shall I say is calling?" you must evaporate out the internal clause "I shall say"; you're left with either the grammatically gorgeous "Who is calling?" or the boner "Whom is calling?"

And finally, since we've done away with the shibboleth about not ending sentences with prepositions, go ahead and use *Who* at the beginning of a question if *Whom* seems unbearably British: "**Who** did you go to the nightclub with?" (Asking "**Whom** did you go to the nightclub with?"—or, worse, "**With whom** did you go to the nightclub?"—will brand you as terminally unhip.)

In spoken English, *whom* anywhere in the sentence is often considered stiff, pretentious. Use what fits your audience best. But err knowingly, and take pleasure in the company of those before you who have done the same: Shakespeare allowed King Lear to ask "To who, my lord?" (rather than the grammatically correct "to whom"), and the translators of the King James Bible allowed "Whom say men that I am?" (should have been *who*, as in "Men say that I am who?").

Now that you've got the *who* and *whom* thing down, you can enjoy this haiku, tweeted on National Grammar Day by Mary Ullmer:

Send not to ask for
whom the bell tolls. It tolls for
who still uses whom.

LAY THIS ERROR TO REST

When Sing and Snore Ernie débuted on toy store shelves, the talking Muppet committed a cardinal sin: He uttered, "It feels good to lay down." Sing and Snore Ernie joined the august company of Byron ("there let him lay") and Bob Dylan ("Lay lady lay") in confusing *lay*, the transitive verb, with *lie*, the intransitive verb. (Granted, Bob Dylan was talking about some serious sinning, but not of the syntactical sort.)

Keep in mind that *lay* needs a direct object; *lie* needs no object. Sing and Snore Ernie meant "It feels good to lie down." After lying down, though, he could have said "Now I lay me down to sleep," and he would have been correct, thanks to the direct object "me" (meaning "myself").

I wish my yoga teacher would get this distinction. Every time he tells us it's time for shavasana, he says, "Now lay on your backs for Shavasana." It's enough to make a corpse turn in the grave.

Lay down your pens

At the San Francisco Writers Grotto, sixty writers share an office space and another thirty lurk on a listserv. We distract ourselves with conversations like this, which all started when Elizabeth Bernstein looked up the difference between *lay* and *lie,* but wasn't satisfied that she had it right. She solicited opinions in an email whose subject header read "Now I lie me down to sleep":

Elizabeth:
I am editing a memoir about a man's five-year struggle with chronic pain. He is lying down throughout this book. He lies on doctors' tables. He lies on the floor of his therapist's office. He lies down in waiting rooms. Or, I should say, he lays?
I know a person lies, and a person lays down an object. But really, in the past, is the correct word "laid"?

Stephanie:
You're asking about the past tense of lie. It's lie, lay, lain.

Gerry:
Then there's the James Frey version:
"I lay in my bed."
"I lie in my memoir."

Justine:
You would have to add "I lied and got laid."

Isaac:
I'm submitting this to the editor of Best American Email Threads.

Connie:
lay needs an object to work. chicken lays an egg then lies down. yesterday chicken laid egg then lay down.

don't overlook the most cliched tourist pun in hawaii, now the inevitable t-shirt: I got lei'd in Hawaii.

Jason:
Okay. But as far as I can tell, based on the current discussion there's nothing wrong with this sentence, a supposedly true excerpt from a church newsletter: "This being Easter Sunday, we will ask Mrs. Lewis to come forward and lay an egg on the altar."

THIS IS SHE, BUT DON'T QUOTE ME ON IT

Do you fret about grammar when telemarketers call? "Hello," you say, answering the phone. "May I speak to the head of the household?" the telemarketer asks. It may sound stuffy to reply "This is she," but it is correct. (Who wants to cozy up to a goddam telemarketer anyway?)

Remember, an S + SV + C sentence puts the subject and the predicate on an equal footing, so a noun complement should be in the subjective, not the objective case. Do not utter "This is her" or "This is him."

A concession to the linguistically loose is, however, in order here. The technically incorrect *It's me* and *That's me* have been part of our DNA since as long as English has been recorded. There's something nice and low-key about them. Maybe we just crave a simple English equivalent of the French *C'est moi*.

The idea that we should say "It is I" and "That is I" came around in the eighteenth century, when some fuddy-duddies were applying Latin grammar rules to English. Until then we didn't even have grammar rules. So go ahead, be ungrammatical if it feels right, and tell your critics you walk in the path of the Anglo-Saxons.

Carnal Pleasures

What would advertising be without the short and declarative? If a tagline sticks in your mind, it's probably because it's a simple sentence. Of course, admen and women spice up their copy with slang and muss up punctuation so as not to seem too straight and narrow. But they're still relying on simple sentences.

Brylcreem's "A little dab'll do ya," from 1966, is straight S + V + DO. So's "Flick Your Bic," with which the ad agency Wells Rich Greene turned the brand known for indestructible pens (*stylos* that withstood flames) into a brand known for fire itself. In one oh-so-seventies spot for the disposable lighter, a woman declares, "Myron and I have a liberated marriage. I flick his Bic as often as he flicks mine." Mmmmm. Direct object as object of desire.

SALON, THE ONLINE MAGAZINE where the digerati meet the literati, held a contest in early 1998 to poke fun at the soullessness of onscreen language. *Salon* challenged readers to consider the error message, written by coders to inform you that you must reboot and start all over. The programmed missive usually brings bad news in worse prose: "abort/retry/fail?" and "404—file not found." (Translation: you have just lost all your work and you are wasting your time.)

Inviting readers to submit error messages, *Salon* required that they be written in haiku form. The best entries were—you guessed it—simple sentences:

> Printer not ready.
> Could be a fatal error.
> Have a pen handy?
> —*Pat Davis*

> Everything is gone;
> Your life's work has been destroyed.
> Squeeze trigger (yes/no)?
> —*David Carlson*

Three things are certain:
Death, taxes, and lost data.
Guess which has occurred.
—*David Dixon*

Chaos reigns within.
Reflect, repent, and reboot.
Order shall return.
—*Suzie Wagner*

First snow, then silence.
This thousand dollar screen dies
so beautifully.
—*Simon Firth*

Yesterday it worked
Today it is not working
Windows is like that
—*Margaret Segall*

Hal, open the file
Hal, open the damn file, Hal
open the, please Hal
—*Jennifer Jo Lane*

Catechism

INTRANSITIVES RULE, OK? In one urban street game, competing groups assert superiority by playing with the slang phrase "Rules, OK?" They insert their own name as a subject of the verb "rules." The game may have originated in the 1930s among violent Razor Gangs in Glasgow. When they weren't slashing each other, the rival Scottish gangs were known to tag each other's turf with "(gang name) Rules, OK?" The tag spread to the world of soccer, giving us "Arsenal Rules, OK?" From there it migrated to children's books (*Titus Rules OK*), and to music

(*C Rules OK* is an album by King Creosote; "Rockabilly rules OK" is part of a Stray Cats song). It even appeared in the world of newspaper headlines: in *The Economist,* "Primogeniture Rules, OK?" was perched next to a photo of two siblings feuding over who should lead their late father's multinational business. Parodies have also cropped up, like "Heisenberg Probably Rules, OK?" and "James Bond rules, OOK?" and "Dyslexics lure, KO." Try coming up with some tags of your own. Go ahead, be cutting—but hold the razors.

VERBS RULE, OK? Identify the verb in each of the following sentences, and figure out whether it is intransitive (S + V), transitive (S + V + DO), ditransitive (S + V + IO + DO), static (S + SV + C), or factive (S + V + DO + OC). Hint: only one is factive.

    i. She gave all her colleagues invitations.
   ii. The days grow shorter in December.
  iii. A seagull, obviously looking for a handout, hovered over the ferry's stern.
   iv. The banana peel stuck to the bottom of the principal's shoe.
    v. The chef made the short ribs divine.
   vi. Bravely, she walked on.
  vii. He felt ridiculous in his Elmo costume.
 viii. Daniel's antics taught the sisters a valuable lesson.

WAKING UP TO SENTENCES: Take five or ten minutes to freewrite about your first five minutes today—your waking moments. Write in a stream of consciousness, and don't stop to correct or rewrite anything. Then analyze your sentences. Did you use simple sentences, or did your thoughts tend to tumble out in a jumbled sequence of clauses? Rewrite the paragraphs using only simple sentences (adjectives, adverbs, and prepositional phrases allowed!).

CHAPTER 11

Phrases and Clauses

Bones

Extending the analogy of the boat sentence a little further, what should we make of the various lines and detritus attached to our vessel's hull, mast, or motor? We might think of adjectives and adverbs as ornaments and flags—unless they are more like barnacles and strings of seaweed. What about phrases and clauses? Sometimes they are necessary rigging, but at times they might resemble tow lines or even anchors, catching on rocks and stopping the boat's movement altogether.

So when do these extras enhance a sentence and when do they drag it down?

Let's focus first on the *phrase,* two or more words that form a kernel of meaning. Phrases can contain nouns and verbs, but they do not have a subject or a predicate. They can help give a sentence depth, detail, and movement, but they can also create clutter. To know the difference, you've got to get a handle on the different types of phrases. Working as a unit within the larger sentence, a phrase can function as a noun, an adjective, or an adverb.

The easiest to identify might be the **noun phrase**, which is just a cluster of words that acts as the subject or direct object of a sentence. *My mother's sister* is a noun phrase.

In a **verb phrase**, the main verb and its helpers work in concert. Take "My mother's sister had been playing cards all her life." There, *had been playing* is a verb phrase.

An **appositive phrase** allows us to tuck in detail without having to add a whole new sentence. It clarifies a nearby noun by renaming it in different words and is usually, though not always, enclosed in commas. I could write *I have an aunt named Sosostris. She loves the tarot.* Or I could write, more succinctly, *My aunt, Sosostris, loves the tarot.* (These identifiers are especially helpful in news articles, offering a quick way to identify a source.)

T. S. Eliot uses an appositive phrase (in italics) in "The Waste Land":

Madame Sosostris, *famous clairvoyante* . . .
Is known to be the wisest woman in Europe,
With a wicked pack of cards.

And in describing one of the clairvoyante's tarot cards, Eliot uses not one, but two appositives:

Here is Belladonna, *the Lady of the Rocks,*
The lady of situations.

In **prepositional phrases**, a preposition such as *on, of, above,* or *near* pairs with a noun (and perhaps an adjective). The entire phrase, in turn, acts as an adjective or adverb in the larger sentence. When a prepositional phrase kicks off a sentence, it is usually followed by a comma: "*In 1913,* Proust wrote *Swann's Way.*"

Swann's Way, in fact, opens with an adverbial prepositional phrase, telling us *when* the narrator used to go to sleep:

For a long time, I went to bed early.

If the syntactical role of a prepositional phrase is to modify other words, the stylistic one is to add nuance and control cadence. Proust might have said "In 1880," "during my childhood in Combray," or "back then"—each of which would have subtly changed the sentence's meaning as well as its music.

Verbal phrases are clusters of words that begin with a particular form of a verb but play a different role in the sentence. These are fun, if dangerous, devices. (For the dangerous part, see **Cardinal Sins**.) A **gerund phrase** acts as a noun (in *Reading in bed makes Buck tired,* the gerund phrase acts as the subject). An **infinitive phrase**, which begins with *to* and the base form of the verb, might be a noun (*To sleep,* perchance *to dream*), an adjective (This is the bed *to sleep in*), or an adverb (This bed is too comfy *to resist*).

The trickiest verbal phrases begin with a participle, the form of a verb that ends either in *-ing* (the present participle) or *-ed* (the past participle) and that is used in sentences as an adjective. **Participial phrases** modify nouns, as in the first line of James Joyce's *Ulysses:*

> Stately, plump Buck Mulligan came from the stairhead, *bearing a bowl of lather* on which a mirror and a razor lay crossed.

The participial phrase *bearing a bowl of lather* modifies Mulligan.

Gerund phrases, remember, also end in *-ing*, but they always behave as nouns: *the whining of the train, the weeping of the robin,* and *the crawling of time* made Hank Williams so lonesome he could cry.

Participling the waters

Participles are limber little suckers. Most often, when they're not part of the verb phrase itself, they're acting as adjectives. They can modify single words ("*the finger-picking* guitarist") or they can be parts of adjectival phrases ("*Finger-picking* his way through 'Honeysuckle Rose,' Led Ka'apana thrilled the crowd"). But sometimes participles contort themselves into prepositions (*according to, concerning, regarding, speaking of*) and even conjunctions (*supposing, provided that, granted that*).

Participles can work on their own, too, suggesting an entire sentence and sparking action. On April 10, 2008, when James Karl Buck and his translator were arrested by the Egyptian police while covering an anti-government protest, Buck was able to tweet one word while being taken away by Egyptian authorities:

Arrested

That lone participle prompted his U.C. Berkeley friends and followers into action, leading the university to hire a lawyer on his behalf. He was released a day later.

Infinitive phrases behave as nouns, adjectives, and adverbs. It's hard to find examples of all three in one place, so let's start with the sentence "To err is human, to forgive divine"; the infinitive phrases *to err* and *to forgive* are nouns. Returning to a paraphrase of Hank Williams in "the robin has lost the will to live," *to live* modifies *will*, so it's an adjective. And in "the lonesome whippoorwill sounds too blue to fly," the phrase *to fly* acts as an adverb (How blue was he?).

An **absolute phrase** differs from these others. It is a full sentence from which the verb has gone AWOL—either morphing into a verbal phrase or disappearing into the mist. In the sentence "The bottle of Zin having been drained, we grabbed the Cab," the absolute phrase suggests a full sentence: *The bottle of Zin has been drained.* The absolute phrase functions as an adjective, but it modifies the entire sentence or clause rather than a single noun within it. Like participial phrases, absolute phrases are set apart from the rest of the sentence by commas.

PARALLEL LINES

Phrases can unstarch sentences and give them grace. They can also, if structured right, help keep track of ideas. Especially in a list, it is helpful to conceive phrases so that they are parallel in structure. (*Politicians speak to reporters, in Congress, and on the stump.*) Parallel phrases flow logically, help readers follow the drift—and often lift an idea into eloquence.

In chapter 6, we looked at parallelism in the 1961 inaugural address of John F. Kennedy. Recall that a string of parallel phrases gave the incoming president some stirring rhetoric ("born in this century, tempered by war, disciplined by a hard and bitter peace, proud of our ancient heritage"). Kennedy's fluid string of phrases works so well because they are so symmetrical—semantically and rhythmically. They work like a rhetorical cascade, one phrase building on another: in each phrase, the adjective (*born, tempered, disciplined, proud*) is followed by a prepositional phrase; the rhythm crescendoes as each phrase stretches a little longer than the previous one.

And almost half a century later, Barack Obama echoed Kennedy in his own first inaugural address: "I stand here today . . . humbled by the task before us, grateful for the trust you have bestowed, mindful of the sacrifices borne by our ancestors."

MORE EXTRAVAGANT THAN A phrase is the **clause**. It contains a subject and a predicate, but, like a phrase, a clause contributes to a larger sentence. (Taking that boat analogy about as far as it can go, call clauses the separate hulls of catamarans and trimarans.)

An **independent clause** *could* stand alone as a sentence, but it finds other clauses clinging to it. Independent clauses might be coupled—linked by a conjunction, a relative pronoun, or a hearty piece of punctuation (a semicolon, say): in "Marriage has many pains, but celibacy has no pleasures," the two independent clauses are joined with the conjunction *but*.

A **dependent clause** *cannot* stand alone; it acts as a noun, adjective, or adverb within the sentence. One kind of dependent clause starts with a subordinate conjunction: in "Marriage, if one will face the truth, is an evil, but a necessary evil," *if one will face the truth* is a dependent clause introduced by the subordinate conjunction *if*.

Another kind of dependent clause starts with a relative pronoun, such as *who, whom, whose, that, which, whoever,* or *whomever*: In "Never say that marriage has more of joy than pain," the relative clause *that marriage has more of joy than pain* acts as the direct object of the verb *say*.

A few points about which there is much confusion: First, the relative pronoun *that* offers nice flexibility; it can stand in for people or for things. On the other hand, the relative pronoun *who* stands in only for people. (If you consider your pets children, you can use *who* for them, too.)

We've saved the most vexing relative pronoun question (*that* or *which*?) for last. When dependent clauses are adjectival—that is, when they describe or define a noun or pronoun—they begin either with *that* or with *which*. Grammarians have probably devoted as much ink to *that* and *which* as they have to anything, but confusion remains—in profusion!

Here's what you need to know: First of all, forget those notions of *which* being more proper. The Brits favor *which*, but *that* predominates in the more relaxed American letters. Use *that* whenever a clause is necessary to understand the meaning of the sentence. In "Elizabeth Taylor could have addressed the questions *that you have about marriage*," the clause is necessary: "Elizabeth Taylor could have addressed the questions" is too vague—we are left wondering what questions she could address. Use *which* whenever the clause adds information but could just as easily be left out of the sentence: "All these questions, *which concern the merits and demerits of independence and dependence*, could have been asked of Liz, you know."

While *that* clauses tend to follow straight after the word they modify and need no punctuation, *which* clauses provide extraneous info and are usually enclosed in commas.

Taking exception

If you're a real grammar masochist—in other words, your eyes have not glazed over, and you are twitching for more—this box is for you.

Some grammarians wax on about "restrictive" and "nonrestrictive" clauses, or "essential" and "nonessential" clauses. All these names just attempt to explain when to use *that* and when to use *which*. Just to reiterate: The information in a *that* clause is restrictive/essential—it is necessary to bake the cake that is the sentence. The information in a *which* clause is nonrestrictive/nonessential—it just ices the cake.

Every now and then *which* is used when *that* is called for grammatically. Clarity trumps grammar. In the proverb "All that glitters is not gold," *that* introduces the restrictive clause. But we swap *that* with *which* when the clause appears in a sentence like "He said that that which glitters is not gold." Three *that*s in a row would only confuse.

Then there is the case of "the delayed which," or—as it is called at *The New Yorker*—the "exceptional which." This term was created by the legendary copy editor Eleanor Gould, in concert with editor William Shawn. The exceptional *which* is intended to bring clarity when the more distant of two nouns in a sentence is modified by a relative clause that would otherwise be introduced by *that*—in other words, a restrictive clause whose relative pronoun is widely separated from its antecedent. Here is a *New Yorker* passage about Italian architects that uses an exceptional *which* first, and an unexceptional one second:

> They know better than to plant something in the heart of a city **which** doesn't fit there. The most exciting convention center in the world currently isn't anywhere near the center of a city. It is the Milan Trade Fair, known as Fiera Milano, **which** was built on the site of an old gas refinery at the intersection of a couple of highways not far from the Milan airport.

Paul Goldberger, the critic who wrote these sentences, told me he had a dim memory of being puzzled about the first *which,* since *that* would have been more logical. He also recollected being told "that the exceptional *which* was justified in this instance because the meaning of the sentence without the clause would be different." Fresher, though, is his memory of being troubled by the editors' decision to delete a sentence about "dressing an architectural wolf in sheep's clothing." That change, Goldberger wrote in an email, was something "we devoted more time to discussing." And there you have it: a Pulitzer Prize–winning writer reminding us that a fight over a metaphor, in the end, matters much more than one over a relative pronoun.

Flesh

TURNING A PHRASE

Phrases can build grace into sentences. Taut declarations lend clarity, but too many of them can start to sound like a Dick-and-Jane story. A strategically placed phrase can turn a staccato burst into a more lyrical sentence. This is what we mean by "turning a phrase"—using our command of language and our mastery of the rhythms of a sentence to affect style as well as substance. Cheryl Strayed, in her memoir *Wild*, describes the primitive kitchen in her family's rustic house, which was outfitted with a Coleman camp stove and a real icebox. The sentence is as spare and functional as the items in the kitchen. And then it's not:

> Each component demanded just slightly less than it gave, needing to be tended and maintained, filled and unfilled, hauled and dumped, pumped and primed, and stoked and monitored.

Those phrases add a world of meaning to the intriguing simple sentence. The parallel construction keeps us from getting lost in the wild.

James Baldwin, in a passage from *Giovanni's Room*, lets a little more wildness creep into his sentences. He consecrates same-sex desire to the page, writing about how an Italian bartender in Paris "had awakened an itch, had released a gnaw in me":

> I realized it one afternoon, when I was taking him to work via the boulevard Montparnasse. We had bought a kilo of cherries and we were eating them as we walked along. We were both insufferably childish and high-spirited that afternoon and the spectacle we presented, two grown men, jostling each other on the wide sidewalk, and aiming the cherry-pits, as though they were spitballs, into each other's faces, must have been outrageous. And I realized that such childishness was fantastic at my age and the happiness out of which it sprang yet more so; for that moment I really loved Giovanni, who had never seemed more beautiful than he was that afternoon.

It's hard to focus on grammar when following a love story, but notice how elegantly Baldwin slips an appositive phrase, two participial phrases, a prepositional phrase, and a subordinate clause into what would have been an otherwise straightforward "the spectacle we presented must have been outrageous."

Isaac Babel puts it well in the short story "Guy de Maupassant": "A phrase is born into the world both good and bad at the same time. The secret lies in a slight, and almost invisible twist."

SHORT, LONG, AND LAYERED

Phrases can soften the staccato rhythm of successive simple sentences. Clauses, though, build complexity into thought. And the way you decide to link those clauses has a tremendous influence on style and tone.

News stories are built on straight, declarative sentences, sometimes joined by coordinating conjunctions. Take this lead from *USA Today* in late 2009:

> Tiger Woods apologized Wednesday for letting his family down and said he regrets "those transgressions with all of my heart."

Those sentences are pretty straightforward and taut. The reporter, Michael McCarthy, might have written his lead as two simple sentences. ("Tiger Woods apologized Wednesday for letting his family down. He said he regrets 'those transgressions with all of my heart.'") But the coordinating conjunction *and* gives the lead fluidity without compromising its evenhandedness.

You can pack a lead with information while keeping the sentences limber. Notice how the same story was written up in *The Wall Street Journal*:

> Three days after Tiger Woods denounced as false the flood of speculation surrounding his auto accident, including news reports of his

alleged infidelity, the golfer on Wednesday apologized for "transgressions" that "let my family down."

The *WSJ* story continues in the same vein, using a relative clause, a subordinate clause, and a participial phrase in the very next sentence. ("Mr. Woods, who hasn't spoken publicly since the crash last Friday, released a statement on his Web site, regretting 'personal behavior' that he didn't specify.") The various phrases and clauses allow the reporter, Corey Dade, to highlight not just the drama of the story but the high-tension tug-of-war between the sports icon and the press.

Dr. Martin Luther King, Jr., was a master of the subordinate clause, as we will see in the next chapter, but even in shorter bursts he recognized the rhetorical value of subordinating conjunctions, as in this sentence he quoted in *Why We Can't Wait*:

> When you are right, you cannot be too radical; when you are wrong, you cannot be too conservative.

Cardinal Sins

LUMPEN LINES

O.K., so you understand the idea of parallelism. Parallel phrasing also helps us memorize certain quotes ("Tune in, turn on, drop out") or remember which button to press when we call an 800 number ("For reservations, press 1. For locations, press 2. For customer service, press 3").

Parallel lines sound so natural that we can forget how unnatural it is to actually create them. Most lesser mortals end up writing sentences that might as well be a game of "one of these things is not like the other."

Here's what you hear when you dial the Fastrak number in the San Francisco Bay Area:

> For account information, including current balance, recent payment information, to verify or update your credit card information, to

change your replenishment method from cash to credit card, or to change your four-digit PIN, press 1.

Those instructions would be easier to follow if they were parallel and arranged from long to short: *To review recent payments, to hear your balance or other account information, to change your four-digit PIN, to verify or update your credit card number, or to change your replenishment method from cash to credit card, press 1.*

Publications that lack copy editors often churn out lumpy sentences. A water district in Massachusetts sent out this endorsement for Sedum, "the perfect drought-tolerant plant":

It is pretty, easy to grow, grows in dense clumps that control weeds, thrives on rainfall alone, and with hundreds of varieties available, there are lots to choose from.

We have adjective, adjective phrase, verb phrase with a relative clause, verb phrase, long prepositional phrase, and independent clause. Sedum may be drought-tolerant, but that sentence needs weeding and watering.

And here's an ad that's so out-of-control there's no medicine to fix it:

Partners Private Care, a subsidiary of Partners Home Care, offers in-home support, such as home health aides for personal care assistance, nursing, and home management, that give you confidence to live on your own.

DANGLING DOOZIES

Some of the most hilarious errors in English result from phrases that aren't properly tracked. The most common and comical sin is called the *dangling participle*. Remember, participles exist so that verbs can modify nouns. Dangling participles are adjectival phrases that have come unmoored from the nouns they are supposed to modify and instead modify the nearest noun they can find. Here's a dangling participle reprinted in *The New Yorker* as a space filler:

> In San Diego, the "in" place for years has been McDini's for corned beef. Thinly sliced and heaped on rye, corned beef lovers won't be disappointed.

When was the last time *you* were thinly sliced and heaped on rye?

Here's another, about an "in" place in Manhattan that no doubt hosted many a birthday party, but not one in which the revelers were wrapped like presents:

> For over a half-century Rumpelmayer's has been one of New York's most popular ice-cream parlors. Decorated with cuddly stuffed animals and trimmed with large pink velvet bows, you feel like you're sitting inside a present.

I once asked readers to send me their favorite dangling participles. One sent a sentence remembered from a fourth-grade lesson, another a dangler from that terrifying grammar textbook, Warriner's. Others sent examples of strange things afoot:

- Hopping from foot to foot, the crosstown bus came into view.
- The girl commented on my big blue eyes seated next to me.
- Donna saw the ball walking by the lake.
- Walking into the mortuary, an open coffin frightened me.
- I found a dollar walking home.

And here's a delicious dangler from a recipe for crullers, a fried and twisted pastry:

> Rolled in brown sugar, I enjoy them for breakfast.

That dangler appeared in a version of a cookbook before the copy editor, ahem, ate it for breakfast.

What do grammar geeks do for fun?

Each year on National Grammar Day (What? You didn't know March 4 was National Grammar Day?), the journalist and freelance editor Mark Allen hosts a haiku writing contest on Twitter. The 2012 winner turned a musing on stranded modifiers into a 5-7-5 poemette. The winner was written by Larry Kunz (@larry_kunz), a technical writer from Raleigh-Durham, North Carolina:

Being a dangler,
Jane knew it would have to come
out of the sentence

Poor Jane. Is being a dangler sort of like being a loser?

One of the several tweets earning special mention came from Tom Freeman (@SnoozeInBrief):

Dangling oddly
I conjured absurdities
With modifiers.

That narrator, clearly, is an ironist, not a loser.

MORE MAYHEM

Prepositional phrases can lead to endless abstraction. Take the cliché "in the eye of my mind": it takes two prepositional phrases and a lot of abstraction to say the same thing as "imagination."

But perhaps more dangerous—and delightful—are prepositional phrases that have drifted away from the word they modify. Mayday!

Here are some favorites from the days when cheapskates hawked their wares in as few words as possible:

> FOR SALE: an Erard grand piano, the property of a lady about to travel in a walnut-wood case with carved legs.

> FOR SALE: Mahogany table by a lady with Chippendale legs.

> LOST: Antique walking stick by an old man with a carved ivory head.

There are many reasons to lament the loss of newspaper classifieds, but one of them is that it just isn't as fun (or as easy) to spot danglers on Craigslist.

A veteran of the Foreign Service posted a comment on one of my *New York Times* columns (in the "Draft" series) that offered a dangler. He explained that when he followed tradition and wrote to the officials at his next post to advise of his travel plans, he unintentionally sent this alarming message: "My wife and I will be flying to post with our cat in an on-board carrying cage." "Ouch," the veteran diplomat added by way of comment. "I hate it when they scratch!"

At least that dangler had some glamour attached to it. Here's an advisory that went out from headquarters to a company that remains anonymous:

> The company's refrigerator holds microwavable lunches for 18 employees frozen in the top compartment.

Ask yourself: who was frozen? After eighteen employees given the deep freeze, let's thaw out by going to Las Vegas. Journalist James Kilpatrick found this sentence in a story in the *Las Vegas Sun* about a young woman who had her breasts surgically enlarged from size 31A to 34C:

> Denise soon applied for and got a plum job at a major Strip casino, earning big tips each day serving drinks in a bikini.

I've heard of drinks served in all kinds of glasses, but how do you get them not to spill from a bikini?

That recalls an intentional prepositional slip by Groucho Marx, in *Animal Crackers*:

I once shot an elephant in my pajamas. How he got into my pajamas I'll never know.

Carnal Pleasures

Because we think in chunks, not just words, phrases and clauses in pidgins and dialects can make for some wacko linguistic odysseys. In that breezy language tango called Spanglish, words, phrases, and entire sentences swing back and forth between English and Spanish. A handy Spanish word might stand in for an English one, or an English word might be hijacked into Spanish—"chilling out" becomes *chileando,* and "email" becomes *emailiar.* Notice the switch-hitting in the lyrics of a Los Lobos song: "Let's go *bailando, noche*'s looking fine, jump into the *carro,* drink a bunch of wine."

Cristina Saralegui, a celebrity on the Univision Network, claims that even her miniature dachshund, Cosa, speaks Spanglish. When Cristina tells her dog, *"Bajate de la cama!"* (Get off the bed!) Cosa ignores her. Only when she insists, *"Cosa, por favor,* get down," does the dog obey. Whether you're a person or a *perro,* the key to Spanglish is fluency not just with single words, but with *groups* of words—phrases—like *Que no?* or *Yo se,* or *Oye, chica.*

In the Hawaiian creole known as Pidgin English, syntax is scrambled, and words from different languages—Hawaiian, Japanese, Chinese, Filipino—are folded into English sentences. The popular song "Manuela Boy" includes this refrain:

Manuela Boy, my dear boy
You no more *hilahila*
No more five cents, no more house
Go Aʻala Paka *hiamoe.*

Hilahila is Hawaiian for "shame"; the phrases in the last line jump from language to language: *Go* is obviously an English imperative ("you go"); *Aʻala Paka* is a hybrid, a transliteration of Aʻala Park; *hiamoe* is Hawaiian for the infinitive phrase "to fall asleep."

The Hawaiian writer Lois-Ann Yamanaka plays with Pidgin English in her novels of life in the fiftieth state. *Wild Meat and the Bully Burgers* quotes the story of Lovey Nariyoshi, a young girl growing up in Hilo, with her patois of Polynesian words (*luna, lanai*), Japanese phrases (*kendo sensei*), and Hawaiian-English hybrids (*haolified, haole-ish*):

> My other neighbor Katy and me sit on her porch across the street from my house. It's really Katy's mother's house with the big jacaranda tree in the front yard and a white wicker swing like the plantation lunas have on their lanais . . . .
>
> Katy says she likes the name Charlene if she has a girl and Charles if she has a boy. Named after her ji-chan who was a kendo sensei at a dojo near the pancake house by the airport.
>
> I give her my suggestions since lately I've been Katy's main visitor. "Autumn, Summer, or Heather for a girl. . . ."
>
> Katy says, "When the baby comes, I let you bathe him and change his diaper like that. But no name him—you too haolified with your names, Lovey. Who you think you? Sometimes you act too haole-ish to me. You crazy—you like be haole or what?" I don't say anything. Katy goes on. "I know I got one boy in here. But I gotta name um."

Catechism

HOW DO YOU PHRASE THAT? Take a few paragraphs of a piece of writing you admire and see if you can find examples of appositive, prepositional, participial, gerund, infinitive, and absolute phrases.

DOWN THE RABBIT HOLE: As a way of testing your grasp of phrases and clauses, identify each of the following phrases (underlined) and clauses [in square brackets]—i.e., say what kind of phrase (appositive, gerund, etc.) or clause (subordinate, relative, independent) it is:

> Alice did not think that it was so very much out of the way <u>to hear the Rabbit say to itself, "Oh dear! Oh dear! I shall be late!"</u>

[When she thought it over afterwards,] it occurred to her [that she ought to have wondered at this,] [but at the time it all seemed quite natural.]

[But when the Rabbit took a watch out of its waistcoat-pocket and looked at it and then hurried on,] [Alice started to her feet.]

It flashed <u>across her mind</u> that she had never before seen a rabbit with either a waistcoat-pocket or a watch to <u>take out of it.</u>

<u>Burning with curiosity,</u> she ran <u>across the field</u> after it and was just in time to see it pop <u>down a large rabbit-hole under the hedge</u>.

In another moment, down went Alice after it, <u>never once considering</u> <u>[how in the world she was to get out again]</u>.

Hint: that last one is a doozy; "considering" kicks off a phrase; "in the world" is another phrase; "how she was to get out again" is a clause.

SENTENCE GENETICS: You might think it impossible to find a case where a relative clause made a passage brilliant, but consider this one, from Dave Eggers's *A Heartbreaking Work of Staggering Genius*:

The author feels obligated to acknowledge that, yes, the success of a memoir—of any book, really—has a lot to do with how appealing its narrator is. To address this, the author offers the following:

1) That he is like you
2) That, like you, he falls asleep shortly after he becomes drunk
3) That he sometimes has sex without condoms
4) That he sometimes falls asleep when he is drunk having sex without condoms
5) That he never gave his parents a proper burial
6) That he never finished college
7) That he expects to die young
8) That, because his father smoked and drank and died as a result, he is afraid of food
9) That he smiles when he sees black men holding babies

Using Eggers as a model, write a string of relative clauses (it's O.K. if you have fewer than nine) expressing the appeal of a certain person—you or anyone in your family. It's O.K. to be playful or over the top.

Then start again, using subordinating conjunctions (*although, because, despite, if, since, while,* etc.) to lay out how your personality does or doesn't reflect that of your parents or your grandparents. The subordinating conjunctions should build some complexity into the paragraph by emphasizing paradoxes, or perhaps cause-and-effect relationships. (*Although my father was a military officer who respected the chain of command, he raised three kids who eschewed every sort of authority.*)

CHAPTER 12

Length and Tone

Bones

Gabriel García Márquez writes unhurried sentences that almost defy parsing. In *Absalom, Absalom!* William Faulkner wrote a 1,288-word sentence, but he used "My mother is a fish" as a complete chapter in *As I Lay Dying*. Gil Scott-Heron could rap, but he could also ramble. Joan Didion can stop us short with simple truths, and she can take us on strolls down labyrinthine corridors.

Trust these great writers: there is no one right way to render an idea. Masters of the sentence play with length, complexity, and tone to settle on sentence style. But different sentences carry different valences, and we can create them not just to get an idea across but also to convey attitude or elicit emotion. Sentences inform us, but they can also touch us.

The best sentences unify their elements—subjects linked to predicates, surprising adjectives, neat adverbs, elegant phrases—into a clear, coursing stream of thought. Sometimes they have compound subjects (more than one Who or What) or compound predicates (more than one So What).

But sometimes a sentence contains more than one subject-predicate pair. Sometimes it embraces clauses that twist and turn and surprise. If so, it qualifies as one of the following:

- **A compound sentence.** When two independent clauses, each detailing a complete action, are hitched by a coordinate conjunction, the two parts balance each other in weight and importance. At the same time, hitching them together brings separate ideas into juxtaposition, as in Mark Twain's "Tell the truth or trump—but get the trick."

  Pay attention to punctuation: independent clauses in a compound sentence require a coordinate conjunction (*for, and, nor, but, or, yet, so*) and a comma or a dash. When you want to bolt the clauses together without the softening influence of a conjunction, use a bracing piece of punctuation like Mark Twain's semicolon in the following: "Training is everything. The peach was once a bitter almond; cauliflower is nothing but a cabbage with a college education."

- **A complex sentence.** Here, one or more dependent clauses lean on an independent clause. What dooms a clause to dependency? Subordinate conjunctions (like *if, since,* or *while*) and relative pronouns (*who, whomever, that*). Take Mark Twain's maxim about the principal difference between a dog and a man: "If you pick up a starving dog and make him prosperous, he will not bite you." The sentence begins with a subordinate clause, *If you pick up a starving dog and make him prosperous,* followed by an independent clause, *he will not bite you.* A complex sentence has an internal dynamic: the clauses have a distinct relationship to each other and allow us to emphasize the relationship of ideas.

  If a subordinate clause begins a complex sentence, it is usually separated from the independent clause by a comma.

- **A compound-complex sentence.** This contains one or more dependent clauses and at least two independent clauses. Mark Twain did these sentences, too: "When angry, count to four; when very angry, swear." *When angry* is a dependent clause leaning on the independent *count to four,* and *when very angry* is a dependent clause leaning on *swear*. This short but intense sentence holds several different ideas, operating on different levels, in place.

Mark Twain's sentences are pretty economical, but most unsimple sentences stretch out a bit. Compound sentences allow us to pack more information into a sentence, and to do so without a lot of herky-jerky simple sentences. Complex sentences allow us to express an idea with some interesting kinks in it. Perhaps we want to draw attention to a cause and its effect, or to express relationships in time, or perhaps we want to put a rhetorical finger on paradox. When we join two clauses with subordinate conjunctions like *because, if, although,* or *since,* we are putting ideas into a kind of hierarchy, subordinating one idea to another.

Balancing acts

Punctuation gets dicey once you leave the world of simple sentences. Keep in mind that whole thoughts—entire clauses—need to be marked off by either punctuation or a conjunction. Here are the five basic ways to punctuate two complete thoughts, with independent clauses indicated by underlining:

- Let the two clauses stand on their own, separated by a period (and thank you, Leo Tolstoy):

   All happy families resemble each other. Each unhappy family is unhappy in its own way.

- Link the two clauses ever so slightly, by using a semicolon instead of a period:

   All happy families resemble each other; each unhappy family is unhappy in its own way.

- Strengthen the linkage by using a coordinate conjunction and a comma between the two clauses:

   All happy families resemble each other, but each unhappy family is unhappy in its own way.

- Subordinate one clause to the other by starting it with a subordinate conjunction:

  Although all happy families resemble each other, <u>each unhappy family is unhappy in its own way.</u>

- Emphasize the paradox by separating the two clauses with a conjunctive adverb:

  <u>All happy families resemble each other;</u> however, <u>each unhappy family is unhappy in its own way.</u>

Flesh

Call them curt, call them to-the-point: Simple sentences are the stuff of "hard-boiled" novelists like Raymond Chandler, writing about the Santa Ana winds in his short story "Red Wind":

> There was a desert wind blowing that night. It was one of those hot dry Santa Anas that come down through the mountain passes and curl your hair and make your nerves jump and your skin itch. On nights like that every booze party ends in a fight.

Joan Didion also employs the technique when describing the same winds in "Los Angeles Notebook," an essay in *Slouching Towards Bethlehem*. She follows a fluid sentence with crisp ones:

> I have neither heard nor read that a Santa Ana is due, but I know it, and almost everyone I have seen today knows it too. We know it because we feel it. The baby frets. The maid sulks.

Those three blunt sentences have the harsh force of the winds Didion names.

To the writer itching to indulge in a long sentence, Mark Twain counsels: "Make sure that there are no folds in it, no vaguenesses, no parenthetical interruptions of its view as a whole; when [you have] done with it, it won't be a sea-serpent with half of its arches under the water, it will be a torch-light procession."

Simple sentences offer the most straightforward way to get to the point quickly and clearly. But when you want your writing to have the stately grace of "a torch-light procession," you can play with syntax and style—with the contrast of short and long, with rhythm and repetition, with pauses and parentheticals, with endings that bang and endings that whimper.

SUSPENSEFUL SENTENCES

Sometimes we don't so much want a seamless flow, or a drum of random ideas punctuated with commas and ellipses, but rather hard pauses, high tension, urgent twists and turns. Then we bring in subordinate clauses.

A seemingly insignificant *as* can provide a nice pivot. A sentence that begins with *if* builds anticipation right in. A string of *whereas*es can lead to a hard and fast law—or an indictment. One Father's Day ad for Scotch uses a series of subordinate clauses (*Because I've known you all my life. Because you let me play cricket on the lawn. Because a red Rudge bicycle once made me the happiest boy on the street . . .*) to build to a firm conclusion (*Because if you don't deserve Chivas Regal, who does?*).

Subordination can also be lighthearted. Groucho Marx understood this, as he demonstrated in this riff from *Duck Soup,* using two simple sentences and three complex ones:

> You'd better beat it. I hear they're going to tear you down and put up an office building where you're standing. You can leave in a taxi. If you can't leave in a taxi, you can leave in a huff. If that's too soon, you can leave in a minute and a huff.

Subordination can also bring drama and gravity. Dr. Martin Luther King, Jr., understood its particular power. One passage in his "Letter from Birmingham Jail" relies on a sequence of *when* clauses that build, ratcheting up the urgency, until King arrives at a powerful *then* clause:

> But **when** you have seen vicious mobs lynch your mothers and fathers at will and drown your sisters and brothers at whim; **when** you have seen hate filled policemen curse, kick and even kill your black broth-

ers and sisters; **when** you see the vast majority of your twenty million Negro brothers smothering in an airtight cage of poverty in the midst of an affluent society; **when** you suddenly find your tongue twisted and your speech stammering as you seek to explain to your six year old daughter why she can't go to the public amusement park that has just been advertised on television, and see tears welling up in her eyes when she is told that Funtown is closed to colored children, and see ominous clouds of inferiority beginning to form in her little mental sky, and see her beginning to distort her personality by developing an unconscious bitterness toward white people; . . . **then** you will understand why we find it difficult to wait. There comes a time when the cup of endurance runs over, and men are no longer willing to be plunged into the abyss of despair.

If you are interested in exploring the rhetorical effects of different sentence structures, including the one employed here by Dr. Martin Luther King, Jr., the critic Stanley Fish, in *How to Write a Sentence and How to Read One,* devotes an entire chapter each to what he calls the "subordinating," the "additive," and the "satiric" styles.

Comedic or commanding, light or lofty, the tone of sentences is set by language, length, phrasing, and style. Mastering tone is a matter of stripping your ideas to the essence, then playing with all these devices to shade your meaning.

VARIETY

The English critic George Saintsbury once compared the act of sentence making—the letting out and pulling in of clauses—to the letting out and pulling in of the slide of a trombone or the "draws" of a telescope.

When Winston Churchill addressed the House of Commons in 1940, after the defeat at Dunkirk, he needed his sentences to put steel in the spine of his countrymen. His peroration illustrates superb sentence musicianship:

We shall not flag or fail. We shall go on to the end. We shall fight in France, we shall fight on the seas and oceans, we shall fight with

growing confidence and strength in the air, we shall defend our island, whatever the cost may be, we shall fight on the beaches, we
shall fight on the landing grounds, we shall fight in the fields and in
the streets, we shall fight in the hills; we shall never surrender.

Churchill starts with two short sentences with full stops. Then he piles
one clause atop another, taking advantage of the rhythm offered to
him by parallel structure. His speech comprises a succession of S + V
sentences and clauses (only "we shall defend our island" stands apart
structurally, with its direct object). In the compelling, swelling third
sentence, Churchill keeps his subject and verb (*we shall fight*) steady
and creates a powerful crescendo. When Churchill breaks his incantation with a half stop (the semicolon) and the words *we shall never surrender*, the structural change underscores his resolve.

You don't always have to be so tidy. Look at what Gabriel García
Márquez unleashes in the opening of *The Autumn of the Patriarch*:

Over the weekend the vultures got into the presidential palace by
pecking through the screens on the balcony windows and the flapping of their wings stirred up the stagnant time inside, and at dawn
on Monday the city awoke out of its lethargy of centuries with the
warm, soft breeze of a great man dead and rotting grandeur.

García Márquez's winding masterpiece comprises three main clauses
(*the vultures got, the flapping of their wings stirred up*, and *the city
awoke*) and innumerable phrases, all befitting his magical-realist style.
The sentence arcs slowly, like the vultures it describes.

Most of us lesser mortals navigate sentence waters less turbulent
than either Churchill's or García Márquez's. We mix short and long,
working that trombone. Even in a story that demands a quiet tone and
humble language, sentence variety prevents the narrative from becoming simplistic. I went for spareness in language but variety in length
for a memory piece published in the *Honolulu Advertiser*. It profiled
Antone Correa, a Portuguese immigrant who toiled for forty-four years
as a laborer on a Hawaiian sugar plantation and thirty more years in his

own backyard. The words are simple, but the sentence structure has all the variety of Papa's potted plants:

> Clearly, Papa had once been handsome. His face, in repose, was still remarkable: eyes sunk deep between prominent cheekbones, a set of enormously bushy gray-black eyebrows, both high forehead and arched nose noble in bearing, skin brown and leathery and stretched taut over his jaw.
>
> But by the time we knew Papa, his body was hinged at the waist and starting to wither. He always wore baggy plantation khakis and a white cotton shirt. I never saw him in a pair of shoes. Instead, he wore leather thongs that crossed over his toes, which bunched together like overgrown tree roots. His legs had weakened: he used a walker to move around the house and the yard. The walker kept his upper body strong. He was barrel-chested, with thick hairy arms and stubby fingers. One of his fingers was a stump, as a result of an accident with a saw. Stump or no, he had a gentle touch.
>
> Despite his difficulty walking, Papa was a tremendous gardener. Beds of flowers and ferns surrounded the house, but Papa spent even more time caring for countless potted plants, on several raised wooden platforms in the backyard. There—in old coffee tins—he sprouted trees and raised vegetables. He was forever sending us home with avocados and bananas.

That description of a simple man mixes simple sentences, a variety of phrases, compound sentences, and one complex sentence.

Take the time to try a sentence one way, then another. The art of sentence making comes down to experimentation, skill, and variety. Just because you can do the three-and-a-half-somersault tuck off the high board doesn't mean you must ditch the gorgeous swan dive. Good sentences can be short and muscular, and they can be long and graceful. Like the imagination, they shift and surprise.

Cardinal Sins

SKEW LINES

To string together phrases and clauses for rhetorical effect, remember that Churchillian rhetoric works because of parallel structure. Parallelism—internal syntactical balance—requires that you use similar phrasing for each element of the list. If you can't keep track of your phrases and clauses, you will end up with linguistic rats' nests instead of elegant parallels.

William Safire caught this infelicity in an ad for Harvard Business School:

> What's innovative, time-tested, diverse, intense, global and develops leaders?

The problem with Harvard's list is that the first five elements are adjectives, and the last is a clause. Not parallel. Not good.

One media critic writing for a national magazine tried to get away with this paragraph on Elvis:

> The symbol of rock and roll rebellion returned a mutant, a maker of dumb Hawaiian beach movies, a troubled superstar stuffing himself with drugs, passing out Cadillac cars like candy bars, with a retinue living in a tacky mansion and, eventually, a Vegas act whose jeweled jumpsuits now come more readily to mind than the quiet, oblivious, oddball kid.

A sharp copy editor tamed that sentence, whose various parts career from appositives to participials to prepositionals. Here's the parallel version; each modifying phrase is anchored by a clear noun phrase:

> The symbol of rock-and-roll rebellion returned to the States a mutant: **a pretty face** gracing dumb Hawaiian beach movies, **a troubled superstar** stuffing himself with drugs, **an aging freak** passing out Cadillac cars like candy bars, **a patriarch** lording over a retinue liv-

ing in a tacky mansion, and, eventually, **a Vegas act** whose jeweled jumpsuits now come more readily to mind than the quiet, oblivious, oddball kid.

RUNAWAYS

Playing with long sentences does not mean ignoring basic rules. There is no excuse for muddy thinking, ill-formed ideas, or flooding streams of consciousness. That's why we just went through all this sentence stuff. If you don't get the structural underpinnings of a sentence, go back to simple subjects and predicates.

This run-on sentence, from an essay by a student in a composition class, starts at a museum and then changes venues without warning:

> The museum has a new exhibit on Egyptian art, canvases by John Singer Sargent, and a Jewish Film Festival is occurring simultaneously.

That can, and should be, broken into two sentences: *The museum has a new exhibit on Egyptian art as well as one featuring canvases by John Singer Sargent. The Jewish Film Festival is occurring simultaneously.*

These sentences, from an essay by a student after a visit to a crocodile farm in Cambodia with his class, needed some help from Copy Editor Dundee:

> When our teacher informed us we were visiting a crocodile farm I ignored my initial confusion over this seeming irrelevance, everything else on our itinerary had been culturally educational or historically relevant, instead I allowed childish excitement to prevail.
>
> Just an hour ago the prospect of watching a ferocious crocodile hunt a live animal exhilarated me, the reality of the situation however, was beginning to set in.

Remember, independent clauses need to be set off by something stronger than a comma.

Run-ons are not uncommon in the political arena. There, though, they can hint at not just a syntactical lack of control, but a desire to obfuscate the facts. Or maybe they just reveal a pol with a loose handle on them.

The run-on queen, for sure, is Tea Party darling Sarah Palin. In July 2009, she resigned as governor of Alaska in the midst of an ethics investigation. She argued that the investigation had already cost her and the state millions of dollars, not to mention endless distraction. That was the noble explanation. She also offered this run-on explanation:

> It may be tempting and more comfortable to just keep your head down, plod along, and appease those who demand: "Sit down and shut up," but that's the worthless, easy path; that's a quitter's way out.

We think she was saying there that she wanted to avoid becoming a lame duck governor, and she was trying to defang criticism about her stepping down midterm. Former Minnesota governor Jesse Ventura took the bait, responding to Palin's decision with these simple sentences: "She told the people of Alaska she wanted to be their governor. And that's a four-year commitment. And now, right in the middle, she quits?"

TOWERS OF BABBLE

As if it weren't bad enough that the Ivory Tower gives us lugubrious nouns, ludicrous adjectives, and pompous prepositional pileups, think of the *sentences* churned out by academics. *Philosophy and Literature,* a journal published by the Johns Hopkins University Press, runs an annual contest for the ugliest, most stylistically awful sentence to come out of scholarly books and articles. Winners include untamable sentences like this one, by Stephen T. Tyman in *The Philosophy of Paul Ricoeur:*

> With the last gasp of Romanticism, the quelling of its florid uprising against the vapid formalism of one strain of the Enlightenment, the dimming of its yearning for the imagined grandeur of the archaic, and the dashing of its too sanguine hopes for a revitalised, fulfilled humanity, the horror of its more lasting, more Gothic legacy has settled in, distributed and diffused enough, to be sure, that lugubriousness is recognisable only as languor, or as a certain sardonic laconicism disguising

itself in a new sanctification of the destructive instincts, a new genius for displacing cultural reifications in the interminable shell game of the analysis of the human psyche, where nothing remains sacred.

That's not a stream of thought; it's a bunch of big words thrown into an Osterizer.

Carnal Pleasures

Trust Madison Avenue to get it that parallelism (and a few other tricks) allows you to create slogans that stick even if they are not simple sentences. In his book *Microstyle: The Art of Writing Little,* the linguist Christopher Johnson points out that it takes only a few words to woo—if they are strung together on the right syntactical filament. Here are some examples of crafty compound sentences, with the coordinating conjunctions (not to mention the subjects) sometimes implied:

> I am stuck on Band-Aid brand, 'cause Band-Aid's stuck on me.
> Fly like a CEO, pay like a temp.
> Better built, better backed.
> Expect more. Pay less.

Those sentences are from, respectively, Johnson & Johnson, Virgin America, Mitsubishi, and Target.

And here's a noncomplicated complex sentence, courtesy of Morton Salt:

> When it rains, it pours.

The *when* at the start of the sentence subordinates that first clause.

Finally, here's a sentence—from Cracker Jack, circa 1919—whose exact type remains elusive:

> The more you eat, the more you want.

Are those really two adjective phrases stuck together as two pieces of caramel corn would be?

AT THE OTHER END of the guilty-pleasures spectrum is a film review by Christopher Orr that ran on Atlantic.com. The film? *The Words*. The verdict? "We're left to ponder whether this lazy literary mindfuck might have worked better on the printed page, only to conclude that, no, the prose is too dreadful." But that verdict is rendered in a pull quote. The bulk of the review itself is one long impenetrable run-on:

> The movie begins with Dennis Quaid (heavy-faced, a bit melancholy) as a famous writer, reading to a rapt, upscale Manhattan audience from his new novel, a novel about a younger writer, played by Bradley Cooper, who marries his college sweetheart (Zoe Saldana) but struggles to find his way into print—his fiction is described as being too "Interior," which is not a sin of which Cooper seems likely to be guilty, in this film or any other—until one day he discovers, implausibly tucked into the seam of an ancient second-hand briefcase, a thick yellowed postwar manuscript, brilliant and unpublished, which he re-types, word for word, and submits under his own name, and which makes him an instant literary sensation, feted with awards and further book contracts, until one day, another day, he is approached in the park by an old man, played by Jeremy Irons (decked out in exhausted, exhausting stubble), who is the true author of the novel that Cooper has stolen, and who tells him the tragic story of his own youth in 1940s Paris. . . .

The review goes on for 587 more words before ending "Oh, and the movie is titled *The Words*. Of course." Touché.

IN *ULYSSES*, JAMES JOYCE'S punctuationless paragraphs and endless sentences worked because of his superior command of cadence. Phrases and clauses did their work—even without commas—and words themselves (*and, O, yes*) became Joyce's punctuation. The Irish novelist's ear was impeccable; it's far easier to spoof him than to best him. So we'll let Joyce, in the ending of *Ulysses,* give us the last word on sentences:

> and the night we missed the boat at Algeciras the watchman going about serene with his lamp and O that awful deepdown torrent O and the sea the sea crimson sometimes like fire and the glorious sunsets and the figtrees in the Alameda gardens yes and all the queer little streets and pink and blue and yellow houses and the rosegardens and the jessamine and geraniums and cactuses and Gibraltar as a girl where I was a Flower of the mountain yes when I put the rose in my hair like the Andalusian girls used or shall I wear a red yes and how he kissed me under the Moorish wall and I thought well as well him as another and then I asked him with my eyes to ask again yes and then he asked me would I yes to say yes my mountain flower and first I put my arms around him yes and drew him down to me so he could feel my breasts all perfume yes and his heart was going like mad and yes I said yes I will Yes.

Catechism

PARALLEL PARTS: Which elements are parallel in the following examples? Identify the kind of phrase or clause echoed:

- I found a way to be a good mother and still be a great mom. (Sunny D ad)
- The loss we felt was not the loss of ham but the loss of pig. (E. B. White, "Death of a Pig")
- What special affinities appeared to him to exist between the moon and women? Her nocturnal predominance: her satellitic dependence: her luminary reflection: her constancy under all her phases, rising and setting by her appointed times, waxing and waning: the forced invariability of her aspect: her indeterminate response to inaffirmative interrogation: her potency over effluent

and refluent waters: her power to enamour, to mortify, to invest with beauty, to render insane, to incite to and aid delinquency: the tranquil inscrutability of her visage: the terribility of her isolated dominant resplendent propinquity: her omens of tempest and of calm: the stimulation of her light, her motion and her presence: the admonition of her craters, her arid seas, her silence: her splendour, when visible: her attraction, when invisible (James Joyce, *Ulysses*).

CATCH MY DRIFT? Are the following political catchphrases phrases, fragments, simple sentences, compound sentences, complex sentences, or a blend of more than one of those:

- **We are all republicans—we are all federalists**—Thomas Jefferson's first inaugural address.
- **Tippecanoe and Tyler too**—popular slogan for Whig Party candidates William Henry Harrison and John Tyler in the 1840 U.S. presidential election.
- **Four score and seven years ago**—Abraham Lincoln, Gettysburg Address.
- **Yesterday, December 7, 1941, a date which will live in infamy**—said by President Franklin D. Roosevelt after the Japanese attack on Pearl Harbor.
- **I shall return**—U.S. general Douglas MacArthur after leaving the Philippines.
- **The buck stops here**—Harry Truman.
- **Ich bin ein Berliner**—said by John F. Kennedy in West Berlin.
- **There you go again**—said by Ronald Reagan to Jimmy Carter, in a 1980 presidential debate.
- **Where's the beef?**—former vice president Walter Mondale, attacking Colorado senator Gary Hart in 1984 Democratic primary debate.
- **Read my lips: no new taxes**—said by George H. W. Bush during the 1988 U.S. presidential election.
- **That giant sucking sound**—Ross Perot in 1992 with regard to

American jobs going to Mexico if the North American Free Trade Agreement (NAFTA) were ratified.

- **It's the economy, stupid**—used during Bill Clinton's 1992 presidential campaign and widely attributed to Clinton adviser James Carville.
- **Yes, we can**—slogan of Barack Obama's 2008 presidential campaign.

Yes, you can figure all this out. Head to the Appendix if you want a little help.

ONE FOOT AFTER THE OTHER, OR A COMPLICATED DANCE? Find two articles on the same news event (a press conference, for example, or a speech by the president), one from the AP or Reuters, one from *The New York Times*. In the case of the AP/Reuters version, look for an article that relies on coordinate conjunctions to join independent clauses. In the case of the *New York Times* version, look for one that relies on subordinate conjunctions. Analyze the difference between the sentences, the paragraphs, the stories. How much information is packed in? Are there S curves? Is there paradox?

FROM DRAFT TO CRAFT: Using stream of consciousness, freewrite for ten or twenty minutes, without pausing, about a mentor or personality who has been a great influence on your life. Don't think about the sentences per se. Just try to write evocatively about the person. After you've finished, craft a character sketch of that person (much like that of Papa Correa). Look carefully at the sentences. Mix long and short, complex and simple. Use subordinate conjunctions to help emphasize paradoxes or, perhaps, cause-effect relationships. Take command of your sentences—if you feel comfortable writing short and long, appositive and absolute, simple and complex, staccato and fluid, you begin to have great freedom in writing sentences that will have an intended effect on the reader. This is the essence of craft!

PART 3

Music

We are born with a natural delight in the music of language. As infants we coo and babble and let consonants roll around in our mouths like mother's milk. As young children, we invent words, mash syllables together, and delight in nonsensical lines. We let ourselves be lulled to sleep by the playful rhymes of Mem Fox ("It's time for bed, little goose, little goose, / The stars are out and on the loose"). We seek out stories with fanciful sounds ("Quickberry / Quackberry / Pick me a blackberry"). We begin to sense the link between what's on the surface, and what's under it ("I meant no harm. I most truly did not. / But I had to grow bigger. So bigger I got. / I biggered my factory. I biggered my roads. / I biggered my wagons. I biggered the loads").

As we mature, our delight in the music of words goes a bit underground, but it's still there. We repeat not just Chaucer's prologue, but also advertising jingles. We let brand names like Chunky Monkey and SurveyMonkey tumble off our tongues. We appreciate the curt sentences of Hemingway as well as those that are long and loose and lyrical. We let ourselves be moved by the moral authority of Nelson Mandela. We follow the Dalai Lama on Facebook. We let Chris Christie voice our outrage after a hurricane, Barack Obama our sorrow after a massacre of children.

Language remains an adventure, if sometimes a somewhat mysterious one: We are drawn to reliable narrators and find that metaphors lift us. We are transported by soaring vowels. The cadence of sentences acts on us like the rhythm of an ancient drum.

The music of language leads us to meaning, to our own humanity.

RELISH EVERY WORD

Prose can be art, possessing all the qualities we associate with its more highfalutin cousin, poetry. Prose, too, can have melody, rhythm, lyricism, and voice. But how do you get there?

To paraphrase Ezra Pound, don't imagine that the art of prose is any simpler than the art of music; spend as much time developing your craft as a pianist spends practicing scales. "Let the neophyte know assonance and alliteration, rhyme immediate and delayed, simple and polyphonic, as a musician would expect to know harmony and counterpoint," Pound argued in his 1913 essay, "A Few Don'ts."

Devour novels. Cue up recordings of famous speeches. Fall in love with poetry. Download episodes of *Deadwood* and *The Wire*. Read your writing aloud.

Cultivate catholic tastes. If you are a lawyer, loll about in the laconic images of Chinese poetry. If you are a novelist prone to the prolix, study the staccato sentences of David Mamet. If you are a lit teacher, take up Tom Clancy. If you write a newsletter for an accounting firm, take up the tango and memorize the words to every song. If you are an advertising copywriter, go for David Foster Wallace. Shake up your sensibilities. Discover the rut you're in, and climb out.

Learn to love other tongues. "Let the candidate fill his mind with the finest cadences he can discover, preferably in a foreign language," commanded Pound. "Saxon charms, Hebridean folk songs, the verse of Dante, and the lyrics of Shakespeare. . . . Dissociate the vocabulary from the cadence. . . . Dissect the lyrics of Goethe coldly into their component sound values, syllables long and short, stressed and unstressed, into vowels and consonants."

Sound a little highbrow? O.K., then, listen to the nightly news on Univision, especially if *no hablas español*.

AIM DEEP, BUT BE SIMPLE

Every now and then, politicians become infatuated with "plain English." Granted, using simple words, short sentences, and a user-friendly conversational style has its merits. Plain English beats the tufts of fuzz many bureaucrats spew forth. But as much as we deserve clarity from our public servants, we should hold our hired rhetoricians to a higher plane than "plain."

If you want an illustration of the simple and the deep, do a search for two speeches from the Senate impeachment trial of President Bill Clinton. Arkansas Democrat Dale Bumpers played the country lawyer ("The American people are now and for some time have been asking to be allowed a good night's sleep. They're asking for an end to this nightmare. It is a legitimate request"). Illinois Republican Henry Hyde played the proud orator ("It's your country—the President is our flag bearer, out in front of our people. The flag is falling, my friends—I ask you to catch the falling flag as we keep our appointment with history"). Both senators found words and cadences to reach beyond the chamber. They were talking to the jury of American citizens.

When occasions call for eloquence, you need poetry, not plain English.

TAKE RISKS

Language offers us a surprising, savage terrain full of pockets and peaks. Shakespeare invented words like crazy. Mark Twain wrote in dialect. Muhammad Ali rapped in rhythmic sentences. Junot Díaz mixes Spanish into his sentences like rum into fruit juice. Nicki Minaj spices her lyrics with slang. Despite this, English teachers still hew to Standard Written English as a paragon of virtue. Don't you hew, too.

American speech, wrote the early-twentieth-century journalist and amateur linguist H. L. Mencken, "at its greatest, lacks restraint and urbanity altogether." The author of *The American Language* notes a friendliness toward "novelties for the mere sake of their novelty," an attitude open to "extravagant raciness."

Extravagant raciness isn't the exclusive province of American English. David Dabydeen, a prizewinning British poet, writes verse in what he calls the "angry, crude, energetic" creole of his native West Indies. In an essay titled "On Not Being Milton: Nigger Talk in England Today," Dabydeen argues that contemporary English poetry is afflicted with "the disease of gentility." Dabydeen champions the work of poets like John Agard, whose "Listen Mr. Oxford Don" thumbs its nose at the very notion of "correct" English:

> Dem accuse me of assault
> on de Oxford dictionary . . .
> I slashing suffix in self-defense
> I bashing future with present tense
> and if necessary
> I making de Queen's English accessory
> to my offence

The patois of British blacks, Dabydeen writes, is like Caliban "tearing up the pages of Prospero's magic book and repasting it in his own order, by his own method, and for his own purpose." And what a purpose it is.

Whether West Indian creole, the idioms of the Deep South, or Lake Wobegonics, nonstandard English remembers the strong link between the spoken and the written, a link getting even stronger in this age of email. Slang, vernacular, the colloquial—all have a place in literary writing. Without abandoning prose with a capital *P*, we can build the musicality of our writing by listening to the street.

Don't settle for the safe.

SEEK BEAUTY

Some language types diss our mother tongue, calling it less musical than those exotic languages—Italian, perhaps, or Tahitian—that drip with mellifluous vowels. But English, rooted in an Anglo-Saxon of crisp consonants and punchy words, leavened by Scandinavian, and spiced by imported words from the Continent and the rest of the world, makes its own kind of music.

The Spanish-born, Paris- and Oxford-educated writer Salvador de Madariaga waxed ecstatic about the beauty of English words in 1928:

> They are marvellous, those English monosyllables. Their fidelity is so perfect that one is tempted to think English words are the right and proper names which acts are meant to have, and all other words are pitiable failures. How could one improve upon *splash, smash, ooze, shriek, slush, glide, squeak, coo*? Is not the word *sweet* a kiss in itself, and what could suggest a more peremptory obstacle than *stop*?

If you want to wallow, like Madariaga, in the simple beauty of English, pick up the Book of Psalms and read them out loud. Memorize the Gettysburg Address and linger on the speeches in the anthology *Lend Me Your Ears*. Or listen to the lyrics of Cole Porter.

On the other hand, don't be a word Nazi. Enjoy the nonstandard syllables of Zora Neale Hurston and Zadie Smith. Enjoy the arch polysyllables of George F. Will. Listen to the twangy metaphors of Jimmie Dale Gilmore.

FIND THE RIGHT PITCH

My parents were educated on the East Coast and insisted on standard English at the dinner table, but we lived on the North Shore of O'ahu, surrounded by sugarcane fields and famous beaches. Every day, my brother and sister and I would flip back and forth between the Queen's (or at least my mother's) English and Pidgin English.

Our elementary school had an annual storytelling contest in which we would memorize and recite a short book. I was better at books than at kickball, so this was a big deal. In sixth grade, I picked Leo Lionni's *Tico and the Golden Wings*. When I told my story, I felt I had my audience in my hands, with my bird voices, dramatic pauses, and stage whispers. Then a classmate told the story of "Ali Baba and the Forty Thieves." *What a cliché*, I thought to myself, though I might not have used that word. How unimaginative! And he was telling the entire story in Pidgin English! A disgrace!

Pretty soon, the students who had sat politely while I told them about Tico and the golden wings started to laugh at the exploits of "dah bruddah Baba." They started to hoot, and holler, and howl. By the time my nemesis sat down, the cafeteria was in a frenzy.

Needless to say, he won.

Storytelling is an exchange between the writer and the reader, the narrator and the audience. The better we know our audience, the more that exchange will crackle. My classmate delivered "Ali Baba and the Forty Thieves" in a style that was perfect for those kids. And his rendition was funny.

Of course, a different audience might have responded to the stately story of Tico. In another crowd, poignancy might trump Pidgin punch lines.

But all great storytelling touches upon a common experience, a shared desire, an ineffable but inescapable emotion. Writing is a conversation. Let's never forget that we need to speak and write like human beings with hearts, and not like the tin woodsman in *The Wizard of Oz* or Hal in the movie *2001*.

Understanding pitch, and being able to adjust it, is especially valuable in an era when information often trumps insight and the flow of data exceeds our capacity to distill—to make it ours and to make it matter. The computer makes it easy to spew out paragraphs; the Kindle, the iPhone, and the iPad make it easy to receive them. But we still need to craft our passages. We want narrators—not newsreaders. We desire stories—not brands, press releases, or tweets. We crave writing that is original, passionate, and personal.

CHAPTER 13

Melody

Bones

We think of melody as the collection of stirring notes that give a tune sweetness. In prose, melody translates into *euphony*—the acoustic effect of words combined to be pleasing and harmonious. Sweet words, euphonious phrasing, sensuous sentences—they affect us as much as meaning does.

Our earliest memories of storytelling—listening to nursery rhymes and fairy tales intoned in the familiar voices of a parent or grandparent—are sense memories. The linguist David Crystal tells us that sound—being a linguist, he calls it "phonological structuring"—is at the very heart of the way we learn language. We pick up and repeat sounds and rhymes and rhythmic patterns. We never lose our love of the way music imitates nature, rolls around in our mouths, makes us laugh, feel sad, or just go "ahhh."

But sound isn't just about pleasure. Our love of the sound of words may go further back; it may be our legacy from the days when all narrative was set to song. In preliterate times, sound helped a listener remember and repeat orally transmitted text. Today, sound and rhythm help us memorize everything from a sonnet to the Pledge of Allegiance. It's an especially important device when we need to grab a listener's or a reader's attention, such as in news headlines or advertising slogans.

What are the poetic devices available to the sound-conscious prose stylist? They include assonance, consonance, rhyme, alliteration, and onomatopoeia:

- **Assonance** repeats vowel sounds within words for effect (*clean . . . neat*). **Consonance** lets the initial consonants of words echo with internal consonants (*Sala-ma-sond*). Dr. Seuss used both devices in this bit from *Yertle the Turtle and Other Stories*: "On the far-away Island of Sala-ma-Sond, / Yertle the Turtle was king of the pond. / A nice little pond. It was clean. It was neat. / The water was warm. There was plenty to eat."

- **Rhyme** sets up an exact correspondence between the final syllable or syllables of words. Dr. Seuss loved rhyming names like *Yertle the Turtle,* and he loved rhyming titles—*Fox in Socks, The Cat in the Hat, Hop on Pop,* and *One Fish Two Fish Red Fish Blue Fish.*

- **Alliteration** refers to the repetition of the initial sound—one or more letters—of words in a phrase or sentence. Dr. Seuss's *Hooray for Diffendorfer Day* combines alliteration (and rhyme) in the title as well as in the text: "Miss Twining teaches tying knots / In neckerchiefs and noodles, / And how to tell chrysanthemums / From miniature poodles. / Miss Vining teaches all the ways / A pigeon may be peppered, / And how to put a saddle / On a lizard or a leopard."

- **Onomatopoeia** may be Greek to you and me, but those twelve letters just mean "name making." Pronounced "onna-motta-pee-ah," the term carries the idea that we can name a thing (or action) by imitating the sounds associated with it. With onomatopoeia, the sound of the word defines it. In *The Lorax,* "Grickle grass" is the name given by Dr. Seuss to the town's unruly tufts. Seuss characters like the Grinch and the Sneetches owe their names to onomatopoeia.

  Zap, zowie, bam, socko, wow, oof, wham, bing, grrr—comics rely as heavily on onomatopoeia as does the kid-book doc. But words used in more serious contexts also rely on sound to convey sense.

The late great word maven William Safire once spent an entire paragraph considering what he called the "imitative word" *plunk*. The verb "came into the language in 1805 to denote plucking a string or striking a hollow object to emit a short, metallic sound," Safire noted in his *New York Times* column. Now it describes the pizzicato sound of a violin. "Toward the end of the century," Safire noted, "*plunk down* appeared, meaning 'to drop abruptly' (plunk it down) or 'to set down firmly' (plunk down a dollar bet) or 'to settle into position' (she plunked herself down in the witness chair)." All of us can, and ought to, delight in plinks and plunks the way Safire did.

Christopher Johnson, in *Microstyle,* writes of studies that show humans perceive sounds with high sonority (with little obstruction or interruption in their pronunciation) as softer, rounder and more feminine than those with low sonority. And so we have L'Oréal, Revlon, Avon. On the other hand, masculine product names include Black & Decker, Craftsman, and Rigid.

The poet Alastair Reid makes up "proper" names for things in his book *Ounce Dice Trice*. He uses alveolar sounds (*t, d, s, l, r,* and *n*—pronounced lightly, with the tongue behind the top front teeth) to give us insects named Twilliter, Limlet, Tilltin, Legliddy, and Tristram.

And what could be a better word for a chattering, flighty, silly person than *flibbertigibbet*?

Onomatomeaning

Some sounds have acquired a meaning of their own.

A short *i* often suggests smallness, as in *little, bit, slim, kid, chit, thin, skinny, imp, shrimp, piddling.*

The sound *fl-* at the start of a word can convey awkward or jerky movement, as in *flounder, flitter, flail, flutter, flip-flop, flurry, fling.*

Alveolar sounds such as *t, d, s, l, r,* and *n* (pronounced lightly, with the tongue behind the top front teeth) suggest smallness and lightness, as in words like *itty-bitty* and *eensy-weensy.*

The hard consonants *b, d, c, k, q, p,* and *t*—especially when followed by *-ash*—represent explosive action, as in *bash, blast, crash, dash, gash, gnash, trash.* Or they suggest sudden noise: *pop, tap, quack, crackle.*

A closing *-sh* often suggests soft, rustling sounds or the flow of water: *swish, hush, flush, gush, rush, slush.*

The nasal *sn-* sound begins many words concerning the nose—or facial contortions: *sneeze, snort, sniff, sniffle, snuff, snarl, snivel, snout, sneer, snicker.*

Finally, *-in, -ing,* and *-ong* are used to convey a bell-like chime, as in *ring, ding, ding-dong, bong, gong, ping,* and Edgar Allan Poe's *tintinnabulation.*

Flesh

Dr. Seuss isn't the only children's writer to play to our love of sound. Think of the Lewis Carroll characters Tweedledee and Tweedledum. Then there's Rudyard Kipling's *Rikki-tikki-tavi,* whose title is all onomatopoeia and whose opening lines make a medley of exotic sounds:

> This is the story of the great war that Rikki-tikki-tavi fought single-handed, through the bathroom of the big bungalow in Segowlee cantonment. Darzee, the tailor-bird, helped him, and Chuchundra, the musk-rat, who never comes out into the middle of the floor, but always creeps round by the wall, gave him advice, but Rikki-tikki-tavi did the real fighting.

Like onomatopoeia, assonance and consonance are hardly just child's play—even adults delight in word combos like *wishy-washy, mishmash, flimflam, riffraff,* and *chitchat.*

Edgar Allan Poe's poem "The Bells" is a classic example of sound in a grown-up poem.

> Hear the sledges with the bells—
> Silver bells!

What a world of merriment their melody foretells!
How they tinkle, tinkle, tinkle,
In the icy air of night!
While the stars that oversprinkle
All the heavens seem to twinkle
With a crystalline delight.

(You have to read a little further to find *tintinnabulation*.)

These sonic devices are obvious in poetry, but we have to look harder to see them in prose, especially because they often work on a subliminal level. What do you notice about the relationship between music and meaning in this opening passage from *Their Eyes Were Watching God* by the novelist Zora Neale Hurston?

> Ships at a distance have every man's wish on board. For some they come in with the tide. For others they sail forever on the horizon, never out of sight, never landing until the Watcher turns his eyes away in resignation, his dreams mocked to death by Time. That is the life of men.

THE GREAT VERBAL IMPROVISATIONALIST Muhammad Ali sparred with assonance and consonance as much as he sparred with other heavyweights: they made his "Rumble in the Jungle" catch on as *the* descriptor for his fight with George Foreman in Zaire. Ali even worked rhyme into his riffs, as in this one, comparing his condition in that fall of 1974 to his condition in 1964 when, as an upstart in professional boxing, he fought Sonny Liston for the first time:

> I'm experienced now. Professional. Jaw's been broke. Been knocked down a couple times. I'm bad! I been chopping trees. I done something new for this fight: I done rassled with a alligator. I done tussled with a whale. I done handcuffed lightning, throwed thunder in jail. That's bad!

In the consonance corner, Ali gives us *rassled* and *tussled*. As far as rhyme goes, who would have expected *whale* and *jail*?

THE SOUND OF SIBILANTS

We think of rhyme as the province of country-western crooners and urban rappers. But we find it infrequently in prose. Alliteration, on the other hand, appears in the titles of best sellers (*Good to Great*) and advertising taglines ("Guinness is good for you"). It can be silly (as in General Mills' "I'm cuckoo for Cocoa Puffs") or serious (as when Francis X. Clines called the conservative online columnist Matt Drudge a "Walter Winchell wannabe").

Sonorous sounds, including alliteration, are alive and well in the best public rhetoric. One of the most striking lines in Barack Obama's second inaugural address, delivered on January 21, 2013, used symbolism, parallelism, and alliteration to link the struggles for equality of women, and blacks, and gays:

> We, the people, declare today that the most evident of truths—that all of us are created equal—is the star that guides us still; just as it guided our forebears through Seneca Falls, and Selma, and Stonewall; just as it guided all those men and women, sung and unsung, who left footprints along this great Mall, to hear a preacher say that we cannot walk alone; to hear a King proclaim that our individual freedom is inextricably bound to the freedom of every soul on earth.

"Stonewall" took the breath away. The repeated s's in "Seneca Falls, and Selma, and Stonewall" called attention to the triad and made the sudden inclusion of gay rights in the list of otherwise unsurprising symbols ever more notable.

SHEEP MAA AND MOTOR CARS GO BEEP BEEP

In *Angela's Ashes*, the Irish-born novelist Frank McCourt captures the colloquial poetry of his father, his clan, and indeed of Ireland itself. McCourt, Sr., is driven to distraction by the questions of his son, raised in New York and abruptly plopped down in the Irish countryside ("What are cows, Dad?"—"Cows are cows, son"—and "What are sheep, Dad?"). The elder McCourt finally erupts in sonorous harmony with the surrounding landscape:

> Is there any end to your questions? Sheep are sheep, cows are cows, and that over there is a goat. A goat is a goat. The goat gives milk, the sheep gives wool, the cow gives everything. What else in God's name do you want to know?
>
> And Malachy yelped with fright because Dad never talked like that, never spoke sharply to us. He might get us up in the middle of the night and make us promise to die for Ireland but he never barked like this. Malachy ran to Mam and she said, There, there, love, don't cry. Your father is just worn out carrying the twins and 'tis hard answering all those questions when you're carting twins through the world.
>
> Dad set the twins on the road and held out his arms to Malachy. Now the twins started to cry and Malachy clung to Mam, sobbing. The cows mooed, the sheep maaed, the goats ehehed, the birds twittered in the trees, and the beep beep of a motor car cut through everything.

WHO'S AFRAID OF VIRGINIA WOOLF?

To the Lighthouse is often cited for Virginia Woolf's stream-of-consciousness writing and her startling metaphors. But take a look at the *sounds* of her words:

> The <u>monotonous</u> fall of waves on the beach, which for the most part beat a measured and <u>soothing tattoo</u> to her thoughts and seemed consolingly to repeat <u>over and over again</u> as she sat with the children the words of some old cradle song, <u>murmured</u> by nature, "I am guarding you, and am your support," but at other times, suddenly and unexpectedly, especially when her mind raised itself slightly from the task actually in hand, had no such kindly meaning, but like a <u>ghostly roll</u> of drums <u>remorselessly</u> beat the measure of life, made one think of the destruction of the island and its engulfment in the sea, and warned her whose day had slipped past in one quick doing after another that it was all ephemeral as a rainbow—this sound which had been ob-

scured and concealed under the other sounds suddenly <u>thundered hollow</u> in her ears and made her look up with an <u>impulse of terror</u>.

Notice how Woolf uses "monotonous," "soothing tattoo," "repeat over and over again," and "murmured" when she's referring to the "kindly meaning" of waves on the beach (and, in turn, to the calming of her thoughts) and then "ghostly roll," "remorselessly beat," "thundered hollow," and "impulse of terror" when she's referring to more ominous forces of nature and of consciousness. The first set of words murmurs with soft syllables, soft consonants, soft vowels. The second set gives us an "uh-oh" with "ghostly roll," followed by the syllables that register like the warning beats of a tympani.

Subtle, but masterful.

Cardinal Sins

We can twist poet Alexander Pope's diktat—"the sound must seem an echo of the sense"—into a caveat for the novice writer: When sound *doesn't* echo sense, the writing misfires.

HEAVYHANDEDNESS

Techniques like rhyme and alliteration work only when they sound natural. They must be used like salt: sparingly. When Spiro Agnew denounced the Eastern liberal establishment as "nattering nabobs of negativism," he may have uttered a quotable phrase, but the alliteration seemed forced. Who talks that way?

Of course, politicos easily fall prey to such follies. Perhaps the worst was Warren Harding's "not nostrums but normalcy, not revolution but restoration, not agitation but adjustment, not surgery but serenity, not the dramatic but the dispassionate, not experiment but equipoise."

Jesse Jackson defends his own rhyming phrases, saying that "Down with dope, up with hope" gets the point across more powerfully than "Off with narcotics, up with sobriety." He's got a point. But rhyme is best when it's surprising, not canned. You almost don't need Jackson around to complete his pat and predictable rhymes ("If my mind can conceive it and my heart can believe it, then I can achieve it").

Johnnie Cochran's unforgettable phrase about the glove—"If it doesn't fit, you must acquit"—may have worked magic on the O.J. jury, but such rhetoric loses its fizz over time. Cochran's too-facile rhyme even inspired a *Seinfeld* parody—in the character of Kramer's lawyer, Jackie Chiles.

FOUL VOWELS

The cable tycoon Ted Turner once ribbed Rupert Murdoch before an audience of media moguls, using a word that was all onomatopoeia: "Time Warner is three times as big as Rupert's company," Turner said. "I'm looking forward to *squishing* him like a bug."

This caused a kerfuffle for news services. Reuters, *Variety,* and the *New York Daily News* spelled the key verb *squash*. But an AP television writer, who had the quote on tape, after all, transmitted the verb as *squish*. William Safire, enthralled, took up the gantlet.

"What do you do to a bug when you step on it?" he asked in his "On Language" column, later anthologized in *Let a Simile Be Your Umbrella*. Safire went on:

> *Squash,* formed from the Vulgar Latin *exquassare*—*ex-* ("out") and *quassare* ("to shake")—was first on the scene in 1565, meaning "to press into a flat mass," and it gained an extended meaning of "to suppress." (Yes, the name of the racquet game comes from the sound of a ball being momentarily mashed, flattened, or squashed by a racquet. No, the vegetable that Martha Stewart grows in her window box comes from a shortening of the Narragansett word *askutasquash*.)
>
> Only a century later, *squish* appeared both as an alternative to *squash* and with special reference to the soft, damp sound made by the act of pressing a boot into the mud. Other variants of this onomatopoeic verb are *squush,* more recently spelled *squoosh,* and *smoosh,* as in "You can try jamming your garment bag into that overhead bin, Buster, but you better not *smoosh* down my fur hat."
>
> The use of the *i* instead of the *a* is widespread: in 1970, Vice Presi-

dent Spiro T. Agnew derided radical liberals as *squishy-soft,* and a few years ago, a telephonic friend of Princess Diana used *Squidgy* as a term of endearment . . .

So which is correct, *squish* or *squash?* Wrong question! When words imitate sounds, latitude is given to variants. If you are pressing, beating, squeezing, or mashing a bug or anything else into a pulp, *squash* is more standard; *squish, squoosh, squush,* and *smoosh* add a sense of the soft sucking sound emitted.

SOUNDS THAT HAVE NO MEANING

Sometimes it's sound that separates a big brand from a big bust. Ford's Ranger and Explorer are direct and no-nonsense; Honda's Odyssey carries great promise. The best names combine meaning, message, and melody: Acura (conveying precise engineering), Jetta (racier than VW's "bug"), and Caravan ("It's a car! It's a van! No, it's a parade!"). Less successful names try for euphony and end up just phony, Toyota's Tercel and Yaris, along with Dodge's Elantra, being prime examples. Some names are conceived as bursts of testosterone, then bloom into doomed alphabet soups: CR-V, ES, STE-AWD, TSi. The Lexus GX470 combines meaningless letters and numbers. One early example, the Datsun 280Z, showed some imagination—a sporty Datsun as dashing as Zorro—but it's been downhill from there.

Then come the boners—betraying an absolute ignorance of the English language. The problem here is not so much a lack of onomatopoeia, but a tin ear for meaning. Would *you* have wanted a Dictator to take you for a ride? (Studebaker, ca. 1927.) They sound, well, ugly.

Wonder why Ford's Nucleon bombed? Both the sound and the connotations are infelicitous. Chevrolet's Nova must have seemed novel to its creators, but say it out loud, and you'll understand why Spanish-speaking consumers thought "no go."

Carnal Pleasures

It is fun to play with sound, and to bend and bruise the rules a bit. In a personal essay on my military family, I invented a verb to convey the distinctive, dark, powerful sound made by a helicopter that touches down in the aftermath of a tsunami in Hawaii in 1957, the year I was born:

Molly, seven months pregnant, decided that if there was going to be a tidal wave, she'd better fix things up. She made the bed, straightened the house, and put on a pert navy skirt and pink-and-blue flowered maternity top. Then she sat in an armchair and started sewing. From there she looked seaward, across an acre of grass dotted with plumeria trees and lined on either side with pink oleander hedges.

At 9, she saw the landlord pacing down at the edge of the property and joined him. "By the time I got down to the edge of the beach," she remembers, "the water had pulled way out, exposing 100 yards of reef. The ocean bottom was hardly as you'd expect—clean and sandy, with lots of lovely exposed coral. It was all roiled up—muddy, oily, slimy. Suddenly, there was a rumble, and Fred and I started to cross the yard. The next thing I knew, the water was crackling at our ankles. We scooted towards the car. I was wearing my diamond ring, and didn't need anything from the house, but I *had* to take Max, the Weimaraner. Soon the water was swirling around the car, heaving debris. We lost our brakes, but Fred managed to get us out of there."

By the time Molly made it home, countless GIs in combat uniforms and black boots were carrying her entire dowry out of the house and shoveling mud. They had been sent from Schofield Barracks, where my father was on duty. "The house and yard were swarming," rememberd Molly. "Everything was covered with muck and salt, so they carried out all our possessions, hosed them down, and loaded them into an Army truck. A corporal was hosing down my grandmother's antique rocking chair."

Suddenly, WHUMP, WHUMP, WHUMP, a helicopter thundered in, hovering overhead long enough to bend and bruise the oleander. It touched down in the long yard, and out stepped Ted Walker, gallant Texan, guardian cousin of my father, decorated veteran of World War II and Korea, commanding general of the 25th Division Artillery. After surveying the wreckage, scooping up a glistening beached ahi, and authorizing the troops to rescue Mrs. Hatlelid's piano, Walker informed Molly that she and Joe and Max would come stay with him in his ample general's quarters at Schofield. Then Walker climbed back into the helicopter and WHUMP, WHUMPED off.

HANKLYN-JANKLIN, AND A CERTAIN HANKERING

The American love of wordplay is shared by anglophones around the world. Some English dialects spoken in India are especially boisterous, with coinages like *Bollywood* (the Bombay-based movie industry) and *Eve-teasing* (sexual harassment). Some terms grow out of the Indian habit of using echo words, such as *rumble-tumble* (scrambled eggs) and *partysharty* (a fete where beer-sheer and chicken-whicken will be ingested).

(For more on Hindi words that have floated into standard English, as well as some of the charming eccentricities of Indian English, check out the book *Hanklyn-Janklin* by the late British expat Nigel Hankin. He collected a whole volume's worth and names the book as a tribute to its 1886 forebear, *Hobson-Jobson*.)

In *The God of Small Things,* the central character, an Indian girl named Rahel, negotiates between English and Malayalam, the native language that the adults in her family use to camouflage talk they don't want children to hear. The author, Arundhati Roy, plays with the *sounds* of English to comic and sometimes ominous effect, as in the moment when bad behavior during an airport meeting with a cousin earns Rahel and her twin brother, Estappen, the wrath of their mother, Ammu.

"Estappen!" Ammu said. And an angry feeling rose in her and stopped around her heart. A Far More Angry Than Necessary feeling. She felt somehow humiliated by this public revolt in her area of jurisdiction. She had wanted a smooth performance. A prize for her children in the Indo-British Behavior Competition.

Chacko said to Ammu in Malayalam, "Please. Later. Not now."

And Ammu's angry eyes on Estha said *All right. Later.*

And Later became a horrible, menacing, goose-bumpy word.

Lay. Ter.

Like a deep-sounding bell in a mossy well. Shivery, and furred. Like moth's feet.

The Play had gone bad. Like pickle in the monsoon.

Roy repeats "Lay. Ter."—as well as other sound improvisations ("A Wake A Live A Lert")—as her novel wends its way to a horrible, menacing, goose-bumpy end.

If sounds give sensuality to prose, few have mastered their charms quite like Vladimir Nabokov. He was one novelist who knew how to turn sensuality into carnality. What could be more lascivious than these lines, which capture Humbert Humbert's obsession with the twelve-year-old Dolores Haze:

Lolita, light of my life, fire of my loins. My sin, my soul. Lo-lee-ta: the tip of the tongue taking a trip of three steps down the palate to tap, at three, on the teeth. Lo. Lee. Ta.

She was Lo, plain Lo, in the morning, standing four feet ten in one sock. She was Lola in slacks. She was Dolly at school. She was Dolores on the dotted line. But in my arms she was always Lolita.

Catechism

SPLISH SPLASH SPLAT: Go sit near a window when it's raining, and listen. (If it's not raining, sit near a fountain or the shore of an ocean, lake, or river.) Write down as many words as you can to describe the sound of the rain. Feel free to make words up. Does it sound one way when it's falling on the roof, another when it's falling on wide leaves, and another when it's dropping into a puddle?

As you listen to the water, pay close attention to the sound itself, and then to the sound of the words you find to describe it. For example, you might use *pound* (a single syllable, heavy with consonants) to describe the rain on a roof, but *splatter* for the sound of rain falling on wide leaves. How is the sound of the water different in each case, and how can that be expressed in the sound of the words you choose?

CRASH, BANG, WALLOP: Find a scene that is a symphony of sound. (A busy street corner? A screeching subway? A quiet courtyard in which each footstep registers?) Tune in to those sounds only. (Ignore the panhandlers, the change of the traffic lights, the people looking at you askance.) Find words that are onomatopoeic in some way, that suggest the sounds themselves. Write sentences whose rhythms evoke the sounds you are hearing.

THE JINGLING AND THE TINGLING: Review the passages in this chapter. Melody often comes in the rewriting; as we polish prose, we see the opportunity to play with sounds within sentences. Rewrite a passage of something you've already written, paying special attention to the way the words work together. Alliteration, assonance, rhyme, and onomatopoeia should not be forced, but it's O.K. here to let the pendulum swing all the way over in the direction of sonority.

CHAPTER 14

Rhythm

Bones

We all know what rhythm means to poetry: it's those dear little dactyls, sure-footed Shakespeare, Wordsworth, "wánder[ing] lónely ás a clóud." But what does rhythm mean to prose? Do we just trade the "da-*dah* da *dah* da-*dah* da-*dah* da-*dah*" of iambic pentameter for the banal "yadda yadda yadda" of *Seinfeld*?

Whatever the genre, rhythm remains essentially *beat*—whether the 4/4 time of rhapsodies or the urgent tempos of rap. Rhythm is repetition, incantation, timing—perhaps comedic, perhaps dramatic. Rhythm is that deep-down sense of music that is as inborn as a heartbeat.

In most poetry, rhythm is reliable and identifiable. It's meter: the arrangement of sounds into set patterns of stressed and unstressed syllables, into longs and shorts. The basic metrical units are called *feet* and consist of at least two syllables; the most familiar feet are the iamb (˘ ´), the trochee (´ ˘), the anapest (˘ ˘ ´), and the dactyl (´ ˘ ˘).

As a prose stylist, you don't really need to memorize the names of metrical feet, but you do need to appreciate their effect. Leonard Bernstein notes, in *The Joy of Music*, that iambic pentameter—the five-foot lines of, say, Shakespearean sonnets—underlies most blues lyrics. The poet Mary Oliver writes that iambic pentameter best reflects the natural rhythm of English: "It fits without stress, makes a full phrase, and leaves little breath at the end."

But if meter is regular and recognizable in poetry, it's unpredictable in prose, varying from line to line with the flow of the words and the undercurrents of meaning. In prose—conversation, oration, and narration—rhythm is a matter of more subtle patterns, of longs and shorts, ins and outs, ups and downs.

Put your best foot forward

Metrical feet can have up to five syllables (as does the dochmiac), but the most common have two or three:

Two-fers	Three-fers
iamb ˘ ´	anapest ˘ ˘ ´
trochee ´ ˘	dactyl ´ ˘ ˘
spondee ´ ´	amphibrach ˘ ´ ˘
pyrrhic (or dibrach) ˘ ˘	tribrach ˘ ˘ ˘
	bacchic ˘ ´ ´
	anti-bacchic ´ ´ ˘
	cretic ´ ˘ ´
	molossus ´ ´ ´

Here's a little ditty, cited in Richard Lederer's *The Miracle of Language*, to help you get a handle on meter. Read it out loud:

The íambs gó from shórt to lóng.
Tróchees síng a márching sóng.
Dáctyls go dáncing as líght as a féather.
But the ánapest's dífferent, you sée, altogéther.

Flesh

When we listen carefully to our writing and reshape its rhythms to our liking, prose can become music. "If we were more studious to write prose that could be read aloud with pleasure to the ear," wrote Sir Arthur Quiller-Couch in 1916, "we should be opening the pores to the ancient sap."

Speaking of the ancient sap, many of the most memorable phrases of the Bible, especially the King James Bible of 1611, are so easily received, remembered, and recited precisely because of their rhythms. Many of those lines unfold in classic iambic and anapestic combinations, like this line from the King James Bible:

> Render therefore unto Caesar the things which be Caesar's, and unto
> God the things which be God's.

(Do you recall how some of the most memorable lines from the inaugural speeches of John F. Kennedy and Barack Obama—cited in chapters 6 and 11, echo that biblical sentence?)

Even when that line was revised for the New English Bible, the rhythms remained:

> Pay Caesar what is due to Caesar, and pay God what is due to God.

(Do you hear the difference, though, in those rhythms?)

Today's jargon-jamming Antipoet might wreck such biblical cadences. It's easy to imagine these words flowing from an MBA, deaf to the long tradition of meter:

> Appropriate to Caesar the things that appertain to that chief executive.

Even if they aren't common in boardrooms and C-suites, really good copywriters and branding experts understand the power of rhythm. Multiple monosyllabic words give a phrase an emphatic rhythm, like the banging of a drum, as in the adage "Loose lips sink ships."

Screenwriters and drama queens also understand the value of metrical schemes. Check out this passage from *Make-Believe Town*, in which the playwright David Mamet recounts the cleansing that poker player David "Chip" Brown took in a round of seven-card stud:

> Chip was in a game with a drunk. He held a pair of aces, and the drunk, after his fourth card, held four diamonds. Chip was an eleven-to-ten favorite to win the hand, but the drunk wouldn't go home. They raised each other thirty-six times, and the drunk caught his fifth diamond, and Chip retired broke.

There it is: the good old iamb ("he héld a páir of áces"; "and Chíp retíred bróke").

Mamet insists that his characters prefer iambic pentameter and that he indulges them, if loosely: "None of us think about it, but we tend to speak that way," Mamet said in an interview on NPR's *Fresh Air*. "I mean, most of the blues is written that way, too: 'I hate to see that evening sun go down.' That's iambic pentameter." Mamet further explained: "Look here, you know, I could sit and talk to you all day, but finally, at the end, what would we say? That you and I had sat and that we spoke, but what we'd spoken of—what would that be? The time, the place, the radio, the day—Okay, so you see here I am on my way to a sonnet that's all iambic pentameter."

Free verse

"Rhyme and meter don't suit my mind or the way it needs to move," the contemporary poet Matthew Zapruder once told the *Los Angeles Times*. "It's like style: it might seem cool every once in a while to wear a vintage suit, but the fact of the matter is it just doesn't work for me." Zapruder says that while he doesn't use such overt formal elements, "there is always a rhythm that develops, subtly, in the voice of the speaker. Maybe something more like a cadence."

For an example of the cadence in Zapruder's poems, see "April Snow" on page 57. "I think, secretly, that my poems actually do rhyme. It's just that the rhyme is what I would call 'conceptual,' that is, not made of sounds, but of ideas that accomplish what the sounds do in formal poetry: to connect elements that one wouldn't have expected, and to make the reader or listener, even if just for a moment, feel the complexity and disorder of life, and at the same time what Wallace Stevens called the 'obscurity of an order, a whole.' "

SENTENCE RHYTHMS

Rhythm is not simply a matter of meter. Sometimes simple **repetition** is used as a device. It might be single words that are repeated for effect, or rhythms within clauses. And sometimes the repetition is enlivened by a twist, as when Jesse Jackson said, "Both tears and sweat are salty, but they render a different result. Tears will get you sympathy; sweat will get you change." The power of that phrase comes not only from the repetition of the words *tears* and *sweat,* but also from the repetition in his phrases.

Jackson was cleverly alluding to earlier orators, including British prime minister Winston Churchill, who told the House of Commons upon replacing Neville Chamberlain in May 1940 (three days after the German invasion of France), "I have nothing to offer but blood, toil, tears, and sweat."

Two decades later, John F. Kennedy charmed the press and the public with a speaking style of neat staccato bursts. When asked how he became a hero, Kennedy replied iambically, "They sank my boat." With the help of speechwriters like Theodore Sorensen, Kennedy's sentences stretched out, his crisp diction complemented by lyrical cadences. President Kennedy's inaugural address in 1961 set up repeating rhythmic patterns that let words and phrases play off each other. Rhythms helped his phrases settle into our national consciousness:

If a free society cannot help the many who are poor, it cannot save the few who are rich.

Let us never negotiate out of fear, but let us never fear to
negotiate.

And so, my fellow Americans, ask not what your country can do
for you; ask what you can do for your country.

In his March 18, 2008, speech on race, during the Democratic primary, Barack Obama echoed this kind of sentence. Starting with the first two phrases of the U.S. Constitution, "We the people, in order to form a more perfect union," Obama later referred to "a union that could and should be perfected over time," and then stated, with echoes of JFK, "This union may never be perfect, but generation after generation has shown that it can always be perfected."

In his second inaugural address, Obama returned to such a rhetorical device. This time he keyed his speech off the Declaration of Independence, with its opening lines "We hold these truths to be self-evident, that all men are created equal, that they are endowed by their Creator with certain unalienable rights, that among these are life, liberty, and the pursuit of happiness." Here's how Obama used repetition again: "For history tells us that while these truths may be self-evident, they have never been self-executing."

SWELLING RHYTHMS

Speeches intended to move audiences need to be ringing, strong, visceral. Repetition and cadence allow orators to articulate moral imperatives and elicit powerful emotions. But repetition in prose is not always so neat, especially in more subtle, less strident passages.

Ernest Hemingway often used seemingly simple word repetition. Sometimes it underscored his theme and verged on incantation (check out the use of *nada* in "A Clean Well-Lighted Place"). At other times, Hemingway built his repetitions into a distinctive pulse. Take, for example, the following description in *For Whom the Bell Tolls*. Robert Jordan, the American hero fighting in a guerrilla band against the Fascists in the Spanish Civil War, makes love with Maria:

Then there was the smell of heather crushed and the roughness of
the bent stalks under her head and the sun bright on her closed

eyes . . . and for her everything was red, orange, gold-red from the sun on the closed eyes. . . . For him it was a dark passage which led to nowhere, then to nowhere, then again to nowhere, once again to nowhere, always and forever to nowhere, heavy on the elbows in the earth to nowhere . . . now beyond all bearing up, up, up and into nowhere, suddenly, scaldingly, holdingly all nowhere gone and time absolutely still and they were both there, time having stopped and he felt the earth move out and away from under them.

This passage uses layers of repetition to build to its syntactic climax. The repeated use of *and* to link the clauses, as well as the chants of *nowhere* and *up, up, up* and *suddenly, scaldingly, holdingly,* and *absolutely* all culminate in the moment when time stops and the earth metaphorically moves out and away from under them.

WRITERS CAN ALSO BUILD rhythm through the subtle and wavelike effects on the reader of long sentence upon short, of quiet pauses and little breaths—or of strong stops and big white spaces.

Virginia Woolf had an uncanny ability to re-create the pulses and trills of the imagination, of characters' delicate inner monologues, and of the blunt punctuations of outer dialogues. Woolf blended thoughts and actions in a flow of images. Passages like this one from *Mrs. Dalloway,* though carefully crafted, reflect the mysterious rhythms of the mental stream:

The hall of the house was cool as a vault. Mrs. Dalloway raised her hand to her eyes, and, as the maid shut the door to, and she heard the swish of Lucy's skirts, she felt like a nun who has left the world and feels fold round her the familiar veils and the response to old devotions. The cook whistled in the kitchen. She heard the click of the typewriter. It was her life, and, bending her head over the hall table, she bowed beneath the influence, felt blessed and purified, saying to herself, as she took the pad with the telephone message on it, how moments like this are buds on the tree of life, flowers of darkness they are, she thought (as if some lovely rose had blossomed for her eyes only); not for a moment did she believe in God; but all the more, she thought, taking up the pad, must one repay in daily life to servants, yes, to dogs and canaries, above all to Richard her husband, who was the foundation of it—of the gay sounds, of the green lights, of the cook even whistling, for Mrs. Walker was Irish and whistled all day long—one must pay back from this secret deposit of exquisite moments, she thought, lifting the pad, while Lucy stood by her, trying to explain how

"Mr. Dalloway, ma'am—"

There's no one way to get to harmonious prose. If Virginia Woolf mastered the music of the elite drawing room, Dr. Martin Luther King, Jr., mastered the music of street demonstrations. On August 23, 1963, he moved the nation in an address from the steps of the Lincoln Memorial. The sentences in his "I Have a Dream" speech, modulating from short to long, are both pointed and poignant. He repeated *one hundred years later* four times, to emphasize the "chains of discrimination." He repeated *now* to explain why civil rights could not wait (*Now is the time to make real the promises of democracy*). His "I have a dream," reiterated over and over, elevated his speech to incantation. His wish that his children be judged "not for the color of their skin but for the content of their character" became an iconic example of alliteration. He pulled out all the stops, and he made them work together with rhythm.

Cardinal Sins

MAKING TEXT HUMDRUM

One reason that preachers have an edge when it comes to rhythm is that they are steeped in the cadences of liturgical texts. Books like the Bible, after all, were written to be read aloud, and their rhythms lend themselves to regular recitation.

Likewise, the traditional Anglican *Book of Common Prayer* was written to be read aloud by a congregation during services. By necessity, its cadences worked. But in modernizing the language of the prayer book, revisers forgot to reorchestrate the music. The twentieth century's tin-eared editors forgot about meter and flattened out rhythms. For centuries, the steady iambic rhythm in the last line of the Nicene Creed softened into delicate anapests: "And He shall come again, with glory, to judge both the quick and the dead."

But the same line, rewritten in the 1970s to be more contemporary, now lurches from iamb to dactyl to anapest:

And he will come again in glory to judge the living and the dead.

Did the revisers deem the wonderfully succinct "quick" too esoteric for modern-day readers? Did they not hear the difference between a dactyl and an anapest?

It's not just clerics who know how to spoil a beautiful phrase. In *What I Saw at the Revolution,* the Republican speechwriter Peggy Noonan spoofs staff editors in the White House by speculating about how they would eviscerate that most rhythmic and powerful of presidential speeches, the Gettysburg Address: "Fourscore and seven years ago" would be changed, Noonan jokes, first to "eighty-seven years ago," then to "long ago," then to "sometime ago"; then it'd be deleted altogether. "Our fathers brought forth upon this continent" would end up "our fathers and mothers created here." "Conceived in liberty" would be ditched (the margin screams: "too much sexual imagery—sounds like we're talking about teen pregnancy"), as would "we cannot dedicate—we cannot consecrate—we cannot hallow this ground" ("too negative? Let's talk about what we *can* do!").

REDUNDANCY IS NOT RHYTHM

It's one thing to understand the power of repetition—quite another to repeat words mindlessly. When Sarah Palin, recalling the chaotic days after she was chosen as the Republican vice presidential nominee in 2008, tried to explain away her flawed performance, here's how she put it:

Time on the ground is very important, and I'd be the first to not necessarily recommend a short amount of time, people need to start making up their minds here pretty soon for that time on the ground, meeting with constituents and having time to pack their suitcases.

Sarah, you wanna tell us one more time how important time on the ground is?

"RHYTHM" IS NO DEFENSE FOR SHODDY JOURNALISM

All this encouragement to build rhythm into your prose requires a caveat. It takes listening and sensitivity (and some talent) to develop an ear for the music of prose. Encouraging "rhythm" is not tantamount to giving a license for mindless repetition or irritating singsong.

A *Wired* reporter once refused this editor's request to insert the name of an official into a political story concerning the National Information Infrastructure because he didn't want to "mess up the rhythm" of his sentence. Aside from the sheer idiocy of such an excuse, the sentence he was protecting was practically a case study in infelicitous meter:

No law enforcement agency has yet proven it needs all these digital trapdoors. "Right now most law enforcement personnel don't have any idea what the NII is"—this according to one official who appeared on the panel.

That rhythm needs to be scrapped, not saved.

LISTLESS LISTS

Parallelism builds rhythm, and nonparallelism kills it. Imagine that Marc Antony had said: "I came for the purpose of burying Caesar, not to praise him." Doesn't exactly roll off the tongue.

Inattentive writers muck up lists badly, throwing imbalanced cadences together and leaving their readers scrambling. The elements of a list should echo each other in length, number of syllables, and rhythm. "A government of the people, by the people, and for the people" works. "A government of the people, that the people create, for the benefit of the people" doesn't.

If it's impossible to craft a list of exactly parallel elements, at least try to let the length of the phrases build so that you end up with a crescendo, not cacophony:

> Have Jell-O brand gelatin. Because it's cool (like ice cream), smooth (like pudding), light (like chiffon pie), refreshing (like sherbet), and it tastes like fruit.

If you must break your neatly parallel pattern, break it at the end. Let the longest or most ungainly phrase tumble out last:

> Disney's *The Lion King* is part pageant, part puppet show, part parade, with a touch of Las Vegas revue thrown in.

Carnal Pleasures

Singers and songwriters live at language's epicenter—from ancient bards like Homer, whose epic narratives were told in song, to the jazzman Cab Calloway, whose comic and sometimes profane patter was a foil for the music of his band. (Calloway the wordman registered the Harlem vernacular in a book, *Mister Hepster's Jive Talk Dictionary*.)

Starting in the sixties, Gil Scott-Heron reinvented the notion of jazz patter, his Black Power rhetoric backed by a bongo in songs like "Whitey on the Moon," in which the narrator "can't pay no doctor's bills" even while society's spent billions sending a man to the moon:

> A rat done bit my sister Nell
> With Whitey on the moon
> Her face and arms began to swell
> And Whitey's on the moon. . . .
> You know, the man just upped my rent last night
> 'Cause Whitey's on the moon
> No hot water, no toilets, no lights,
> But Whitey's on the moon.

Scott-Heron is up to more than just patter. Sure, the blunt language and street syntax make his story seem uncrafted and conversational. But the repetition of "Whitey's on the moon" (albeit with slightly different phrasing each time) lets him build on his theme with each new utterance. The narrative is more proselike than singsong, but if you count the syllables in each line, you'll see that Scott-Heron has his rhythm down cold: every other line is close to eight syllables, and the intervening ones are all six.

Folksingers, too, let narrative unfold in bursts of rhythm. Think of all those stories Bob Dylan has told over the years, from "Lonesome Death of Hattie Carroll" to "Not Dark Yet." Some of his lyrics are pure poetry, some plainly prosaic. The "music" comes from the rhythm of the words.

The best romantic put-down in country music—Butch Hancock's "She said 'Babe, you're just a wa-ave, you're not the water"—is a nice combo of iambs and anapests.

Rap is the latest twist on this tradition of narrative song. Call rap "storytelling with a beat," "sonic bricolage," or, as one critic prefers, "an endless stream of rhythmic verbal jazz," stories of the street use the gritty medium for serious discourse. Forget correct syntax. Forget iambic pentameter. This is rhyme and rhythm used to pack a point. This is pure language-as-music.

Hip-hop has gained notoriety for the brutal and misogynistic rhymes of gangsta rap like that of Tupac Shakur ("William Bennett, Delores Tucker, / you's a motherfucker; / instead of trying to help a nigger, / you destroy a brother"). Or the profane and chaotically spelled lines of Nicki Minaj ("I tell them bitches anyway / 'Cause we don't care what none of them galopies say / You can't stop me, I'mma fulfil my prophecy / I do it, I did it, the proper way").

But rappers like Public Enemy's Chuck D churn out authoritative and history-conscious polemics. (Chuck D calls rap "black America's CNN.") Public Enemy's best-known hit, "Fight the Power," unfolds like a 1989 update of "Whitey on the Moon," and "Louder than a Bomb" takes on subjects like the government's treatment of the black community:

CIA, FBI
All they tell is lies

And when I say it they get alarmed
'Cause I'm louder than a bomb

Some narrative songs roll out in prose. They break the rules, but in different ways from rap and hip-hop. In *Wild: From Lost to Found on the Pacific Crest Trail*, Cheryl Strayed's tough but lyric prose lurches from profane to profound as she describes an eleven-hundred-mile solo hike she undertook at age twenty-six after her mother died, her marriage failed, and her life disintegrated:

> What if I forgave myself? I thought. What if I forgave myself even though I'd done something I shouldn't have? What if I was a liar and a cheat and there was no excuse for what I'd done other than because it was what I wanted and needed to do? What if I was sorry, but if I could go back in time I wouldn't do anything differently than I had done? What if I'd actually wanted to fuck every one of those men? What if heroin taught me something? What if yes was the right answer instead of no? What if what made me do all those things everyone thought I shouldn't have done was what also had got me here? What if I was never redeemed? What if I already was?

Strayed's *What if*s relentlessly peel back the layers of her self-doubt as she deconstructs her insecurities one at a time to work through past pain.

In *The Things They Carried*, the novelist Tim O'Brien reinforces the weight, the routine, the wretched burdens of soldiers in Vietnam. In a simple list of items, O'Brien does more than just play with parataxis and anaphora, repetition and rhythm. He weighs the reader down with words just as the men were weighed down with weapons. The repetition here becomes almost a chant, the eerie chorus of a soldier's marching song gone somehow wrong. The rhythms are as inescapable as their gruesome task:

> The things they carried were largely determined by necessity. . . . P-38 can openers, pocket knives, heat tabs, wristwatches, dog tags, mosquito repellent, chewing gum, candy, cigarettes, salt tablets, packets

of Kool-Aid, lighters, matches, sewing kits, Military Payment Certificates, C rations, and two or three canteens of water. Together, these items weighed between 15 and 20 pounds, depending upon a man's habits or rate of metabolism. Henry Dobbins, who was a big man, carried extra rations; he was especially fond of canned peaches in heavy syrup over pound cake. Dave Jensen, who practiced field hygiene, carried a toothbrush, dental floss, and several hotel-sized bars of soap he'd stolen on R&R in Sydney, Australia. Ted Lavender, who was scared, carried tranquilizers. . . .

Some things they carried in common. . . . They shared the weight of memory. They took up what others could no longer bear. Often, they carried each other, the wounded or the weak. They carried infections. They carried chess sets, basketballs, Vietnamese-English dictionaries, insignia of rank, Bronze Stars and Purple Hearts, plastic cards imprinted with the Code of Conduct. They carried diseases, among them malaria and dysentery. They carried lice and ringworm and leeches and paddy algae and various rots and molds. They carried the land itself—a powdery orange-red dust that covered their boots and fatigues and faces. They carried the sky. The whole atmosphere, they carried it, the humidity, the monsoons, the stink of fungus and decay, all of it, they carried gravity.

Catechism

NAMING RHYTHMS: Plato said that "music and rhythm find their way into the secret places of the soul." Start acquainting yourself with rhythm by listening to the rhythms of very different music—African drums, Hawaiian slack-key guitar, chamber music, hip-hop. Find words to describe the rhythm, specifically, and not just the genre of the music, the sound of the instruments, or the meaning of the lyrics. Is it percussive? Fluid? Irregular? Even? Rough? Lurching? Like an incantation? Like a lullaby?

REVISING RHYTHMS: Take a paragraph of something you've previously written. Does the writing have a rhythm? Play with different rhythms in your words and your sentences to heighten what you are trying to express.

PSYCHOLOGY THROUGH RHYTHM: Let's take another look at the passages by Ernest Hemingway on pages 126 and 248. The paragraph from "Hills Like White Elephants" is followed by this bit of dialogue, as the man and the girl order two glasses of Anis del Toro:

> The man called "Listen" through the curtain. The woman came out from the bar.
>> "Four reales."
>> "We want two Anis del Toro."
>> "With water?"
>> "Do you want it with water?"
>> "I don't know," the girl said. "Is it good with water?"
>> "It's all right."
>> "You want them with water?" asked the woman.
>> "Yes, with water."
>> "It tastes like liquorice," the girl said and put the glass down.
>> "That's the way with everything."

Notice the repetition of certain words (especially *water*) as well as the rhythm of the sentences—the short staccato dialogue and the fluid description. Now compare that with the passage from *For Whom the Bell Tolls* on page 248. How do the very different sentence rhythms of each passage create very different effects (in the first case a tense conversation between a man and a woman on the skids, in the second a dreamlike, stream-of-consciousness description of lovemaking)?

TRY THIS EXERCISE IN conveying psychology through rhythm: Observe two people in a park, at a ballpark, or on a dance floor. Are their movements quick and jerky or graceful and fluid? If the former, write a series of staccato sentences (short words, hard sounds, and short sentences). Eavesdrop. Is their conversation brusque or baroque? If the latter, write a series of sentences with a more lyrical, languid, or liquid rhythm (polysyllabic words, softer sounds, stretched-out sentences).

CHAPTER 15

Lyricism

Bones

The lyre—the small harp of the ancient Greeks—haunts the term *lyricism,* harking back to the days when narratives were accompanied by strings. Lyric poetry in ancient times was often set to music, but in modern times the genre refers more to emotionally expressive lines set to a certain rhythmic scheme. I use the word here to refer to the expressive side of the equation, and in particular to the way that words can be used to evoke images, memories, and sensations.

You might say, though, that the ultimate lyrical writing still happens when the poetically inclined put words to heartbreakingly beautiful melody. Think Billie Holiday, early Bob Dylan, Joni Mitchell, Jimmie Dale Gilmore.

Or think country-western balladeers like Hank Williams, who mainline lust, love, and lonesomeness in their unforgettable lines:

Hear that lonesome whippoorwill
He sounds too blue to fly
The midnight train is whining low
I'm so lonesome I could cry

Did you ever see the night so long
When time goes crawling by

The moon just went behind a cloud
To hide its face and cry

Williams's lyricism springs mostly from vivid descriptions that work on
our reservoir of feelings and associations. In the first stanza, he does it
through adjectives and imagery: the lonesome whippoorwill, the midnight train. In the second he relies on metaphor, turning Time into
a crawling animal. He endows the whippoorwill and the moon with
human feelings, just in case we don't make the connections.

Prose can be as lyrical as a country-western croon, if you work your
words so that they convey deep emotions and direct thoughts. Let your
imagination leap and your words sing. Lyricism as I define it springs
from connotation, imagery, and metaphor:

- **Connotation** seeks felicitous words with layers of meaning and
  resonances beyond the concrete. One reason many Christians
  cling sentimentally to the King James Bible is the poetry in its
  words. In phrases like "Neither cast ye your pearls before swine,"
  the words have connotations that were lost in the New English
  Bible of 1961, with its "Do not feed your pearls to pigs." *Feed* in
  the modern version cannot even imagine the nuances of *cast,* and
  pig trades the suggestion of evil and moral depravity of *swine* for
  the generic term for the barnyard animal.
- **Imagery** relies upon the re-creation in words of a concrete visual
  image, tapping deep feelings through visual descriptions. Images
  are our link to memory, to the imagination, to the collective unconscious. An image, though vivid, means only what it literally is:
  a marigold, an Appaloosa, a black Underwood typewriter. Jonathan Raban uses imagery to help us see a landscape on the Great
  Plains: "The earth was almost black, the grass and sage were em-
  erald green."
- **Metaphor** is a way of talking about one thing by describing something else. Metaphors compare disparate things—surprising us,
  revealing deeper truths and providing unexpected insights. (We
  are using "metaphor" here as a catchall term including simile,
  symbol, and analogy.) When William Finnegan describes the Feb-

ruary surf at Ocean Beach, he uses metaphor: "The first wall of sandy, grumbling white water felt like a barrel of gritty ice cubes poured down my back." Metaphor can also be expressed implicitly; Finnegan calls offshore winds, those that blow from land to sea, "the wonder drug of surfing" and compares them to an artist's implement: "On a good day, their sculptor's blade, meticulous and invisible, seems to drench whole coastlines in grace."

Metaphor can convey psychology as well as topology and oceanography, as in this M.F.K. Fisher quote: "Once at least in the life of every human, whether he be brute or trembling daffodil, comes a moment of complete gastronomic satisfaction."

Lyricism turns words into sensory figments, whether pictures, smells, or sounds. It makes an idea visceral; it links the here and now with memory; it summons the imagination and invites it to sit down and join us.

More on metaphor

Metaphor and **simile** involve comparisons between unlike things. In *simile* the comparison is expressed through words such as *like, as, than, similar to,* and *resembles* ("louder than a bomb"). In *metaphor,* the comparison is expressed when a figurative term is substituted for a literal term. In *Bad Land,* as Jonathan Raban imagines a train leaving North Dakota in 1909, he compares the landscape with fungi: "With the sun sinking fast toward the horizon, the train crept through a sudden irruption of badlands terrain, past mushrooms of sandstone on stalks of pale gray clay." When describing the perfect spring weather of a week in June almost a century later, he uses simile: "Every creek and coulee brimmed with water like milky cocoa."

Personification is a particular type of metaphor in which an inanimate object or an idea is represented in human terms. Raban personifies trees when he gives them knees instead of trunks: "Water swirled round the knees of the cottonwoods and filled the irrigation ditches."

Symbol refers to the use of one thing to mean much more than what it is. A lightbulb is a trite symbol for an idea. "The Road Not Taken" was Robert Frost's symbol for the consequences of choice. The ruins of houses "skewed and splayed" that dotted the landscape surveyed by Raban symbolize the dashed dreams of long-ago emigrants:

> Their windows, empty of glass, were full of sky. Strips of ice-blue showed between their rafters. Some had lost their footing and tumbled into their cellars. All were buckled by the drifting tonnage of Montana's winter snows, their joists and roofbeams warped into violin curves.

Analogy and **extended metaphor** involve a web of comparisons. Sentences might be likened to boats, for example (see page 149), or a man walking in the cold might be compared to a walking skeleton.

Flesh

In prose, a single word can be enough to make a passage lyrical. When a reporter slips an image into a lede, he or she takes the story beyond the Who What When Where into the How and Why. In 1989, J. Michael Kennedy and Bob Baker conveyed the drama and horror of a plane crash near Sioux City through this unforgettable imagery:

> A crippled United Airlines DC-10 crashed a half-mile short of a runway while trying to make an emergency landing Wednesday afternoon, bursting into a cartwheeling fireball that broke into what one eyewitness described as "15,000 pieces."

That "cartwheeling fireball," together with the snapshot of "15,000 pieces," made the *Los Angeles Times* opening stand out from the hundreds of ledes printed across the country about the disaster in an Iowa cornfield.

Metaphor might also be a swift phrase or a deft stroke that zeroes in on a character or a subject. Novelist James Salter, in *A Sport and a*

Pastime, used "the silence of a folded flag" to describe the quiet of an afternoon in provincial France. Mary Karr, in her memoir *Cherry,* lets an adolescent summer of "stultifying" idleness become "a long scroll of papyrus onto which something longed to be writ." Uwem Akpan's short story "Baptizing the Gun" features a protagonist who lets a shady character join him in his car, then regrets it: "My stomach feels like a grater, and my insides hurt as if they'd been shredded."

Metaphor can work especially well in describing character. Jane Austen, when she describes Pemberley in *Pride and Prejudice,* lets the estate—and in particular its stream—speak acres about its owner, Mr. Darcy:

> It was a large, handsome stone building, standing well on rising ground, and backed by a ridge of high woody hills;—and in front, a stream of some natural importance was swelled into greater, but without any artificial appearance. Its banks were neither formal nor falsely adorned. Elizabeth was delighted. She had never seen a place for which nature had done more, or where natural beauty had been so little counteracted by an awkward taste.

Henry Louis Gates, Jr., used a knot of comparisons to portray basketball legend Michael Jordan as an archetype: "The man is both hulking and suave, and it's easy to see why he has become a totem of black masculinity; he makes Bill Cosby look like Uncle Ben." Later in the same *New Yorker* profile, Gates gives an account of Jordan's contentious contract negotiations with Chicago Bulls general manager Jerry Reinsdorf: "Jordan, considered strictly as an athlete, is the Second Coming, and Reinsdorf, considered strictly as a mogul, is a second-rater. It's as if Pat Robertson were making Jesus punch a time card."

Since we're talking sports, let's not leave out that metaphor machine Jim Harbaugh, the head coach for the San Francisco 49ers. His tight end and long snapper Brian Jennings, Harbaugh once told the *San Francisco Examiner,* "is like a Jedi Knight of snapping the football. He's not a Padawan learner. He's not an apprentice. He's a full-fledged Jedi Knight." Harbaugh casts his metaphoric eye inward, too. Well, sort of: "I don't believe in peeling back the onion and looking at the soul," he has said. "Transparent as a baggie. I'm thinking about this week's game and this week alone."

WITH EXTENDED METAPHOR, A writer develops an image through successive lines, as in Virginia Woolf's essay "A Room of One's Own." Based upon two papers she read to an arts society, Woolf addresses the complicated issue of "women and fiction." Woolf writes that she "sat down on the banks of a river and began to wonder what the words meant":

> To the right and left bushes of some sort, golden and crimson, glowed with the colour, even it seemed burnt with the heat, of fire. On the further bank the willows wept in perpetual lamentation, their hair about their shoulders. There one might have sat the clock round lost in thought. Thought—to call it by a prouder name than it deserved—had let its line down into the stream. It swayed minute after minute, hither and thither among the reflections and the weeds, letting the water lift it and sink it, until—you know the little tug—the sudden conglomeration of an idea at the end of one's line: and then the cautious hauling of it in, and the careful laying of it out. Alas, laid on the grass how small, how insignificant this thought of mine looked; the sort of fish that a good fisherman puts back into the water so that it may grow fatter and be one day worth cooking and eating.

Woolf extends her metaphor: an idea begins as a fish gently tugging at the end of the line, then becomes prey—something with which the thinker toys—then shifts yet again—to a disappointment, or perhaps a promise of fatter fish to come.

Cardinal Sins

Many competent passages lack not only "the silence of a folded flag" but the boisterousness of one unfurling. If the words are precise and evocative, a passage can still stir us without lyrical devices. Yet there is often disappointment when a short story or long article lacks the sudden surprise of a glittering image, or the evocative power of a fine metaphor.

That said, if you use metaphor, it has to be good. No, it has to be perfect. Just as there is nothing so awe-inspiring as a metaphor that sparks the imagination, there is nothing so dispiriting as an inept one—or a hopeless cliché. Let the metaphor maker beware.

TIN-EAR-ICAL

Sometimes writers stretching for the lyrical founder on infelicities. "We know what it feels like to feel like a square wheel," says poet Jane Hirschfield in a crisply delivered TED talk about metaphor, "but not what it's like to be tired as a whale."

The combinations may not jibe, like a description of a cybergang member whose eyes were "black as blueberries." When it comes to bad metaphors, the eyes have it. David Mamet, in *Make-Believe Town*, mocks the screenwriter who gushed, "She has a pair of eyes that makes you think of olives in a plate of milk." Bet you wouldn't want to *taste* a combo of olives and milk. Who would want to behold it?

Sometimes writers paste adjectives onto metaphors without thinking through the concomitant image. Stop and use some brain cells before resorting to a phrase like "the biggest bottleneck." "Most troublesome," maybe. A media critic once described an excitable Microsoft executive as "speaking at the hypertext speed of the information revolution." *Hypertext* speed? Since when is hypertext—a system of coding text that links electronic documents with each other—*speedy*? A music critic for the *Wilmington News Journal* once heralded "the synergistic combination of the European style with the Russian melodic fertilizer which Tchaikovsky managed to spread across the orchestral field." Now that's a tin ear.

DEAD METAPHORS

Metaphors must be original, invented by the writer for the story at hand. A metaphor has the shelf life of a fresh vegetable. *The hammer and the anvil* and *no axe to grind* once were vivid, because people once actually used anvils and axes. They are used unthinkingly by writers today who may not even be aware of their original meaning. Such ignorance leads to common errors like "tow the line" instead of "toe the line" (the athlete's practice of standing as close as possible to the starting line before a race).

When a Silicon Valley venture capitalist once bragged about a partnership with a Parisian bank that "provides us with a European beachfront to help our U.S. companies establish overseas partners," he was using a dead metaphor. Perhaps he needed a trip out of California—to Normandy?—to learn the difference between *beachfront* and *beachhead*.

Dead metaphors don't always spring from such obvious ignorance. The poet Donald Hall once told me he regretted using "the barn dies" in one of his poems, because that's a dead metaphor—a barn can "rot" and it can "fall down," he pointed out, but it can't "die."

A CLICHÉ NO LONGER MAKES A "CLICK"

Cliché is, first, a word so trite that it has lost all power, and second, a phrase that is so common any sentient adult can complete it without thinking, if given just the first two words.

The English word came to us in the nineteenth century from the French, where it is the past participle of *clicher,* or "to click." In French printer's jargon, *cliché* (which mimicked the sound of a mold striking molten metal) was a synonym for *stéréotype,* which in turn evolved from the Greek for "solid impression." A stereotype was a printing plate that duplicated typography and that was used by the printer in lieu of the original.

So a cliché is a word or phrase used over and over again in lieu of an original. In *vast majority*, the adjective *vast* is trite. The bottom line on *bottom line* is that the combo is hackneyed.

Most clichés started life as startling metaphors. Shakespeare coined many of them: "my salad days" (in *Antony and Cleopatra*), "neither rhyme nor reason" (*As You Like It*), "to the manner born" (*Hamlet*), "knit his brows" (*Henry IV, Part 2*), "it was Greek to me" (*Julius Caesar*), "play fast and loose" (*King John*), "pomp and circumstance" (*Othello*), "with bated breath" (*The Merchant of Venice*), "fool's paradise" (*Romeo and Juliet*), and my favorite, "brevity is the soul of wit" (*Hamlet* again).

But rather than just *liking* Shakespeare, you owe it to your readers to *make like* Shakespeare. Coin your own metaphors.

MIXED METAPHORS

One problem with clichés is that they come out automatically, without thought. If you're going to use one, don't forget to ponder it first. Buried within may be a mixed metaphor. When a woman in Ireland came to President Clinton's defense in 1998, she argued: "If everybody's washing were hung out, there would be skeletons in all their closets."

When Boyle Roche, a member of the British Parliament in the nineteenth century, said, "Mr. Speaker, I smell a rat; I see him floating in the air; I hear him rustling in the breeze, but I shall nip him in the bud," he turned a rat into a bird into a leaf into a rose. Mixed Metaphor City.

A century later, John McCain seemed torn about whether to compare President Bill Clinton's 2000 State of the Union speech to a "two-hour marathon," dirty linen, or General Tso's Chicken. "What you should do is give a vision for America," he said, "not give a laundry list that looks like a Chinese menu with one from column A and one from column B."

When funding for an interstate highway was being debated in the Centennial State, a resident of Golden was quoted in the *Denver Post*:

> It distracts from the goal, and the goal is so big—we're hunting elephants with a BB gun. If we don't all get behind fixing the hole in the hull, we're all going down. And that team spirit isn't there.

That guy needs metaphors like he needs a hole in the hull.

The New Yorker collects slips of the pen from reputable newspapers all over the country, reprinting them under the heading "Block That Metaphor." Here is an all-time favorite:

> Like a giant sheet of carbon paper, South Florida spreads its familiar arms from baseball camp to baseball camp, catching time in a bottle

and wrapping the Boys of Springtime in a velvet glove of comfortable déjà vu.

The New Yorker also snagged this headline from the *Tulsa World*:

Step Up to the Plate and Fish or Cut Bait

Don't let mixed metaphors get a stranglehold on you, even if they rhyme.

Carnal Pleasures

Lyricism doesn't have to be lofty: it can also be lowbrow. And funny. Politics has given us some metaphorical howls: Teddy Roosevelt accused his predecessor, William McKinley, of showing "all the backbone of a chocolate éclair," while Harold Ickes, Franklin Roosevelt's secretary of the interior, declared that Louisiana's Huey Long was "suffering from halitosis of the intellect." Then there was Secretary of State John Milton Hay's put-down of William Jennings Bryan as "a half-baked, glib little briefless jack-leg lawyer."

Some writers cleverly subvert clichés, giving them a second life. When Diane Ackerman says of the rain forest, "the meek inherit nothing," she plays off the established phrase ("the meek shall inherit the earth"), making her own more striking. When the *Washington Post* columnist Mark Shields, a regular metaphor machine, refers not to "smoking guns" in trumped-up investigations, but to "smoking water pistols," he creates a fresh metaphor out of a stale one. (If you still need convincing of Shields's rhetorical genius, consider this metaphor: "Everybody in Washington is an ethical eunuch and a moral leper who would steal a hot stove and go back for the smoke.")

Businesses often tweak clichés into clever names; think of all those hair salons with names like The Mane Attraction, About Faces, A Head of Our Times, and Shear Delight.

IN BLACK ENGLISH, INVECTIVE riffs called "doing the dozens" kid others about intellectual deficiencies, physical shortcomings, or, especially, "your mamma." The rhythmic, often rhyming ripostes—also called "signifying" or "sounding"—demand an ability to ad-lib in metaphor:

> Your mamma's so old she used to drive chariots to high school.
> Your mamma's so mean you have to take two trains and a bus to get on her good side.
> Your hair is so short it's like blowing dust off a jug.
> Your teeth are so yellow you put the sun out of business.
> You so ugly you look like you fell outta the ugly tree and hit every branch on the way down.

As much as we love biting metaphors, the greatest pleasure is watching one unfold elegantly over an entire passage of great prose. How many times have writers tried to describe biting cold? Here's Jonathan Raban on the cold of Montana, with its "shocking and insulting quality, like a boot in the face." On a minus-27-degree night, Raban decides to walk the nine-tenths of a mile from a restaurant back to the Edgewater Red Lion Inn:

> I had never felt my bones *as* bones before—the dry clacking of the joints of the skeleton. My kneecaps, thin and brittle as sand-dollars, came to my attention first, followed by my wrists, knuckles, shoulder-blades and ankles. I rattled as I walked, my trouser-legs flapping round bare white shinbones.
>
> For the first few blocks, I was Captain Scott, bravely leading the way across the icecap. Then I became poor Titus Oates, with his enormous frostbitten foot. "Well, said Oates, leaving Scott's tent at 80°08'S, "I am just going outside, and I may be some time."
>
> . . . The walking skeleton at last gained the hotel car park, enormous, rimed with frost—the final glacier. Keep going, chaps; almost there. I wanted a flag to plant.

But for my all-time favorite metaphor, here's Vladimir Nabokov, in *Pnin*. The protagonist, a middle-aged professor, returns from the dentist, contemplating the psychological effect of a new set of dentures:

A warm flow of pain was gradually replacing the ice and wood of the anesthetic in his thawing, still half-dead, abominably martyred mouth. After that, during a few days he was in mourning for an intimate part of himself. It surprised him to realize how fond he had been of his teeth. His tongue, a fat sleek seal, used to flop and slide so happily among the familiar rocks, checking the contours of a battered but still secure kingdom, plunging from cave to cove, climbing this jag, puzzling that notch, finding a shred of sweet seaweed in the same old cleft; but now not a landmark remained, and all there existed was a great dark wound, a terra incognita of gums which dread and disgust forbade one to investigate. And when the plates were thrust in, it was like a poor fossil skull being fitted with the grinning jaws of a perfect stranger.

It takes true imagination to turn a tongue into a fat sleek seal on the familiar rocks.

Catechism

GHOSTING RIGHT PAST THE LOGICAL MIND: Want a metaphor refresher? Listen to Jane Hirschfield's TED talk "The Art of the Metaphor," available on YouTube. Not only does it explain the device clearly, it does so with the poet's own delightful words: "Metaphors think with the imagination and the senses," she says. "The hot chili peppers in them explode in the mouth and the mind. They're also precise." Metaphors get under your skin, she says, "by ghosting right past the logical mind."

LOLL ABOUT IN SOME LYRICS: Take a look at your favorite songs and see if the composer uses metaphors in the lines. If you come up empty-handed, try these three:

- "I Want a Little Sugar in My Bowl" by Bessie Smith
- "Shelter from the Storm" by Bob Dylan
- "Just a Wave, Not the Water" by Butch Hancock

OBJECT OF MY AFFECTION: Wander around your house looking at different household objects. Find ones that are either a symbol or a metaphor for something else (a lamp, a huge bathtub, a bookshelf, the Nike swoosh?). Now focus on the thing you would grab first if your house were on fire. Freewrite about it: Describe it as concretely as you can. Tell the story of how you came to it—or it to you. Why is it so precious? After you have written your paragraph, think about whether the possession is a metaphor. Consider making the link between the object and its deeper meaning explicit—either in a line of the essay or in its title.

TAKE A WALK ON THE WILD SIDE: Take a foray in inclement weather—shocking and insulting cold, or stultifying heat, or a tempest of Shakespearean proportions. Using Jonathan Raban's description of the Montana cold as a model, find a metaphor and extend it.

CHAPTER 16

Voice

Bones

The word *voice* most commonly refers to the timbre produced by a person's vocal cords—whether nasal or velvety or harsh or soothing. Among literary types, *voice* refers to the effect of a writer's words on the page—whether the gonzo dispatches of Hunter S. Thompson or the graceful sentences of Alma Guillermoprieto. Voice is the *je ne sais quoi* of spirited writing. It separates brochure from brilliance, memo from memoir, a ship's log from *The Old Man and the Sea*. The best writers stamp prose with personality; their timbre and tone are as recognizable on the page as their voices on the phone.

The writer leaves us with a sense that we are listening to a skilled raconteur rather than passing our eyes over ink on paper. This involves more than just following the simplistic command "Write the way you talk": voice involves more than accurate transcription. Capturing the zing of conversation requires attentive listening and painstaking revision. It comes from connection, from the narrator subtly reaching out to the reader and saying, "We're in this together."

Conversation was *the* critical element in Robert Frost's poetry, and it formed the basis of a theory of language that he applied to both poetry and prose. "I was after poetry that talked," the New England poet once said. The poet believed that language allows a "correspondence" between writer and reader:

> If my poems were talking poems—if to read them you heard a voice—that would be to my liking! . . . Whenever I write a line it is because that line has already been spoken clearly by a voice within my mind, an audible voice.
>
> I have unconsciously tried to do just what Chaucer did when the language was young and untried and virile. I have sought only those words I had met up with as a boy in New Hampshire, working on farms during the summer vacations. I listened to the men with whom I worked. . . . When I started to carry their conversation over into poetry, I could hear their voices, and the sound posture differentiated between one and the other.

That "audible voice" within gives prose strength, the sense of a person speaking naturally. (This quote, describing the evolution of Frost's effort to convert colloquial speech into art, appears in an essay by Peter J. Stanlis in *Modern Age* quarterly.)

Strong voice comes when writers play with the full palette available to them and make clear choices: literary English (formally correct, rich in vocabulary, complex in sentence structure, and, at its best, flowing with stately grace); conversational English (ranging from high-minded palaver to lowbrow banter); jargon (the professional patois of doctors, lawyers, and corporate chiefs); and colloquial, idiomatic English (the language of the street, whether Spanglish, Pidgin English, or Valley Girl chatter).

What's magical about voice is the way we, as readers, recognize it.

Flesh

"The pen must at length comply with the tongue," Samuel Johnson wrote in the preface to his dictionary, and among the writers of his time who mastered the art of unaffected written conversation were the poet John Dryden and the parodist Jonathan Swift. Across the Atlantic and into the next century, the literary evangelist Walt Whitman was bent on developing a distinctly American voice, reflecting "the liberties and the brawn of These States." But it took Mark Twain to limn the rhythms and vocabulary of American English in prose at once literary and colloquial. (T. S. Eliot ranked Twain with Dryden and Swift as "one of those rare writers who have brought their language up to date, and in so doing, 'purified the dialect of the tribe.'")

In *Huckleberry Finn,* Twain zestily explored the new American vernacular, using what he called "the Missouri Negro dialect, the extremist form of the backwoods Southwestern dialect, the ordinary 'Pike County' dialect, and four modified varieties of this last." Elsewhere, Twain dabbled in "Injun-English" and the slang of prospectors in California and Nevada, as well as "the vigorous new vernacular of the occidental plains and mountains." Here's a sample, from "The Celebrated Jumping Frog of Calaveras County":

> Well, thish-yer Smiley had rat-tarriers, and chicken cocks, and tomcats, and all them kind of things, till you couldn't rest, and you couldn't fetch nothing for him to bet on but he'd match you. He ketched a frog one day, and took him home, and said he cal'lated to educate him; and so he never done nothing for three months but set in his back yard and learn that frog to jump. And you bet you he *did* learn him, too. He'd give him a little punch behind, and the next minute you'd see that frog whirling in the air like a doughnut—see him turn one summerset, or maybe a couple, if he got a good start, and come down flat-footed and all right, like a cat. He got him up so in the matter of ketching flies, and kep' him in practice so constant, that he'd nail a fly every time as fur as he could see him. Smiley said all a frog wanted was education, and he could do 'most anything—and I believe him.

BEHIND THE BYLINE

At its most risky, voice swings, it swears, it swivels at the hip. The movie critic Pauline Kael wrote in a chatty, urgent, impassioned voice. Writing about *Last Tango in Paris*, she mixed references to the playwright August Strindberg, schlockmeisters, and the writer Norman Mailer, among others. Her language went from lyrical to lurid: "The colors in this movie are late-afternoon orange-beige-browns and pink—the pink of flesh drained of blood, corpse pink." Sometimes she was downright plainspoken: "This is a movie people will be arguing about, I think, for as long as there are movies."

The science writer Mary Roach has evolved a distinctive, wry style of reporting: "The human head is of the same approximate size and weight as a roaster chicken," she writes in the first line of *Stiff: The Curious Lives of Human Cadavers*. "I have never before had occasion to make the comparison, for never before today have I seen a head in a roasting pan."

Voice can be boisterous. *Angela's Ashes*, the memoir of the Limerick-born writer Frank McCourt, brims with Irish authenticity:

> There may be a lack of tea or bread in the house but Mam and Dad always manage to get the fags, the Wild Woodbines. They have to have the Woodbines in the morning and anytime they drink tea. They tell us every day we should never smoke, it's bad for your lungs, it's bad for your chest, it stunts your growth, and they sit by the fire puffing away. Mam says, If 'tis a thing I ever see you with a fag in your gob I'll break your face. They tell us the cigarettes rot your teeth and you can see they're not lying. The teeth turn brown and black in their heads and fall out one by one. Dad says he has holes in his teeth big enough for a sparrow to raise a family.

McCourt's strong voice is rooted in vocabulary true to his characters (*fags, 'tis, gob*) and in his ability to recapture the metaphors that spring from his father's lips as easily as songs about dying for Ireland.

But voice can be understated, too. E. B. White may seem to possess the most seemingly natural, effortless voice possible, but that doesn't mean it's not carefully crafted. Here's the opening to his 1941 essay "Once More to the Lake":

> One summer, along about 1904, my father rented a camp on a lake in Maine and took us all there for the month of August. We all got

ringworm from some kittens and had to rub Pond's Extract on our arms and legs night and morning, and my father rolled over in a canoe with all his clothes on; but outside of that the vacation was a success and from then on none of us ever thought there was any place in the world like that lake in Maine. I have since become a salt-water man, but sometimes in summer there are days when the restlessness of the tides and the fearful cold of the sea water and the incessant wind which blows across the afternoon and into the evening make me wish for the placidity of a lake in the woods.

Anyone raised on *Charlotte's Web* and *Stuart Little* finds comfortable familiarity in that last passage. E. B. White, and his contemporaries James Thurber and Lewis Thomas, write in such understated voices that their work seems effortless. Now *that's* illusion of the highest order. Writing in a natural conversational voice takes serious work.

Cardinal Sins

VANILLA VOICE

The first, if not the worst, sin writers commit when it comes to voice is the absence of one. Much writing is marked by a fatal blandness, resulting from words that are too fuzzy, or vague, or abstract. Instead of sensing a storyteller behind the words, we get the Tin Woodsman, without heart or affect.

June Casagrande, in *It Was the Best of Sentences, It Was the Worst of Sentences,* blames this flaw on the laziness and cowardice of writers who don't take the time to find the right words. Rather than reading that a character heard a noise, she writes, or that a burglar stole some things, or that your CEO implemented a new procedure, "I want loud thuds and Omega wristwatches. I want e-mail surveillance and sudden firings. Tell me that your CEO is cracking down on personal phone calls." The failure to find the right words, of course, is sometimes a deeper failure of observation or imagination on the part of the writer. But it leaves the reader cold.

Sometimes the problem isn't just a lack of detail, or imprecise diction. It's too much detail—of the wrong kind. Stay away from nonsense noun pileups like "interactive facilitated sessions with direct feedback and reinforcement materials" or "nonviolent and nonage-identified behavior issues." These words lack cadence or any semblance of personal voice. Instead they grind like an avalanche of concrete blocks.

WRITING OFF KEY

Voice can't be co-opted cavalierly. It must be true. And it must truly reach out to your silent partner, your reader. Respect this reader. Entice this reader. Don't shut anyone out.

Skilled writers subtly shift tone and voice for different audiences. An engineer might use formal and scientifically exact prose when delivering a paper to colleagues, but if he appears on "Science Friday," he must translate his ideas into terms accessible to the average radio listener on lunch break. Bill Nye the Science Guy uses another voice altogether to present ideas to his audience of children and teachers.

Unfortunately, some scientists and academics aren't able to adjust their voices for the crowd. They use too many puffed-up words—too many nouns ending in *-tion,* too many verbs ending in *-ize,* too many adjectives ending in *-wide.* Take, for example, this mouthful that opens *Signatures of the Visible,* written by the comp lit professor Fredric Jameson:

> The visual is *essentially* pornographic, which is to say that it has its end in rapt, mindless fascination; thinking about its attributes becomes an adjunct to that, if it is unwilling to betray its object; while the most austere films necessarily draw their energy from the attempt to repress their own excess (rather than from the more thankless effort to discipline the viewer).

Prose like this is so endemic in academia that some professors make a sport of lampooning each other's excesses. The judges of an academics' "Bad Writing" contest sponsored by the journal *Philosophy and Litera-*

ture gave the award to Jameson's passage one year, saying that reading it was like "swimming through cold porridge." The Duke University doc does have a respectable academic following, the judges noted.

Adjusting your voice to the crowd may seem like compromise to a professor, but it's practically the job description of a politician. Yet candidates get into trouble when they don't understand narrative voice. Al Gore was an admitted policy wonk but his starchy language ("information superhighway") branded him as wooden. ("He's so boring, his Secret Service code name is . . . Al Gore," the vice president quipped about himself at a Gridiron Dinner in 1994.) Mitt Romney, when asked at a 2012 presidential debate about equality for women, damaged his standing among female voters when he referred to receiving "binders full of women" when he was a governor of Massachusetts and seeking cabinet candidates. That was downright dehumanizing.

And it's no less dehumanizing in a business context. CEOs need to remember that they work with and for people. Repeating a word like "stakeholder" can drive a stake into the heart of the very real person it refers to. An international bank once advertised for a "customer journey re-engineering manager," but it's hard to imagine a real person wanting such a job.

Then there's tech talk, which might well be called "Spock Talk." Microsoft described a new browser that (at least in England) "delivers a richer, faster, and more business-ready Web experience. Architected to run HTML 5, the beta enables developers to utilise standardised mark-up language across multiple browsers." That snippet, wrote Lucy Kellaway in the *BBC News Magazine,* proves "one of the great mysteries of capitalism"—that "no invisible hand . . . joins good language and good profits. If anything, the hand pushes the two apart."

THE FALSE FIRST PERSON

Some novice writers mistake the first person pronoun *I* for voice. While personal narrative does usually rely on strong voice for success, not all narratives need be personal, and many become muddied by the ill-considered use of the first person. Some writing is way too up-close-and-personal for its own good.

In "Africa Rising," a report on that continent that ran in *Wired* magazine, the word *I* appears 235 times, the word *Africa* a mere 78. John Perry Barlow's "report" is far too solipsistic—it is more about him than about Africa:

> I am not ready. Indeed, I am afraid, and fear is not a common afflic-tion of mine. I'm not afraid of being killed, nor of any of the projected African perils that have my loved ones so spooked. I figure their hor-rific images are mostly mediamagoria. I think I'm afraid of becoming someone else, which is, I suppose, a sort of death. I feel as if I am setting out on quest for the next version of myself, much as I did nine years ago when I closed down my first life and went venturing off to Silicon Valley. Now I'm due for a new mission, but it's an odyssey I don't know how to prepare for.

Whether you're doing reportage or crafting a résumé, pay attention to voice. The line between self-expression and self-indulgence can be hard to discern. Test every temptation to use *I*, and try other devices if you care about voice. Even in something as mundane as a cover letter for a job, be polite, but remember it's *you* the person on the other end wants to know about, not a boilerplate professional. Don't speak like a PR flack. Be yourself. Try mixing formal and informal diction. Go for an occasional surprise.

PHONEY TONES

In *Simple and Direct,* Jacques Barzun describes what he calls the "pseudo-Hemingway" tone: writing that creates an impression of headlong speed punctuated by frequent shocks, full of fragments and crime-story clichés. One student of Barzun's nailed the "pseudo-Hemingway" tone in this parody:

> I saw her first. She was tall, blond. She looked good. She smiled. I stepped back. She came up close. She smelled good. She put her arms

around me. I kissed her. She raised an eyebrow. I nodded. We were engaged.

Remember, "being earnest" does not mean mimicking Hemingway.

There are other phony tones to avoid. Journalists with too much hubris and too little control often adopt a pseudo-investigative tone when they are just reporting the news. PR flacks can fill a press release with breathless description and a few too many exclamation points. An editor at a Boston magazine once received this offer from a book publicist:

> You're making it through the holidays, whew! But the next hurdle has a great big red heart marking the date—Valentine's Day—and it looks like you'll be spending it alone. Feel like throwing in the towel and having a pity party? Don't you dare!

The press release went on to offer an article from a self-esteem expert and author telling us how to "pamper the most important person in your life—YOU!" That voice was just over the top.

Carnal Pleasures

Is email a new literary form? Is texting? Tweeting? Whether or not you think so, you have to admit that they brim with voice. A cross between speaking and writing, these messages involve conversational bits enlivened by immediacy and urgency. Partly because it's *not* face-to-face, partly because we use it in a spontaneous way, email is closer to phone conversations than to sober memos and magazine articles. It is chatty, colloquial, intimate.

Texts and tweets are not composed in long hours of reflection and revision but in blunt bursts and on-the-fly fragments. The "rules" of writing never took hold in cyberspace, so these 140-character communiqués are to stories what interjections are to sentences. (Think raw, typo-laden, impassioned, unpolished.)

The voices in the best news tweets lack self-consciousness. Their brisk sentences and transposed letters smack of urgency, like these bulletins from the streets during the Arab Spring:

@tarekshalaby (Tarek Shalaby)

VIVA LA REVOLUCION!!! RT@SultanAlQassemi: MY GOD! MY GOD! This is AMAZING.

@mosaaberizing (Mosa'ab Elshamy)

Dear people watching Arabs Got Talent, there's a better show going on called Tunisia's Got Freedom. Watch that.

@Gsquare86 (Gigi Ibrahim)

A MAN IN #EGYPT SET HIMSELF ON FIRE CHANTING AGAINST STATE SECURITY IN FRONT OF PARLAIMENT AT 9:00 AM TODAY #Sidibouzid #Revolution attempt?

News stories in the U.S. get attention, too. Elon James White, a stand-up comedian and founder of the Brooklyn Comedy Company and the Black Comedy Experiment, tweeted this nanostory after Occupiers blocked the Brooklyn Bridge in 2011:

@elonjames (Elon James White)

"Oh? The NYPD are treating you badly? Violent for no reason? Weird."—Black People

White's ironic voice comes through loud and clear in those 140 characters.

LITERARY VOICE CAN CUT deep, like a small but efficient knife. Ruth Reichl (@ruthreichl) came to Twitter after years of writing and editing feature stories and clever cutlines at *Gourmet* magazine, *The New York Times,* and the *Los Angeles Times*. Occasionally her haikulike tweets refer to news events (like the disaster at the Fukushima nuclear power plant in Japan), but more are part meteorological commentary, part recipe ideas:

> Scrambled weather. Lightning forecast. Earthbound way to start the day: buttered oatmeal, fresh berries, river of thick cream. So soothed.
>
> Terrifying morning. Nuclear catastrophe looms. Making a cup of tea, slicing a golden lemon, cooking one perfect araucana egg. Breathing.
>
> Very old lady begging in the subway. Gave her money, muffins, coffee. Tears.
>
> Home to bracingly spicy sesame noodles. Such sadness here too.

Reichl has many imitators on Twitter, but none who can pack so much compassion, joy, and precision in so tight a space.

WHEN A WRITER HAS developed his or her own voice, we read the text, however long or short, with a sense of recognition. "Ah, yes, I know this voice," we say to ourselves, even before reading the Twitter handle or the byline. Joan Didion has one of those voices. So does Susan Orlean. Then there's Mark Leibovich of *The New York Times*. Here's a Leibovich lead from November 8, 2006, just after the Republicans received, as President George W. Bush called it, a "thumpin'" in the midterm elections:

> It was one of those once-a-decade days in Washington where news, rumor and recrimination crackled in every direction. But the wounded

> duck at the center of it all, President Bush, offered by far the day's most mesmerizing spectacle.
>
> He looked worn at his must-see midday news conference, in need of a haircut, good night's sleep, better makeup job, hug, vacation in Crawford or some combination thereof. The grooves across his forehead were dark and articulated, his voice slightly hoarse. He wore a maroon tie, the color of blood.

Those sentences practically scream *voice*. It's partly Leibovich's word choice: "wounded duck" suggests "lame duck" plus the humiliation of the loss. The bad hair, the bad makeup—all wry details. Then there's the tie. It might have been "red" or even "maroon," but with "the color of blood" Leibovich gamely inserts a little subjectivity into the story.

MADE-UP VOICES

In fiction, literary voice manifests in two quite different ways. Sometimes the writer is, like the New Journalist Tom Wolfe or Mark Twain before him, a veritable ventriloquist, playing with the vernacular of different characters. Julian Fellowes finds the words to express a valet's stoic moral authority and a dowager's intractable snobbery in *Downton Abbey*. Then there's doing the dozens, Downton style. When the Maggie Smith character, Lady Violet Grantham, hears that her daughter-in-law's American mother will be visiting from the United States, she remarks:

> I'm so looking forward to seeing your mother again. When I'm with her, I'm reminded of the virtues of the English.

(Her granddaughter's very decent fiancé, Matthew Crawley, obtusely asks, "But isn't she American?" This gives Lady Violet another opportunity to get in a dig. "Exactly," she retorts.)

At another extreme is David Simon, the HBO wunderkind, who is a master at finding the voice of characters as different as a Baltimore drug lord and a Polish teamster, in *The Wire*, or as a jaded lawyer and a bighearted jazz musician, in *Treme*.

Some writers play with the poetry of nonstandard English. Junot Díaz lays down an eclectic narrative voice that shifts from the barrios of the Caribbean to the New Jersey 'hood. Díaz, born in the Dominican Republic, plies his own brand of language in short stories like "The Sun, the Moon, the Stars":

I don't even want to tell you where we're at. We're in Casa de Campo. The Resort That Shame Forgot. The average asshole would love this place. It's the largest, wealthiest resort on the Island, which means it's a goddam fortress, walled away from everybody else. *Guachimanes* and peacocks and ambitious topiaries everywhere. Advertises itself in the States as its own country, and it might as well be. Has its own airport, thirty-six holes of golf, beaches so white they ache to be trampled, and the only Island Dominicans you're guaranteed to see are either caked up or changing your sheets. Let's just say my *abuelo* has never been here, and neither has yours. This is where the Garcías and the Colóns come to relax after a long month of oppressing the masses, where the *tutumpotes* can trade tips with their colleagues from abroad. Chill here too long and you'll be sure to have your ghetto pass revoked, no questions asked. . . .

Every fifty feet there's at least one Eurofuck beached out on a towel like some scary pale monster that the sea's vomited up. They look like philosophy professors, like budget Foucaults, and too many of them are in the company of a dark-assed Dominican girl. I mean it, these girls can't be no more than sixteen, look *puro ingenio* to me. You can tell by their inability to communicate that these two didn't meet back in their Left Bank days.

Díaz's startling narrative voice emerges first out of vocabulary that embraces Spanish words (*tutumpotes*) and slang (*caked up* and *chill here*) and profane inventions (*Eurofuck*). It also plays with sentence fragments ("The Resort That Shame Forgot") and crude syntax ("these girls can't be no more than sixteen") to reflect the way characters really talk. Díaz also adopts an informal point of view ("Let's just say my *abuelo* has never been here, and neither has yours") and gets in some highbrow-lowbrow disses ("beaches so white they ache to be trampled" and "They look like philosophy professors, like budget Foucaults"). Sum total: distinctive voice.

Catechism

ODE TO A TAPE RECORDER: Transcribing talk is not tantamount to writing, but it offers one technique to cultivate voice. Some writers do start by speaking their ideas into tape recorders, to let their voices flow, to then be able to hear themselves. Others read their lines aloud, over and over, recasting any word or sentence that does not roll off the tongue. Anything that makes you cringe when you read it aloud needs rewriting.

EPISTOLARY VOICE: Collect a few letters you have written to friends. Find a series of your emails—or posts on Facebook—that express something of who you are and how you like to keep in touch with people. Compare the letters with the emails or posts. What is the same in all these forms, and what differs? Look in particular at **style** (the vocabulary, the length of the sentences), **tone** (the attitude, be it earnest, excited, pissed off, or ironic), and **voice** (the overall sense of *you* that comes through the words).

FAMILY TIES: Write a short journalistic sketch of a sibling or a cousin. Do the usual work of finding precise and evocative details, but describe your character objectively. Once it's written, rewrite it two separate times, playing with tone and voice in each rewrite. Change the attitude, trying both reverence and irreverence. Change the point of view, from third person to first or second. Find words to express the intimacy, or distance, or lightheartedness, or grief, or frustration of the relationship. Think about diction, sentence dynamics, and pitch. When you're done, decide which best showcases your own narrative voice.

Epilogue

From the King James Bible to the lyrics of hip-hop—you might say we've gone from "sin and syntax" to "sin and syncopation." No matter the genre, all storytellers are engaged in the same struggle: how to use words, grammar, and music to describe the human condition.

"Remember that you are a human being with a soul and the divine right of articulate speech," wrote George Bernard Shaw. "That your native tongue is the language of Shakespeare and Milton and the Bible; and don't sit there crooning like a bilious pigeon."

Sin and Syntax has tried to coax, coach, and cajole you out of biliousness. Of course, there is much more to making memorable prose than linguistic facility. You also need worthy ideas, you need to tell stories with strong plots, and you need to cast and control the right characters. When it comes to developing these narrative skills, though, no book can help you. Experience is the ultimate master.

Ernest Hemingway once advised prose artists to "Write hard and clear about what hurts." It's good advice. But to follow it, you must stop reading.

Appendix

Here you will find answers and keys to some of the exercises in the Catechism sections. For more, see www.sinandsyntax.com/catechisms.

CHAPTER 2:

Pronouns

THE GOURMET POINT OF VIEW

- "A hungry stomach seldom scorns plain food." (Horace) THIRD PERSON
- "Eat, drink, and be merry." (The Bible) SECOND PERSON / IMPERATIVE MOOD
- "A bachelor's life is a fine breakfast, a flat lunch, and a miserable dinner." (Francis Bacon) THIRD PERSON
- "First we eat, then we do everything else." (M.F.K. Fisher) FIRST PERSON PLURAL
- "Probably one of the most private things in the world is an egg before it is broken." (M.F.K. Fisher) THIRD PERSON
- "A good cook is like a sorceress who dispenses happiness." (Elsa Schiaparelli) THIRD PERSON
- "I come from a family where gravy is considered a beverage." (Erma Bombeck) FIRST PERSON SINGULAR

CHAPTER 3:

Verbs

THESE VERBS ARE MADE FOR . . . :

Blind Gary Davis:	"Lord I Feel Just Like Goin' On"	**STATIC, DYNAMIC**
Elizabeth Cotton	"Mama, Nobody's Here but the Baby"*	**STATIC**
Howlin' Wolf	"Moanin' at Midnight"	**DYNAMIC**
George Strait	"All My Exes Live in Texas"	**DYNAMIC**
Memphis Minnie	"If You See My Rooster (Please Run Him Home)"	**DYNAMIC, DYNAMIC**
Robert Johnson	"I Believe I'll Dust My Broom"	**DYNAMIC, DYNAMIC**
Lee Hazlewood	"These Boots Are Made for Walkin'"	**DYNAMIC**
Led Zeppelin	"The Song Remains the Same"	**STATIC**
The Rolling Stones	"(I Can't Get No) Satisfaction"	**DYNAMIC**
The Seeds	"Can't Seem to Make You Mine"	**STATIC**

*See the static *is* buried in the contraction *Nobody's*?

CHAPTER 4:

Adjectives

ADJECTIVE ALERT

Italics: obvious adjective

Boldface: proper noun as adjective

Small caps: possessive pronoun

Underscore: odd adjective

Met Johnny while at the gate in Honolulu: <u>20</u>, *mixed-race* (*black, American Indian,* and *some* sort of *white*), *beanpole-like.* He's *naive* and *streetsmart* at the *same* time, a <u>fetching</u> combination of <u>wide-eyed</u> curiosity and *hard-luck* stories. *Raised in Berkeley,* he went to **Malcolm X** Elementary, worked at **Johnson's** Barbershop on Sacramento, went to Hawaii to cut hair with HIS uncle, had HIS *brand-new* equipment robbed. He's headed home to get HIS *old* equipment and see HIS *three-day-old* brother. He wants to go back to Honolulu, where he and HIS uncle cut hair "off of Likelike." I sensed something truly *sweet* about him, answered HIS *funny* questions about *Hawaiian* history ("is it *true* they had warriors, but the *white* man had guns?"), gave him a *brief* history of Queen Lili'uokalani, told him to visit **'Iolani** Palace when he goes back. Took a gamble and offered him a ride home. Bruce was *dubious,* but then as *taken in* as I had been. We left him at HIS *mother's* house, where a *pink* Karmann-Ghia and a **VW** bus <u>painted</u> with flowers were standing guard. He put <u>Bruce's</u> number into one of HIS *two* iPhones—the *work* one—and told Bruce he'd give him a haircut anytime—*cheaper* than SuperCuts, and *better.*

CHAPTER 8:

Interjections

PARSE THIS!

Parsing is not always an exact science. Where one person sees a pronoun, another might see an adjective. Even the dictionary lists different possibilities for different words. But here is a liberal key to the parsing, remembering these abbreviations:

N = noun   P = pronoun

V = verb   Aj = adjective

Av = adverb   Pp = preposition

C = conjunction   I = interjection

Pp N   Pp Aj   N   Aj* N   V   Aj Pp   N   Pp V   N   Pp
On Tuesday, in broad daylight, the coon arrived, heavy with young, to take possession of

Aj* N Pp Aj* N   C P   V   P/Aj N   Pp   N   C   P   V Aj* Aj   N
the hole in the tree, but she found another coon in possession, and there was a grim fight

Av Pp Aj* N   Aj* Aj   N   V C C P   V Pp P   C P/Aj Aj   N   V
high in the branches. The new tenant won, or so it appeared to me, and our old coon came

Pp Aj* N Pp   N   C   V Av** Pp Aj   N   Pp   V   P/Aj N   C   V
down the tree in defeat and hustled off into the woods, to examine her wounds and make

P/Aj   N   Pp P/Aj   N   P V   Aj Pp P C P V Pp P/Aj P   V   V   Pp
other plans for her confinement. I was sorry for her, as I am for any who are evicted from

P/Aj   N   Pp Aj*   N   C   N   Av Aj* Aj   N   Pp N C   N
their haunts by the younger and stronger—always a sad occasion for man or beast.

*The or a is also an article, a kind of adjective.
**Off can also be considered a particle, as it is part of a phrasal verb.

CHAPTER 12:

Length and Tone

CATCH MY DRIFT?

The task here is to identify whether the following political catchphrases are phrases, fragments, simple sentences, compound sentences, complex sentences, or a blend of more than one. If you're feeling confident, identify the sentence pattern in the simple sentences:

- **We are all republicans—we are all federalists**—Thomas Jefferson's first inaugural address. TWO SIMPLE SENTENCES (S + SV + C) LINKED BY A DASH
- **Tippecanoe and Tyler too**—popular slogan for Whig party candidates William Henry Harrison and John Tyler in the 1840 U.S. presidential election. PHRASE (BROWNIE POINT IF YOU SAID "NOUN PHRASE")
- **Four score and seven years ago**—Abraham Lincoln, Gettysburg Address. PHRASE (GOLD STAR IF YOU IDENTIFIED IT AS AN ADVERBIAL PHRASE)
- **Yesterday, December 7, 1941, a date which will live in infamy**—said by President Franklin D. Roosevelt after the Japanese attack on Pearl Harbor. SENTENCE FRAGMENT (KUDOS IF YOU RECOGNIZE THE RELATIVE CLAUSE EMBEDDED IN IT AND DOUBLE KUDOS IF YOU NOTE THAT AMERICANS TEND TO PREFER *THAT* OVER *WHICH* IN CASES LIKE THIS)
- **I shall return**—U.S. general Douglas MacArthur after leaving the Philippines. SIMPLE SENTENCE (S + V)
- **The buck stops here**—Harry Truman. SIMPLE SENTENCE (S + V)
- **Ich bin ein Berliner**—said by John F. Kennedy in West Berlin. SIMPLE SENTENCE: I AM A BERLINER (S + SV + C)
- **There you go again**—said by Ronald Reagan to Jimmy Carter, in a 1980 presidential debate. SIMPLE SENTENCE (S + V)

- **Where's the beef?**—former vice president Walter Mondale, attacking Colorado senator Gary Hart in 1984 Democratic primary debate. SIMPLE SENTENCE (S + SV + C)
- **Read my lips: no new taxes**—said by George H. W. Bush during the 1988 U.S. presidential election. SIMPLE SENTENCE FOLLOWED BY A SENTENCE FRAGMENT. "(YOU) READ MY LIPS: THERE WILL BE NO NEW TAXES" WOULD BE TWO SIMPLE SENTENCES, S + V + DO AND S + SV + C).
- **That giant sucking sound**—Ross Perot in 1992 with regard to American jobs going to Mexico if the North American Free Trade Agreement (NAFTA) were ratified. PHRASE (GOLD STAR IF YOU SAID "NOUN PHRASE.")
- **It's the economy, stupid**—used during Bill Clinton's 1992 presidential campaign and widely attributed to Clinton adviser James Carville. SIMPLE SENTENCE (S + SV + C)
- **Yes, we can**—slogan of Barack Obama's 2008 presidential campaign. SIMPLE SENTENCE (S + V)

Acknowledgments

This book, more than most, reflects the energies not of one author but of many creative misbehavers. My thanks go first to the writers who have so inspired me, especially those whose words you see within these covers.

In casting my net wide for examples of wicked and winning syntax, I was helped by many language scamps, including Jack Baba, Martha Baer, Wallace Baine, Katy Butler, Frank Clancy, Ilana DeBare, Alex Frankel, Mark Frauenfelder, Jesse Freund, Sam Kane, Yukari Iwatani Kane, Tim McGee, Tim Patrick, Jennica Peterson, Keris Salmon, Brad Wieners, and Gary Wolf.

My students in a grammar class at Harvard University Extension impressed me with their pluck and found examples of both bad ads and terrific leads that sneaked into this second edition and into the materials I offer to teachers. Thanks especially to Colleen Glenn, Elise Hahl, Tasha Miller, Laurie Owen, and Tsuey-Rong Wu.

Colleagues at the San Francisco Writers Grotto, where the second edition was written, engage in regular repartee about the ins and outs of great writing, and they allowed me to include an especially entertaining Yahoo! Groups conversation here. Laura Fraser and Matthew Zapruder deserve special thanks, as each made an excerpt available and as each engaged with me in spirited conversation about pronouns and poetry.

My researcher on the first edition, Julie Greenberg, proved she could track down anything—even an almost forgotten 1969 Jell-O commercial. Meri Brin helped secure permissions. On the second edition, Josie Hodson and Ava Sayaka Rosen lent a hand, as did Kailani Moran, who became my Excel goddess. Special praise goes to Gianmaria Franchini, who chased down obscure manuscripts, wandered around the Web in search of brand names, and hoofed it to the library to make sure all facts were in place.

Speaking of the library, I thank Renée Tarshis and Peter Warhit in particular of the San Francisco Main Library for their unbridled curiosity and unrelenting helpfulness. Abby Yochelson and others at the Library of Congress answered weird questions without batting an eye—including one about cherry pips.

Friends and colleagues read parts of the manuscript and saved me from most of my own excesses. On the first edition, Micki Esken-Meland, Hollis Heimbouch, Emily McManus, and Mary Beth Protomastro were especially generous. Jessie Scanlon brought to bear a withering wit and a purple pen. On the second edition, Tristan Saldaña made his line edits in Track Changes, and in turquoise. Anne Paniagua reached back to remember what nuns and French teachers taught her about sentence structure. My mother, Molly Mayher, has been correcting my grammar and tightening my sentences since grade school, and continued the tradition.

Many thanks to my editors—first Suzanne Oak at Broadway Books, then Stephanie Knapp at Three Rivers Press. Both line-edited astutely. The book also benefited greatly from the guidance of Matthew Martin and from the attentions of copy editors Rosalie Wieder and Emily DeHuff. The latter also contributed a few killer examples. Zach Greenwald adds "smarts" and "wit" to the job description of his role as production editor; I cannot thank him enough for the changes he made, both minuscule and mighty. The designers, Pei Loi Koay and Maria Elias, made me look especially good.

I owe a special debt to two grammar divas. Karen Elizabeth Gordon first sent me spinning in 1984, when I bought her *Transitive Vampire*, and she has been both mentor and muse. Kate Brubeck, a gifted teacher and generous soul, gave me invaluable help on the second edition, helping me think through the catechisms and turning me on to the delights of the quotative *like*.

Also in the special-debt department is my longtime agent, Wendy Lipkind. Though Wendy never saw the second edition, she encouraged me to do it. My current agent, David Black, made it happen. Thanks also to Sarah Smith for her graceful assistance.

Some other spirits animate this text, even if they missed its latest iteration. My aunt and godmother, Eleanor Mayher Hackett, who started giving me books of poetry before I could talk, scoured the first edition. My father, Joseph Ganahl, made me fall in love with storytelling as I listened to his ghost stories, family tales, and self-deprecating jokes. Up until our very last conversation, he and I were discussing the nuances of nouns.

Finally, my deepest thanks go to Bruce Lowell Bigelow. He has seen me through both editions and knows all my sins.

Index

Extra Resources for Teachers

Are you a teacher seeking a fresh way to inspire writing students of all ages? Two suites of lesson plans to accompany *Sin and Syntax* are available for teachers to purchase. They are intended to take you through two separate semester-long courses.

The first focuses on grammar and good writing. Its exercises and writing prompts correspond to the "Words" and "Sentences" sections of *Sin and Syntax*. The second focuses more on the "Music" section of the book, encouraging writers to explore their own voices and to experiment with literary devices like word choice, tone, melody, metaphor, rhythm, and style.

The materials are suitable for high school, college, and professional-level students, with some suggestions for how to adapt them for even younger writers.

You'll find links to the lesson plans and other resources in the "Talking School" section of sinandsyntax.com.